PIMLICO

175

PORTRAIT
OF THE ARTIST
AS A
BAD CHARACTER

Cynthia Ozick is a member of the American Academy of Arts and Letters and has won various prizes and awards for her novels, short stories, poems and essays. Her books include *The Pagan Rabbi and Other Stories*, *Bloodshed and Three Novellas*, *Trust* (a novel), *The Messiah of Stockholm* (a novel), *The Shawl* (a novella and story), *Art & Ardour* (essays) and *Metaphor & Memory* (essays). *What Henry James Knew*, her most recent collection of essays, is a companion volume to *Portrait of the Artist as a Bad Character*. Her work has been translated into most major languages.

PORTRAIT
OF THE ARTIST
AS A BAD
CHARACTER

and Other Essays on Writing

———

CYNTHIA OZICK

PIMLICO

PIMLICO
An imprint of Random House
20 Vauxhall Bridge Road, London SW1V 2SA

Random House Australia (Pty) Ltd
20 Alfred Street, Milsons Point, Sydney
New South Wales 2061, Australia

Random House New Zealand Ltd
18 Poland Road, Glenfield
Auckland 10, New Zealand

Random House South Africa (Pty) Ltd
PO Box 337, Bergvlei 2012, South Africa

Random House UK Ltd Reg. No. 954009

First published by Pimlico 1996

1 3 5 7 9 10 8 6 4 2

Papers used by Random House UK Limited are natural,
recyclable products made from wood grown in sustainable
forests. The manufacturing processes conform to the
environmental regulations of the country of origin

Printed and bound in Great Britain by
Mackays of Chatham plc, Chatham, Kent

ISBN 0–7126–7484–5

A Drugstore in Winter

THIS IS ABOUT reading; a drugstore in winter; the gold leaf on the dome of the Boston State House; also loss, panic, and dread.

First, the gold leaf. (This part is a little like a turn-of-the-century pulp tale, though only a little. The ending is a surprise, but there is no plot.) Thirty years ago I burrowed in the Boston Public Library one whole afternoon, to find out— not out of curiosity—how the State House got its gold roof. The answer, like the answer to most Bostonian questions, was Paul Revere. So I put Paul Revere's gold dome into an "article," and took it (though I was just as scared by recklessness then as I am now) to the *Boston Globe*, on Washington Street. The Features Editor had a bare severe head, a closed parenthesis month, and silver Dickensian spectacles. He made me wait, standing, at the side of his desk while he read; there was no bone in me that did not rattle. Then he opened a drawer and handed me fifteen dollars. Ah, joy of Homer, joy of Milton! Grub Street bliss!

The very next Sunday, Paul Revere's gold dome saw print. Appetite for more led me to a top-floor chamber in Filene's department store: Window Dressing. But no one was in the least bit dressed—it was a dumbstruck nudist colony up there, a mob of naked frozen enigmatic manikins, tall enameled skinny ladies with bald breasts and skulls, and legs and wrists and necks that horribly unscrewed. Paul Revere's dome paled beside this gold mine! A sight—mute numb Walpurgisnacht—easily worth fifteen dollars. I had a Master's degree (thesis topic: "Parable in the Later Novels of Henry James") and a job as an advertising copywriter (9 a.m. to 6

1

p.m. six days a week, forty dollars per week; if you were male and had no degree at all, sixty dollars). Filene's Sale Days—Crib Bolsters! Lulla-Buys! Jonnie-Mops! Maternity Skirts with Expanding Invisible Trick Waist! And a company show; gold watches to mark the retirement of elderly Irish salesladies; for me the chance to write song lyrics (to the tune of "On Top of Old Smoky") honoring our Store. But "Mute Numb Walpurgisnacht in Secret Downtown Chamber" never reached the *Globe*. Melancholy and meaning business, the Advertising Director forbade it. Grub Street was bad form, and I had to promise never again to sink to another article. Thus ended my life in journalism.

Next: reading, and certain drugstore winter dusks. These come together. It is an aeon before Filene's, years and years before the Later Novels of Henry James. I am scrunched on my knees at a round glass table near a plate glass door on which is inscribed, in gold leaf Paul Revere never put there, letters that must be read backward: YƆAMЯAHꟼ WƎIV ꓘЯAꟼ There is an evening smell of late coffee from the fountain, and all the librarians are lined up in a row on the tall stools, sipping and chattering. They have just stepped in from the cold of the Traveling Library, and so have I. The Traveling Library is a big green truck that stops, once every two weeks, on the corner of Continental Avenue, just a little way in from Westchester Avenue, not far from a house that keeps a pig. Other houses fly pigeons from their roofs, other yards have chickens, and down on Mayflower there is even a goat. This is Pelham Bay, the Bronx, in the middle of the Depression, all cattails and weeds, such a lovely place and tender hour! Even though my mother takes me on the subway far, far downtown to buy my winter coat in the frenzy of Klein's on Fourteenth Street, and even though I can recognize the heavy power of a quarter, I don't know it's the Depression. On the trolley on the way to Westchester Square I see the children who live in the boxcar strangely set down in an empty lot some distance from Spy Oak (where a Revolutionary traitor was hanged—served him right for siding with redcoats); the lucky boxcar children dangle their stick-legs from their train-house maw and wave; how I envy them! I envy the orphans of the Gould Foundation, who have their own private swings and seesaws. Sometimes I imagine I am an orphan, and my father is an impostor pretending to be my father.

My father writes in his prescription book: *#59330 Dr. O'Flaherty Pow .60/ #59331 Dr. Mulligan Gtt. 65/ #59332 Dr. Thron Tab .90.* Ninety cents! A terrifically expensive medicine; someone is really sick. When I deliver a prescription around the corner or down the block. I am offered a nickel tip. I always refuse, out of conscience; I am, after all, the Park View Pharmacy's own daughter, and it wouldn't be seemly. My father grinds and mixes powders, weighs them out in tiny snowy heaps on an apothecary scale, folds them into delicate translucent papers or meticulously drops them into gelatin capsules.

In the big front window of the Park View Pharmacy there is a startling display—goldfish bowls, balanced one on the other in amazing pyramids. A German lady enters, one of my father's cronies—his cronies are both women and men. My quiet father's eyes are water-color blue, he wears his small skeptical quiet smile and receives the neighborhood's life-secrets. My father is discreet and inscrutable. The German lady pokes a punchboard with a pin, pushes up a bit of rolled paper, and cries out—she has just won a goldfish bowl, with two swimming goldfish in it! Mr. Jaffe, the salesman from McKesson & Robbins, arrives, trailing two mists: winter steaminess and the animal fog of his cigar,* which melts into the coffee smell, the tarpaper smell, the eerie honeyed tangled drugstore smell. Mr. Jaffe and my mother and father are intimates by now, but because it is the 1930s, so long ago, and the old manners still survive, they address one another gravely as Mr. Jaffe, Mrs. Ozick, Mr. Ozick. My mother calls my father Mr. O, even at home, as in a Victorian novel. In the street my father tips his hat to ladies. In the winter his hat is a regular fedora; in the summer it is a straw boater with a black ribbon and a jot of blue feather.

What am I doing at this round glass table, both listening

---

* Mr. Matthew Bruccoli, another Bronx drugstore child, has written to say that he remembers with certainty that Mr. Jaffe did not smoke. In my memory the cigar is somehow there, so I leave it.

and not listening to my mother and father tell Mr. Jaffe about their struggle with "Tessie," the lion-eyed landlady who has just raised, threefold, in the middle of that Depression I have never heard of, the Park View Pharmacy's devouring rent? My mother, not yet forty, wears bandages on her ankles, covering oozing varicose veins; back and forth she strides, dashes, runs, climbing cellar stairs or ladders: she unpacks cartons, she toils behind drug counters and fountain counters. Like my father, she is on her feet until one in the morning, the Park View's closing hour. My mother and father are in trouble, and I don't know it. I am too happy. I feel the secret center of eternity, nothing will ever alter, no one will ever die. Through the window, past the lit goldfish, the gray oval sky deepens over our neighborhood wood, where all the dirt paths lead down to seagull-specked water. I am familiar with every frog-haunted monument: Pelham Bay Park is thronged with WPA art—statuary, fountains, immense rococo staircases cascading down a hillside, Bacchus-faced stelae—stone Roman glories afterward mysteriously razed by an avenging Robert Moses. One year—how distant it seems now, as if even the climate is past returning— the bay froze so hard that whole families, mine among them, crossed back and forth to City Island, strangers saluting and calling out in the ecstasy of the bright trudge over such a sudden wilderness of ice.

In the Park View Pharmacy, in the winter dusk, the heart in my body is revolving like the goldfish fleet-finned in their clear bowls. The librarians are still warming up over their coffee. They do not recognize me, though only half an hour ago I was scrabbling in the mud around the two heavy boxes from the Traveling Library—oafish crates tossed with a thump to the ground. One box contains magazines—*Boy's Life*, *The American Girl*, *Popular Mechanix*. But the other, the other! The other transforms me. It is tumbled with storybooks, with clandestine intimations and transfigurations. In school I am a luckless goosegirl, friendless and forlorn. In P.S. 71 I carry, weighty as a cloak, the ineradicable knowledge of my scandal—I am cross-eyed, dumb, an imbecile at arithmetic; in P.S. 71 I am publicly shamed in Assembly because I

4

am caught not singing Christmas carols; in P.S. 71 I am repeatedly accused of deicide. But in the Park View Pharmacy, in the winter dusk, branches blackening in the park across the road, I am driving in rapture through the Violet Fairy Book and the Yellow Fairy Book, insubstantial chariots snatched from the box in the mud. I have never been *inside* the Traveling Library; only grownups are allowed. The boxes are for the children. No more than two books may be borrowed, so I have picked the fattest ones, to last. All the same, the Violet and the Yellow are melting away. Their pages dwindle. I sit at the round glass table, dreaming, dreaming. Mr. Jaffe is murmuring advice. He tells a joke about Wrong-Way Corrigan. The librarians are buttoning up their coats. A princess, captive of an ogre, receives a letter from her swain and hides it in her bosom. I can visualize her bosom exactly—she clutches it against her chest. It is a tall and shapely vase, with a hand-painted flower on it, like the vase on the secondhand piano at home.

I am incognito. No one knows who I truly am. The teachers in P.S. 71 don't know. Rabbi Meskin, my *cheder* teacher, doesn't know. Tessie the lion-eyed landlady doesn't know. Even Hymie the fountain clerk can't know—though he understands other things better than anyone: how to tighten roller skates with a skatekey, for instance, and how to ride a horse. On Friday afternoons, when the new issue is out, Hymie and my brother fight hard over who gets to see *Life* magazine first. My brother is older than I am, and doesn't like me; he builds radios in his bedroom, he is already W2LOM, and operates his transmitter, (*da-di-da-dit, da-da-di-da*) so penetratingly on Sunday mornings that Mrs. Eva Brady, across the way, complains. Mrs. Eva Brady has a subscription to *The Writer*; I fill a closet with her old copies. How to Find a Plot. Narrative and Character, the Writer's Tools. Because my brother has his ham license, I say, "I have a license too." "What kind of license?" my brother asks, falling into the trap. "Poetic license," I reply; my brother hates me, but anyhow his birthday presents are transporting: one year *Alice in Wonderland, Pinocchio* the next, then *Tom Sawyer*. I go after Mark Twain, and find *Joan of Arc* and my first satire, *Christian Science*. My mother surprises me with *Pollyanna*, the admiration of her Lower East Side childhood, along with *The Lady of the Lake*. Mrs. Eva Brady's daughter Jeannie has outgrown her Nancy Drews and Judy Boltons, so on rainy afternoons I cross the street and borrow them, trying not to march away with too many—the child of immigrants, I worry that the Bradys, true and virtuous Americans, will judge me greedy or careless. I wrap the Nancy Drews in paper covers to protect them. Old Mrs. Brady, Jeannie's grandmother, invites me back for more. I am so timid I can hardly speak a word, but I love her dark parlor; I love its black bookcases. Old Mrs. Brady sees me off, embracing books under an umbrella; perhaps she divines who I truly am. My brother doesn't care. My father doesn't notice. I think my mother knows. My mother reads the *Saturday Evening Post* and the *Woman's Home Companion*; sometimes the *Ladies' Home Journal*, but never *Good Housekeeping*. I read all my mother's magazines. My father reads *Drug Topics* and *Der Tog*, the Yiddish daily. In Louie Davidowitz's house (waiting our turn for the rabbi's lesson, he teaches me chess in *cheder*) there is a piece of furniture I am in awe of: a shining circular table that is also a revolving bookshelf holding a complete set of Charles Dickens. I borrow *Oliver Twist*. My cousins turn up with *Gulliver's Travels*, *Just So Stories*, *Don Quixote*, Oscar Wilde's *Fairy Tales*, uncannily different from the usual kind. Blindfolded, I reach into a Thanksgiving grabbag and pull out *Mrs. Leicester's School*, Mary Lamb's desolate stories of rejected children. Books spill out of rumor, exchange, miracle. In the Park View Pharmacy's lending library I discover, among the nurse romances, a browning, brittle miracle: *Jane Eyre*. Uncle Morris comes to visit (*his* drugstore is on the other side of the Bronx) and leaves behind, just like that, a three-volume Shakespeare. Peggy and Betty Provan, Scottish sisters around the corner, lend me their *Swiss Family Robinson*. Norman Foti, a whole year older, transmits a rumor about Louisa May Alcott; afterward I read *Little Women* a thousand times. Ten thousand! I am no longer incognito, not even to myself. I am Jo in her "vortex"; not Jo exactly, but some Jo-of-the-future. I am under an enchantment: who I truly am must be deferred, waited for and waited for. My father, silently filling capsules, is grieving over his mother in Moscow. I write letters in Yiddish to my Moscow grandmother, whom I will never know. I will never know my Russian aunts, uncles, cousins. In Moscow there is suffering, deprivation, poverty. My mother, threadbare, goes without a new winter coat so that packages can be sent to Moscow. Her fiery justice-eyes are semaphores I cannot decipher.

Some day, when I am free of P.S. 71, I will write stories; meanwhile, in winter dusk, in the Park View, in the secret bliss of the Violet Fairy Book, I both see and do not see how these grains of life will stay forever, papa and mama will live forever, Hymie will always turn my skatekey.

Hymie, after Italy, after the Battle of the Bulge, comes back from the war with a present: *From Here to Eternity*. Then he dies, young. Mama reads *Pride and Prejudice* and every single word of Willa Cather. Papa reads, in Yiddish, all of Sholem Aleichem and Peretz. He reads Malamud's *The Assistant* when I ask him to.

Papa and mama, in Staten Island, are under the ground. Some other family sits transfixed in the sun parlor where I read *Jane Eyre* and *Little Women* and, long afterward, *Middlemarch*. The Park View Pharmacy is dismantled, turned into a Hallmark card shop. It doesn't matter! I close my eyes, or else only stare, and everything is in its place again, and everyone.

A writer is dreamed and transfigured into being by spells, wishes, goldfish, silhouettes of trees, boxes of fairy tales dropped in the mud, uncles' and cousins' books, tablets and capsules and powders, papa's Moscow ache, his drugstore jacket with his special fountain pen in the pocket, his beautiful Hebrew paragraphs, his Talmudist's rationalism, his Russian-Gymnasium Latin and German, mama's furnace-heart, her masses of memoirs, her paintings of autumn walks down to the sunny water, her braveries, her reveries, her old, old school hurts.

A writer is buffeted into being by school hurts—Orwell, Forster, Mann!—but after a while other ambushes begin;

sorrows, deaths, disappointments, subtle diseases, delays, guilts, the spite of the private haters of the poetry side of life, the snubs of the glamorous, the bitterness of those for whom resentment is a daily gruel, and so on and so on; and then one day you find yourself leaning here, writing at that self-same round glass table salvaged from the Park View Pharmacy—writing this, an impossibility, a summary of how you came to be where you are now, and where, God knows, is that? Your hair is whitening, you are a well of tears, what you meant to do (beauty and justice) you have not done, papa and mama are under the earth, you live in panic and dread, the future shrinks and darkens, stories are only vapor, your inmost craving is for nothing but an old scarred pen and what, God knows, is that?

WASHINGTON SQUARE, 1946

... this portion of New York appears to many persons the
most delectable. It has a kind of established repose which is
not of frequent occurrence in other quarters of the long, shrill
city; it has a riper, richer, more honorable look than any of
the upper ramifications of the great longitudinal thorough-
fare—the look of having had something of a social history.

HENRY JAMES, *Washington Square*

I FIRST CAME down to Washington Square on a colorless
February morning in 1946. I was seventeen and a half years
old and was carrying my lunch in a brown paper bag, just
as I had carried it to high school only a month before. It
was—I thought it was—the opening day of spring term at
Washington Square College, my initiation into my freshman
year at New York University. All I knew of N.Y.U. then
was that my science-minded brother had gone there; he had
written from the Army that I ought to go there too. With
master-of-ceremonies zest he described the Browsing Room
on the second floor of the Main Building as a paradisal
chamber whose bookish loungers leafed languidly through
magazines and exchanged high-principled witticisms between
classes. It had the sound of a carpeted Olympian club in
Oliver Wendell Holmes's Boston, Hub of the Universe, strewn
with leather chairs and delectable old copies of *The Yellow
Book*.

On that day I had never heard of Oliver Wendell Holmes
or *The Yellow Book*, and Washington Square was a faraway
bower where wounded birds fell out of trees. My brother

9

had once brought home from Washington Square Park a baby sparrow with a broken leg, to be nurtured back to flight. It died instead, emitting in its last hours melancholy faint cheeps, and leaving behind a dense recognition of the minute explicitness of mortality. All the same, in the February grayness Washington Square had the allure of the celestial unknown. A sparrow might die, but my own life was luminously new: I felt my youth like a nimbus.

Which dissolves into the dun gauze of a low and sullen city sky. And here I am flying out of the Lexington Avenue subway at Astor Place, just a few yards from Wanamaker's, here I am turning the corner past a secondhand bookstore and a union hall; already late, I begin walking very fast toward the park. The air is smoky with New York winter grit, and on clogged Broadway a mob of trucks shifts squawking gears. But there, just ahead, crisscrossed by paths under high branches, is Washington Square; and on a single sidewalk, three clear omens; or call them riddles, intricate and redolent. These I will disclose in a moment, but before that you must push open the heavy brass-and-glass doors of the Main Building, and come with me, at a hard and panting pace, into the lobby of Washington Square College on the earliest morning of the freshman year.

On the left, a bank of elevators. Straight ahead, a long burnished corridor, spooky as a lit tunnel. And empty, all empty. I can hear my solitary footsteps reverberate, as in a radio mystery drama: they lead me up a short staircase into a big dark ghost-town cafeteria. My brother's letter, along with an account of the physics and chemistry laboratories (I will never see them), has already explained that this place is called Commons—and here my heart will learn to shake with the merciless newness of life. But not today; today there is nothing. Tables and chairs squat in dead silhouette. I race back through a silent maze of halls and stairways to the brass-and-glass doors—there stands a lonely guard. From the pocket of my coat I retrieve a scrap with a classroom number on it and ask the way. The guard announces in a sly croak that the first day of school is not yet; come back tomorrow, he says.

A dumb bad joke: I'm humiliated. I've journeyed the whole way down from the end of the line—Pelham Bay, in the northeast Bronx—to find myself in desolation, all because of a muddle: Tuesday isn't Wednesday. The nimbus of expectation fades off. The lunch bag in my fist takes on a greasy sadness. I'm not ready to dive back into the subway—I'll have a look around.

Across the street from the Main Building, the three omens. First, a pretzel man with a cart. He's wearing a sweater, a cap that keeps him faceless—he's nothing but the shadows of his creases—and wool gloves with the fingertips cut off. He never moves; he might as well be made of papier-mâché, set up and left out in the open since spring. There are now almost no pretzels for sale, and this gives me a chance to inspect the construction of his bare pretzel poles. The pretzels are hooked over a column of gray cardboard cylinders, themselves looped around a stick, the way horseshoes drop around a post. The cardboard cylinders are the insides of toilet paper rolls.

The pretzel man is rooted between a Chock Full o' Nuts (that's the second omen) and a newsstand (that's the third).

The Chock Full: the doors are like fans, whirling remnants of conversation. *She will marry him. She will not marry him.* Fragrance of coffee and hot chocolate. *We can prove that the senses are partial and unreliable vehicles of information, but who is to say that reason is not equally the product of human limitation?* Powdered doughnut sugar on their lips.

Attached to a candy store, the newsstand. Copies of *Partisan Review*: the table of the gods. Jean Stafford, Mary McCarthy, Elizabeth Hardwick, Irving Howe, Delmore Schwartz, Alfred Kazin, Clement Greenberg, Stephen Spender, William Phillips, John Berryman, Saul Bellow, Philip Rahv, Richard Chase, Randall Jarrell, Simone de Beauvoir, Karl Shapiro, George Orwell! I don't know a single one of these names, but I feel their small conflagration flaming in the gray street: the succulent hotness of their promise. I mean to penetrate every one of them. Since all the money I have is my subway fare—two nickels—I don't buy a copy (the price of *Partisan* in 1946 is fifty cents); I pass on.

11

I pass on to the row of horses on the north side of the Square. Henry James was born in one of these, but I don't know that either. Still, they are plainly old, though no longer aristocratic: haughty last-century shabbies with shut eyelids, built of rosy-ripe respectable brick, down on their luck. Across the park bulks Judson Church, with its squat squarish bell tower; by the end of the week I will be languishing at the margins of a basketball game in its basement, forlorn in my blue left-over-from-high-school gym suit and mooning over Emily Dickinson:

> There's a certain Slant of light,
> Winter Afternoons—
> That oppresses, like the Heft
> Of Cathedral Tunes—

There is more I don't know. I don't know that W. H. Auden lives just down *there*, and might at any moment be seen striding toward home under his tall rumpled hunch; I don't know that Marianne Moore is only up the block, her doffed tricorn resting on her bedroom dresser. It's Greenwich Village—I know *that*—no more than twenty years after Edna St. Vincent Millay has sent the music of her name (her best, perhaps her only, poem) into these bohemian streets: bohemia, the honey pots of poets.

On that first day in the tea-leafed cup of the town I am ignorant, ignorant! But the three riddle-omens are soon to erupt, and all of them together will illumine Washington Square.

Begin with the benches in the Park. Here, side by side with students and their loose-leafs, lean or lie the shadows of the pretzel man, his creased ghosts or doubles: all those pitiables, half-women and half-men, neither awake nor asleep, the discountable, the repudiated, the unseen. No more notice is taken of any of them than of a scudding fragment of newspaper in the path. Even then, even so long ago, the benches of Washington Square are pimpled with this hell-tossed crew, these Mad Margarets and Cokey Joes, these volcanic coughers, shakers, groaners, tremblers, droolers, blasphemers, these public urinators with vomitous breath and rusted teeth—

stumps, dead-eyed and self-abandoned, dragging their make-shift junkyard shoes, their buttonless layers of raggedy ratfur. The pretzel man with his toilet paper rolls conjures and spews them all—he is a loftier brother to these citizens of the lower pox, he is guardian of the garden of the jettisoned. They rattle along all the seams of Washington Square. They are the pickled City, the true and universal City-below-Cities, the wolfish vinegar-Babylon that dogs the spittled skirts of bohemia. The toilet paper rolls are the temple-columns of this sacred grove.

Next, the whirling doors of Chock Full o' Nuts. Here is the marketplace of Washington Square, its bazaar, its roiling gossip parlor, its matchmaker's office and arena—the outermost wing, so to speak, evolved from the Commons. On a day like today, when the Commons is closed, the Chock Full is thronged with extra power, a cello making up for a missing viola. Until now, the fire of my vitals has been for the imperious tragedians of the *Aeneid*; I have lived in the narrow throat of poetry. Another year or so of this oblivion, until at last I am hammer-struck with the shock of Europe's skull, the bled planet of death camp and war. Eleanor Roosevelt has not yet written her famous column announcing the discovery of Anne Frank's diary. The term "cold war" is new. The Commons, like the college itself, is overcrowded, veterans in their pragmatic thirties mingling with the reluctant dreamy young. And the Commons is convulsed with politics: a march to the docks is organized, no one knows by whom, to protest the arrival of Walter Gieseking, the German musician who flourished among Nazis. The Communists—two or three readily recognizable cantankerous zealots—stomp through with their daily leaflets and sneers. There is even a Monarchist, a small poker-faced rectangle of a man with secretive tireless eyes who, when approached for his views, always demands, in perfect Bronx tones, the restoration of his king. The engaged girls—how many of them there seem to be!—flash their rings and tangle their ankles in their long New Look skirts. There is no feminism and no feminists; I am, I think, the only one. The Commons is a tide: it washes up the cold war, it washes up the engaged girls' rings, it washes up the several philosophers and the numerous poets. The philosophers are all Existentialists; the poets are all influenced by "The Waste Land." When the Commons overflows, the engaged girls cross the street to show their rings at the Chock Full.

Call it density, call it intensity, call it continuity: call it, finally, society. The Commons belongs to the satirists. Here, one afternoon, is Alfred Chester, holding up a hair, a single strand, before a crowd. (He will one day write stories and novels. He will die young.) "What is that hair?" I innocently ask, having come late on the scene. "A pubic hair," he replies, and I feel as Virginia Woolf did when she declared human nature to have "changed in or about December 1910"—soon after her sister Vanessa explained away a spot on her dress as "semen."

In or about February 1946 human nature does not change; it keeps on. On my bedroom wall I tack—cut out from *Life* magazine—the wildest Picasso I can find: a face that is also a belly. Mr. George E. Mutch, a lyrical young English teacher twenty-seven years old, writes on the blackboard: "When lilacs last in the dooryard bloom'd," and "Bare, ruined choirs, where late the sweet birds sang," and "A green thought in a green shade"; he tells us to burn, like Pater, with a hard, gem-like flame. Another English teacher—his name is Emerson—compares Walt Whitman to a plumber; next year he will shoot himself in a wood. The initial letters of Washington Square College are a device to recall three of the Seven Deadly Sins: Wantonness, Sloth, Covetousness. In Commons they argue the efficacy of the orgone box. Eda Lou Walton, sprightly as a bird, knows all the Village bards, and is a Village bard herself. Sidney Hook is an intellectual rumble in the logical middle distance. Homer Watt, chairman of the English Department, is the very soul who, in a far-off time of bewitchment, hired Thomas Wolfe.

And so, in February 1946, I make my first purchase of a "real" book—which is to say, not for the classroom. It is displayed in the window of the secondhand bookstore between the Astor Place subway station and the union hall, and for weeks I have been coveting it: *Of Time and the*

14

River. I am transfigured; I am pierced through with rapture; skipping gym, I sit among morning mists on a windy bench a foot from the stench of Mad Margaret, sinking into that cascading syrup: "Man's youth is a wonderful thing: it is so full of anguish and of magic and he never comes to know it as it is, until is it gone from him forever . . . And what is the essence of that strange and bitter miracle of life which we feel so poignantly, so unutterably, with such a bitter pain of joy, when we are young?" Thomas Wolfe, lost, and by the wind grieved, ghost, come back again! In Washington Square I am appareled in the "numb exultant secrecies of fog, fog-numbed air filled with solemn joy of nameless and impending prophecy, an ancient yellow light, the old smoke-ochre of the morning . . ."

The smoke-ochre of the morning. Ah, you who have flung Thomas Wolfe, along with your strange and magical youth, onto the ash heap of juvenilia and excess, myself among you, isn't this a lovely phrase still? It rises out of the old pavements of Washington Square as delicately colored as an eggshell.

The veterans in their pragmatic thirties are nailed to Need; they have families and futures to attend to. When Mr. George E. Mutch exhorts them to burn with a hard, gemlike flame, and writes across the blackboard the line that reveals his own name,

> The world is too much with us; late and soon,
> Getting and spending, we lay waste our powers,

one of the veterans heckles, "What about getting a Buick, what about spending a buck?" Chester, at sixteen, is a whole year younger than I; he has transparent eyes and a rosebud mouth, and is in love with a poet named Diana. He has already found his way to the Village bars, and keeps in his wallet Truman Capote's secret telephone number. We tie our scarves tight against the cold and walk up and down Fourth Avenue, winding in and out of the rows of secondhand book-shops crammed one against the other. The proprietors sit reading their wares and never look up. The books in all their thousands smell sleepily of cellar. Our envy of them is speckled with longing; our longing is sick with envy. We are the sorrowful literary young.

Every day, month after month, I hang around the newsstand near the candy store, drilling through the enigmatic pages of *Partisan Reviews*. I still haven't bought a copy; I still can't understand a word. I don't know what "cold war" means. Who is Trotsky? I haven't read *Ulysses*; my adolescent phantoms are rowing in the ablative absolute with *pius* Aeneas. I'm in my mind's cradle, veiled by the exultant secrecies of fog.

Washington Square will wake me. In a lecture room in the Main Building, Dylan Thomas will cry his webwork syllables. Afterward he'll warm himself at the White Horse Tavern. Across the corridor I will see Sidney Hook plain. I will read the Bhagavad Gita and Catullus and Lessing, and, in Hebrew, a novel eerily called *Whither*? It will be years and years before I am smart enough, worldly enough, to read Alfred Kazin and Mary McCarthy.

In the spring, all of worldly Washington Square will wake up to the luster of little green leaves.

ALFRED CHESTER'S WIG:

IMAGES STANDING FAST

THE OTHER DAY I received in the mail a card announcing the retirement of an old friend, not an intimate, but an editor with whom, over the years, I have occasionally been entangled, sometimes in rapport, sometimes in antagonism. The news that a man almost exactly my contemporary could be considered ready to retire struck me as one more disconcerting symptom of a progressive unreality. I say "one more" because there have been so many others. Passing my reflection in a shop window, for instance, I am taken by surprise by a striding woman with white hair. She is still wearing the bangs of her late youth, but there are shocking pockets and trenches in her face; she has a preposterous dewlap; she is no one I can recognize. Or I am jolted by a generational pang: the discovery that the most able and arresting intellects currently engaging my attention were, when I was first possessed by the passions of mind they have brilliantly mastered, little children.

All the same, whatever assertively supplanting waves may lap around me—signals of redundancy, or of superannuation—I know I am fixed. Or, rather, it is not so much a fixity of self as it is of certain exactnesses, neither lost nor forgotten: a phrase, a scene, a voice, a moment. These exactnesses do not count as memory, and even more surely escape the net of nostalgia or memoir. They are Platonic enclosures, or islands, independent of time, though not of place—in short, they irrevocably *are*. Nothing can snuff them. They are not like candle flames, liable to waver or sputter, and not

17

like windows or looking glasses that streak or cloud. They have the quality of clear photographs or of stone friezes, or of the living eyes in ancient portraits. They are not subject to erasure or dimming.

Upon one of these impermeable Platonic islands, the image of Alfred Chester stands fast. It is likely that this name—Alfred Chester—is no longer resonant in literary circles. As it happens, the editor in question—the one who is now retiring—was among the first to publish Chester. And Chester had his heyday. He knew Truman Capote, or said he did, and Susan Sontag and Paul Bowles and Princess Marguerite Caetani, the legendary aristocrat who sponsored a magazine called *Botteghe Oscure*. He wrote energetically snotty reviews that swaggered and intimidated—the kind of reviews that many young men (and very few young women) in the fifties and sixties wrote, in order to found a reputation. But his real calling was for fiction; and anyhow it was a time when reputations were mainly sought through the writing of stories and novels.

There is another reason, by the way, why these reflections cannot be shrugged off simply as a "memoir," that souvenir elevation of trifles. A memoir, even at its best, is a recollection of what once was: distance and old-fashionedness are taken for granted. But who and what Chester was, long ago, and who and what I was, have neither vanished nor grown quaint. Every new half-decade sprouts a fresh harvesting of literary writers, equally soaked in the lust of ambition, equally sickened (or galvanized) by envy. There is something natural in all this—something of nature, that is. The snows of yesteryear may be the nostalgic confetti of memoir, but last year's writers are routinely replaced by this year's: the baby carriages are brimming over with poets and novelists. Chester, though, has the sorrowful advantage of being irreplaceable, not so much because of his portion of genius (he may not, when all is said and done, deserve this term), as because he was cut down in the middle of the trajectory of his literary growth—so there is no suitable measure, really, by which to judge what he might have been in full maturity. He never came to fruition. He died young.

Or relatively young. He was forty-two. Well, Keats was twenty-five, Kafka forty, and, in truth, we are satisfied: no one feels a need for more Keats or more Kafka. What is there is prodigy enough. It might be argued that Chester had plenty of time to achieve his masterpieces, if he was going to achieve them at all—and yet it is difficult, with Chester, to assent to this. He rarely sat still. Time ran away with him, and hauled him from America to Europe to North Africa, and muddled him, and got in his way. His dogs—repulsive wild things he kept as pets—got in his way. His impatient and exotic loves got in his way. His fears and imaginings got in his way. Finally—the most dangerous condition for any writer—it was the desolation of life itself that got in his way: moral anguish, illness, helpless and aimless wanting, relentless loneliness, decline.

All this I know from the hearsay of that small accumulation of letters and essays and other testimony by witnesses to his latterday bitterness, and the suffering it led to. By then, Chester and I were long since estranged—or merely, on my part, out of touch. I am as certain as I can be of anything that I was never in Chester's mind in the last decade of his life; but he was always in mine. He was a figure, a presence, a regret, a light, an ache. And no matter how remote he became, geographically or psychologically, he always retained the power to wound. He wounded me when he was in Paris. He wounded me when, in 1970, we were both in Jerusalem. And once—much, much earlier—in an epistolary discussion of what we both termed "the nature of love," I wounded him terribly; so terribly that, after those letters were irretrievably written, and read, and answered, our friendship deteriorated. Paris, Tangier, Jerusalem. He lived in all these fabled cities, but I knew him only in New York. I knew him only at—so to speak—the beginning. "In my beginning is my end" was not true for Chester; and having been there at the beginning, I am convinced that he was intended for an end utterly unlike the one he had. I have always believed this—that his life as he was driven to conduct it was a distortion, not a destiny. I even believed that if Chester and I had not been so severely separated, I might have persuaded him (how he would have scoffed at such arrogance) away from what was never, in my view, inevitable.

Unless you count the wig. Chester was the wig's guardian. He was fanatically careful of it in the rain—he wore a rain hat if rain was expected, or, if it was not, covered his head with his coat. He was also the wig's prisoner and puppet; it gave him the life he had, and perhaps the life he eventually chose.

So it is possible, even likely, that I am wrong in my belief—a conviction four decades old—that Chester was not meant to die drugged, drunken, desolate, in the company of a pair of famished wild dogs. It may be—if you count the wig as the beginning—that his end *was* in his beginning, after all. It may be that that orange-yellow wig he so meticulously kept from being rained on determined Chester's solitary death.

Most people called him "Al," and, later, "Alfred." As far as I can tell, except for Mr. Emerson I am the only one who ever called him "Chester," and of course I still call him that. "Chester" has a casual and natural sound to it, and not merely because it can pass as a given name. I go on saying "Chester" because that is how I first heard him referred to. Mr. Emerson regularly said "Chester." Me he called, according to the manners of the time, "Miss." On the other hand, it was not quite the manners of the time; it was a parody of the time before our time; sarcasm and parody and a kind of thrillingly sardonic spite were what Mr. Emerson specialized in. Mr. Emerson's own first name was not accessible to us; in any case, I cannot recollect it. Like Chester in Jerusalem a quarter of a century on, Mr. Emerson either was or was not a suicide. In the summer following our semester with him, the story went, Mr. Emerson stepped into a wood and shot himself. The wood, the shotgun, the acid torque of Mr. Emerson's mouth at the moment of extinction—they all scattered into chill drops of conjecture, drowned in the roil of the thousands of ex-soldiers who were flooding New York University that year. The only thing verifiable in the rumor of Mr. Emerson's suicide was the certainty of his absence: he never came back to teach in the fall.

Mr. Emerson's class was freshman composition, and it was

in this class, in 1946, that Chester and I first met. We were starting college immediately after the war—the Second World War, which my generation, despite Korea and Vietnam, will always call, plainly and unqualifiedly, "the war." The G. I. Bill was in full steam, and Washington Square College—a former factory building that housed the downtown liberal arts branch of N.Y.U.—had reverted to assembly-line procedures for the returning swarms of serious men still in army jackets and boots, many of them New Yorkers, but many of them not: diffident Midwesterners with names like Vernon and Wendell, wretchedly quartered in Long Island Quonset huts together with old-fashioned wives and quantities of babies. To the local teenagers just out of high school, they seemed unimpassioned and literal-minded—grave, patient, humorless old men. Some of them actually *were* old: twenty-seven, thirty-two, even thirty-five. The government, in a historic act of public gratitude, was footing the bill for the higher education of veterans: the veterans, for their part, were intent on getting through and getting jobs. They were nothing if not pragmatic. They wanted to know what poetry and history were *for*.

The truth is, I despised these anxious grownups, in their seasoned khaki, with their sticky domestic worries and ugly practical needs. I felt them to be intruders, or obstacles, or something worse: contaminants. Their massive presence was an affront to literature, to the classical vision, to the purity of awe and reverence, to *mind*. They had an indolent contempt for contemplation, for philosophy, for beauty. There were so many of them that the unventilated lecture halls, thronged, smelled of old shoes, stale flatulence, boredom. The younger students sprawled or squatted in the aisles while the veterans took mechanical notes in childishly slanted handwriting. Their gaze was thickened, dense, as if in trance, exhausted: when, in the first session of the term, a professor of Government (a required course), quoting Aristotle, startled the air with the words "Man is by nature a political animal," they never looked up—as if "animal," used like that, were not the most amazing syllables in the world. Nothing struck them as new, nothing enchanted them, nothing could astonish them. They were a mob of sleepwalkers, heating up the packed corridors and crammed staircases with their sluggish breath and the perpetual fog of their cigarette smoke, inching like a languid deluge from one overcrowded classroom to another. They were too old, too enervated, too indifferent. In the Commons I would hear them comparing used cars. They were despoiling my youth.

And youth was what I was jealous of: youth in combination with literary passion. Nowadays one can hardly set down this phrase—"literary passion"—without the teasing irony of quotation marks representing abashed self-mockery: the silly laughter of old shame. Of course the veterans were, in their sensible fashion, right; they had survived the battle-grounds of catastrophic Europe, had seen mortal fragility and burned human flesh up close, and were preparing for the restoration of their lives—whereas I, lately besotted by the *Aeneid*, by "Christabel," by Shelley's cloud and Keats's nightingale, was an adolescent of seventeen. Chester, though, was not. He was not, as I was, heading for eighteen. He was sixteen still: I envied him for belonging to the other side of the divide. He had the face of a very young child. His skin was as pure and unmarked as a three-year-old's, and he had a little rosy mouth, with small rosy lips. His lips were as beautifully formed as a doll's. His pretty nose was the least noticeable element of his pretty face: the most noticeable was the eyelids, which seemed oddly fat. It took some time—weeks or perhaps months—to fathom that what distinguished these eyelids, what gave them their strangeness, was that they were altogether bald. Chester had neither eyebrows nor eyelashes. He was a completely hairless boy.

He was, besides, short and ovoid, with short active fingers like working pencil erasers. His pale eyes were small and shy; but they had a rapid look, akin to hiding—a kind of skip, a quickstep of momentary caution. We stood at the blackboard in a mostly empty classroom, doodling with the chalk. The veterans, those wearily cynical old men, began straggling in, swallowing up the rows of chairs, while Chester and I made tentative tugs at each other's credentials. He identified himself as a writer. Ordinarily I was skeptical about such claims:

high school had already proved the limitations of the so-called "flair." He told me the name of his high school. I told him the name of mine. I knew without his mentioning it that he had arrived by subway from Brooklyn: I knew it because he had one of the two varieties of Brooklyn speech I could recognize. The first was exceedingly quick: the other was exceedingly slow, dragging out the vowels. Chester's talk sped, the toe of the last sentence stumbling over the heel of the next. A flying fleck of spittle landed on my chin: he was an engine of eagerness. I was, in those days, priggishly speech-conscious, having been subdued by the Shavian Pygmalions of my high school Speech Department, under whose eyes, only a couple of weeks earlier, I had delivered the graduating address. These zealous teachers, missionaries of the glottis and the diaphragm, had effectively suppressed the miscreant Northeast Bronx dentalizations of Pelham Bay—a fragrant nook of meadows and vacant lots overgrown with cattails and wild flowers, archaeologically pocked with the ruins of old foundations: building starts cut off by the Depression, and rotting now into mossy caverns. I lived at the subway's lowest vertebra—the end of the Pelham Bay line: but the ladies of the Speech Department (all three of whom had nineteenth-century literary names, Ruby, Olive, Evangeline) had turned me into a lady, and severed me forever from the hot notes of New York. Chester, rapidfire, slid up and down those notes—not brashly, but minstrel-like, ardent, pizzicato. I saw into him then—a tender, sheltered, eager child. And also: an envious hungry writing beast, and not in embryo. In short, he was myself, though mine was the heavier envy, the envy that stung all the more, because Chester was sixteen and I was not.

The veterans were invisible. We dismissed them as not pertinent. What *was* pertinent was this room and what would happen in it. Here were the veterans, who were invisible; here was a resentful young woman who was to vanish within the week; here was Chester; and Mr. Emerson; and myself, the only surviving female. The young woman who deserted complained that Mr. Emerson never acknowledged her, never called on her to speak, even when her hand was conspicu-

23

ously up. "Woman hater," she spat out, and ran off to another course section. What it came to, then, when you subtracted the veterans, was three. But since Mr. Emerson was what he was—a force of nature, a geological fault, a gorge, a thunderstorm—what it came to, in reality, was two. For Chester and for me, whatever it might have been for the veterans in their tedious hordes, there was no "freshman composition." A cauldron perhaps; a cockpit. Chester and I were roped-off roosters; or a pair of dogs set against each other—pitbulls; or gladiators obliged to fight to the death. All this was Mr. Emerson's scheme—or call it his vice or toy—arbitrarily settled on after the first assignment: a character study, in five hundred words.

On the day the papers were returned, Mr. Emerson ordered me to stand in front of the class—in front of Chester, in effect— and read aloud what I had written. There was an explicit format for these essays: an official tablet had to be purchased at the university bookstore, with blanks to fill in. Then the sheets had to be folded in half, to make a rectangle. The face of the rectangle was for the instructor's grade and comment.

"Read that first sentence!" Mr. Emerson bawled.

I looked down at my paper. There was no grade and no comment.

" 'Gifford was a taciturn man,' " I read.

"Louder! Wake up those sleeping soldiers back there! And keep in mind that I'm a man who's deaf in one ear. What's that goddamn adjective?"

"Taciturn."

"Where'd you swipe it from?"

"I guess I just thought of it," I said.

"Picked it up someplace, hah? Well, what in hell's it *mean*?"

It was true that I had only recently learned this word, and was putting it to use for the first time.

"Does it mean quiet?" I choked out.

"Don't ask *me*, miss. I'm the one that's supposed to do the goddamn asking."

"I think it means quiet."

ALFRED CHESTER'S WIG: IMAGES STANDING FAST

"You think! *I* think you got it out of some trash heap. Read on," he commanded.

He let me continue, quavering, for another paragraph or so. Then his arm shot out like a Mussolini salute.

"All right, miss. Sit! Now you! Chester!"

Chester stood. The somnolent veterans were surprised into alertness: they stared across at the ringmaster and his livestock. Now the rapid Brooklyn voice began—a boy's voice, a boy's throat. The little pink lips—that rosy bouquet—stretched and pursed, looped and flattened. Chester read almost to the end; Mr. Emerson never interrupted. Humiliated, concentrating, I knew what I was hearing. Behind that fragile mouth, dangerous fires curled: a furnace, a burning bush. The coarse cap of false orange-yellow hair shook—it narrowed Chester's forehead, lifted itself off his nape, wobbled along the tops of his ears. He was bold, he was rousing, he was loud enough for a man deaf in one ear. It was ambition. It was my secret self.

"That's enough. Sit, Chester!" Mr. Emerson yelled. "Gentlemen, you'll never find a woman who can write. The ladies can't do it. They don't have what it takes, that's well known. It's universal wisdom, and I believe in it. All the same," he said, "these two, Chester and the lady, I'm not the fool that's going to let them drop back into the pond with the catfish."

After that Chester and I had separate writing assignments—separate, that is, from the rest of the class. Mr. Emerson may have been a woman hater, but it was the veterans he declined to notice and looked to snub. His teaching (if that is what it was) was exclusively for the two of us. It was for our sakes—"that plumber," he sneered—that he disparaged Walt Whitman. It was for our sakes that he devoted minutes every day—irascible still, yet reverential—to praising *Brideshead Revisited*, the Evelyn Waugh bestseller he was reading between classes. And sometimes *in* class: while the veterans slid down in their seats like a silent communal pudding, Mr. Emerson opened to where he had left off and fell into a dry recital:

I was always given the room I had on my first visit; it was next to Sebastian's, and we shared what had once been a dressing-room and had been changed to a bathroom twenty years back by the substitution for the bed of a deep, copper, mahogany-framed bath, that was filled by pulling a brass lever heavy as a piece of marine engineering; the rest of the room remained unchanged; a coal fire always burned there in winter. I often think of that bathroom—the water colours dimmed by steam and the huge towel warming on the back of the chintz armchair—and contrast it with the uniform, clinical little chambers, glittering with chromium-plate and looking-glass, which pass for luxury in the modern world.

Dry, but there was a suppressed rapture in it—rapture for the brass lever, for the water colours (in their transporting British spelling) dimmed by steam. It was clear that Mr. Emerson himself, an unhappy man with tired eyes—they often teared—did not like the modern world; perhaps he would not have liked any world, even one with picturesque coal fires. In the grip of some defenseless fatigue, he gave way to fits of yawning. His snarl was inexhaustible; also comically unpredictable. He took a sardonic pleasure in shock. Certainly he shocked me, newly hatched out of the decorous claims of Hunter High (finishing-school-cum-Latin-prep), where civilization hung on the position of a consonant struck upon the upper gums (never against the teeth), and mastery of the ablative absolute marked one out for higher things. Mr. Emerson said "goddamn," he said "hell," he even alluded, now and then, to what I took to be sexual heat.

It was not that I was ignorant of sexual heat: I had already come upon it in the *Aeneid*; there it was, in Dido and Aeneas. Dido on her pyre, burning for love! And here it was again, between Agnes and Gerald in the dell, in *The Longest Journey*, the early E. M. Forster novel that was included in our freshman composition curriculum. The first paragraphs alone—well before sexual heat made its appearance—were undiluted pleasure:

"The cow is there," said Ansell, lighting a match and holding it out over the carpet. No one spoke. He waited till the end of the match fell off. Then he said again,"She is there, the cow. There, now."

"You have not proved it," said a voice.

"I have proved it to myself."

"I have proved to myself that she isn't," said the voice. "The cow is *not* there." Ansell frowned and lit another match.

"She's there for me," he declared. "I don't care whether she's there for you or not. Whether I'm in Cambridge or Iceland or dead, the cow will be there."

It was philosophy. They were discussing the existence of objects. Do they exist only when there is someone to look at them? or have they a real existence of their own? It is all very interesting, but at the same time it is difficult. Hence the cow. She seemed to make things easier. She was so familiar, so solid.

None of this was familiar in the spring of 1946; E. M. Forster was an unknown name, at least to me; philosophy lay ahead; nothing was solid. Rickie and Ansell were lost in Mr. Emerson's mercurial derisions. For years afterward I remembered only Rickie's limp. Much later I began to read *The Longest Journey* over and over again, until ultimately I had certain passages by heart. In class it was hardly discussed at all. It appeared to hold no interest for Mr. Emerson, and Chester and I never spoke of it. It was not what we read that counted for Mr. Emerson, anyhow; it was what we wrote. Chester and I wrote—were intended to write—as rivals, as yoked competitors under the whip. "Got you that time, didn't she? Made you look small, didn't she?" he chortled at Chester; and, the following week, to me: "Males beat females, it's in the nature of things. He's got the stuff, the genuine shout. He's wiped you out to an echo, miss, believe me." Sometimes he made no comment at all, and gave back our papers, along with the weekly work of the rest of the class, with no more than a cocky glare. That left us stymied; there was no way to find out who had won over the other. Since Mr. Emerson

27

never graded what Chester and I turned in (he routinely graded the others), the only conclusion was that we were both unworthy. And the next week he would be at it again: "She knocked you off your high horse, hah, Chester?" Or: "You'd better quit, miss. You'll never be in the running." All that term we were—Chester and I—a pair of cymbals, ringing and striking in midair; or two panting hares, flanks heaving, in a mad marathon; or a couple of legs-entangled wrestlers in a fevered embrace. It was as if—for whatever obscure reason—Mr. Emerson were some sly, languid, and vainglorious Roman emperor presiding over the bloody goings-on in the Colosseum of his classroom, with the little green buds of Washington Square Park just beginning to unfold below the college windows.

What came out of it, beside a conflagration of jealousy, was fraternity. I loved Chester; he was my brother; he was the first real writer of my generation I had ever met, a thing I knew immediately—it was evident in the increasingly rococo noise of his language, and in Mr. Emerson's retributive glee. If promoting envy was Mr. Emerson's hidden object in instigating the savagery of Chester's competitiveness with me, and mine with him, it is conceivable that it was his own envy Mr. Emerson suffered from, and was picking at. It is not unheard-of for older would-be writers to be enraged by younger would-be writers. The economy of writing always operates according to a feudal logic: the aristocracy blots out all the rest. There is no, so to speak, middle class. The heights belong, at most, to four or five writers, a princely crew; the remainder are invisible, or else have the partial, now-and-then visibility that attaches to minor status. Every young writer imagines only the heights; no one aspires to be minor or invisible, and when, finally, the recognition of where one stands arrives, as it must, in maturity, one either accepts the limitations of fate or talent, or surrenders to sour cynicism. Whether Mr. Emerson was embittered by chances lost or hope denied, or by some sorrowful secret narrowing of his private life, it was impossible to tell. Whichever it was, it threw Chester and me, red in tooth and claw, into each other's arms. It also made us proud: we had been set aside and declared to be of noble blood. (All this, of course, may be retrospective hubris. Perhaps Mr. Emerson saw us as no more than what we were: a couple of literary-minded freshmen whose strenuousness an attentive teacher was generously serving and cultivating.)

We took to walking up and down Fourth Avenue in the afternoons, the two of us, darting into one after another of those rows and rows of secondhand bookstores the long straight street was famous for. The cheapest books were crammed into sidewalk racks under awnings, to protect them from the rain. It seemed always to be raining that spring, a tenderly fickle drizzle and fizz that first speckled and then darkened the pavement and made Chester hood the crown of his head with his jacket. We drilled into back rooms and creaked down wooden basement steps: everywhere those thousands of books had the sewery smell of cellar—repellent, earthen, heart-catching. In these dank crypts, with their dim electric bulbs hanging low on wires over tables heaped with comatose and forgotten volumes, and an infinity of collapsing shelves along broken-plastered brick walls labeled "Theosophy," "History," "Poetry" (signs nailed up decades back, faded and curled by dampness), one could loiter uninterrupted forever. The proprietor was somewhere above, most likely on a folding chair in the doorway, hunched over a book of his own, cozily insulated from the intrusions of customers, bothering nobody and hoping not to be bothered himself. Gradually the cellar smell would be converted, or consecrated, into a sort of blissful incense; nostrils that flinched in retreat opened to the tremulous savor of books waiting to be aroused, and to arouse. Meandering in the skinny aisles of these seductive cellars, Chester and I talked of our childhoods, and of our noses. I admired Chester's nose and deplored my own. "Yours isn't so bad, just a little wide," he said kindly. He told me of his long-ago childhood disease; he did not name it, though he explained that because of it he had lost all his hair. He did not say that he wore a wig.

There was something Hansel-and-Gretelish about our excursions, so brotherly and sisterly, so childlike and intimate, yet prickly in their newness. Fresh from an all-girls high school. I had never before conversed with a boy about books and life. I had never before gone anywhere with a boy. Boys were strangers, and also—in my experience, if not in principle—as biologically unfathomable as extraterrestrials. Though I had a brother, there was a divide between us: he had ascended to college when I was in grade school, and at this hour was still in the army. At home, with my parents at work in their pharmacy, I had the house to myself: I sat at my little wooden Sears, Roebuck desk (a hand-me-down from my brother, the very desk I am using right now), and fearfully pressed out my five hundred words for Mr. Emerson, jealous of what I imagined Chester might be contriving on the same subject, and burning against him with a wild will. I wanted more than anything to beat him; I was afraid he would beat me. When I listened to him read his paper aloud, as Mr. Emerson occasionally had us do even well into the semester, a shrewdly hooked narrative turn or an ingenious figure of speech or some turbulently reckless flash of power would afflict me like a wound. He was startling, he was robust, he was lyrical, he was wry, he was psychological, he was playful, he was scandalous. He was better than I was! In one respect, though, I began to think I was stronger. We were equally attracted to the usual adolescent literary moonings: to loneliness, morbidity, a certain freakishness of personality. But I felt in myself stirrings of history, of idea, something beyond the senses; I was infatuated with German and Latin, I exulted over the Reformation. I supposed it meant I was more *serious* than Chester—more serious, I presumed, about the courses we were enrolled in. Chester was indifferent to all that. Except for English classes, he was careless, unexcited. He was already on his way to bohemianism (a term then still in its flower). I, more naively, more conventionally, valued getting an A; I pressed to excel, and to be seen to excel. I thought of myself as a neophyte, a beginner, an apprentice—it would be years and years (decades, aeons) before I could accomplish anything worth noticing. I regarded my teachers not as gods, but as those who wore the garments of the gods. I was as conscious of my youth as if it were a sealed envelope, and myself a coded message inside it, indefinitely encased, arrested, waiting. But Chester was poking through that envelope with an impatient fist. He was becoming gregarious. He was putting his noisiness to use.

And still he was soft, susceptible. He was easily emotional. I saw him as sentimental, too quickly inflamed. He fell soppily in love at a moment's glance. And because we were brother and sister, I was his confidante; he would tell me his loves, and afterward leave me feeling resentful and deserted. I was not one of the pretty girls; boys ignored me. Their habitual reconnoitering wheeled right over me and ran to the beauties. And here was Chester, no different from the others, with an eye out for looks—flirting, teasing, chasing. Nearly all young women seemed extraordinary that spring: archaic, Edwardian. The postwar fashion revolution, appropriately called the New Look, had descended, literally descended, in the form of long skirts curling around ankles. All at once half the population appeared to be in costume. Only a few months earlier there had been a rigid measure for the length of a skirt: hems were obliged to reach precisely, uncompromisingly, to the lower part of the knee. What else had that meant but an irreversible modernity? Now the girls were all trailing yards and yards of bright or sober stuff, tripping over themselves, delightedly conspicuous, enchanted with their own clear absurdity. Chester chased after them; more often they chased after Chester. When I came to meet him in the Commons nowadays, he had a retinue. The girls moved in on him; so did the incipient bohemians; he was more and more in the center of a raucous crowd. He was beginning to display himself—to accept or define himself—as a wit, and his wit, kamikaze assaults of paradox or shock, caught on. In no time at all he had made himself famous in the Commons—a businesslike place, where the resolute veterans, grinding away, ate their sandwiches with their elbows in their accounting texts. Chester's success was mine. He was my conduit and guide. Without him I would have been buried alive in Washington Square, consumed by timidity.

He journeyed out to visit me twice—a tediously endless subway trip from the bowels of Brooklyn to Pelham Bay. We walked in the barren park, along untenanted crisscross paths, down the hill through the big meadow to the beach. I was proud of this cattailed scene—it was mine, it was my childhood, it was my Brontëan heath. Untrammeled grasses, the gray keen water knocking against mossy stones. Here I was master. Now that Chester was celebrated at school, I warmed to the privilege of having him to myself, steering him from prospect to prospect, until we were light-headed with the drizzly air. At the end of the day, at the foot of the high stair that led to the train, we said goodbye. He bent toward me— he was taller than I, though not by much—and kissed me. The pale perfect lips and their cold spittle rested on my mouth; it was all new. It had never happened before, not with any other boy. I was bewildered, wildly uncertain: I shrank back, and told him I could not think of him like that—he was my brother. (Ah, to retrieve that instant, that Movietone remark learned from the silver screen of the Pilgrim Theater, half a mile down the tracks! To retrieve it, to undo it, to wipe it out!) He wormed his blunt white fingers into his jacket pockets and stood for a while. The el's stanchions shook. Overhead the train growled and headed downtown. Two puddles lay against his lower eyelids, unstanched by the missing lashes. It was the same, he said, with Diana; it was just the same, though Diana wasn't a brute, she hadn't said it outright. He didn't want to be anyone's brother—mine, maybe, but not Diana's. I knew Diana, a brilliant streak in the Commons excitements: in those newfangled long skirts she had a fleet, flashing step, and she wore postwar nylons and neat formal pumps (unrenovated, I was still in my high school sloppy joes and saddle shoes). Diana was one of the beauties, among the loveliest of all, with a last name that sounded as if it had fallen out of a Trollope novel, but was actually Lebanese. In after years I happened on a replica of her face on the salvaged wall of an ancient Roman villa, with its crimson tones preserved indelibly: black-rimmed Mediterranean eyes fixed in intelligence, blackly lit; round cheeks and chin, all creamy pink. An exquisite ur-Madonna. Diana had a generous heart, she was vastly kind and a little shy, with a penetrating attentiveness untypical of the young. Like many in Chester's crew, she was single-mindedly literary. (She is a poet of reputation now.) Chester yearned; and more than anyone, Diana was the object and representation of his yearning.

But I yearned, too. The word itself—soaked in dream and Poesy—pretty well embodies what we were, Chester and I, in a time when there was no ostensible sex, only romance, and the erotic habits of the urban bookish young were confined to daring cafeteria discussions of the orgone box (a contrivance touted by Wilhelm Reich), and severely limited gropings at parties in the parental domicile. One of these parties drew me to Brooklyn—it was my first look at this fabled place. The suburban atmosphere of Flatbush took me by surprise—wide streets and tall brick Tudor-style houses flawed only by being set too closely together. The party, though given by a girl I will call Carla Baumblatt, was altogether Chester's: he had chosen all the guests. Carla would not allow us to enter through the front door. Instead, she herded us toward the back yard and into the kitchen. She had managed to persuade her parents to leave the house, but her mother's admonishments were all around: Carla worried about cigarette ashes, about food spilling, about muddy shoes. She especially worried about the condition of the living room rug; someone whispered to me that she was terribly afraid of her mother. And soon enough her mother came home: a tough, thin, tight little woman, with black hair tightly curled. Carla was big and matronly, twice her mother's size. She had capacious breasts that rode before her, and a homely mouth like a twist of wax, and springy brown hair, which she hated and attempted to squash down. She was dissatisfied with herself and with her life; there was no movie rhapsody in it. An argument began in the kitchen, and there was Carla, cowed by her tiny mother. Curiously, a kitchen scene turns up in Chester's first novel, *Jamie is My Heart's Desire*, published in England in 1956, a decade after Carla's party—the last time she ever tried to give a party at home. The narrator describes a young woman's "largeness": "I have always felt that her body was the wrong one, that it was an exaggerated contrast with her personality, and that one must disregard it in order to know Emily at all. It is her fault I have believed this so long, for in all her ways she had negated the strength and bigness her figure shows, and substituted weakness and dependency and fright, so that one imagines Emily within as a small powerless girl." When Carla reappeared in the living room after quarreling with her mother, she seemed, despite her largeness, a small powerless girl: she was as pale as if she had been beaten, and again warned about dirtying the carpet.

In the middle of that carpet a young woman lay in a mustard glow. Her head was on a fat cushion. Her mustard-colored hair flowed out over the floor. Her mustard-colored New Look skirt was flung into folds all around. She was sprawled there like an indolent cat. Now and again she sat up and perched her chin on her elbow—then the dark trough between her breasts filled with lamplight. She had tiger's eyes, greenly chiaroscuro, dappled with unexpected tinsel flecks. Her name was Tatyana; she gave out the urgency of theater, of Dostoyevsky, of sea gulls. A circle of chairs had somehow grouped in front of her; she had us all as audience, or as a body of travelers stung by a spell into fixity. Carla, stumbling in from the kitchen, seemed devoured by the sight: it was the majesty of pure sexuality. It was animal beauty. Carla's plump stooped shoulders and plump homely nose fell into humility. She called to Chester—they were old neighborhood friends, affectionate old school friends. The familial currents that passed between them had the unearned rhythms of priority. I resented Carla: she had earlier claims than I, almost the earliest of all. I thought of her as a leftover from Chester's former life—the life before Mr. Emerson. It was only sentimentality that continued to bind him to her. She was a blot on his escutcheon. She had no talents other than easy sociability; away from home, in the Commons, she was freely companionable and hospitable: she would catch hold of me in the incoming lunch crowd and wave me over to her table. But we did not like each other. On Chester's account we pretended congeniality. Worse yet, Carla dissembled bookishness; it was an attempt to keep up. In April, on my eighteenth birthday, she astonished me with a present; it was Proust,

Cities of the Plain, in the Modern Library edition. Carla was so far from actual good will that her gift struck me as an intrusion, or an act of hollow flattery, or an appeasement. I owned few books (like everyone else, I frequented the public library), and wanted to love with a body-love the volumes that came permanently into my hands. I could not love a book from Carla. When I eventually undertook to read *Cities of the Plain*, it was not the copy she had given me. I have Carla's copy in front of me now, still unfondled, and inscribed as follows: "*Ma chère—c'est domage que ce livre n'est pas dans l'originale—mais vous devriez être une si marveilleuse linguiste comme moi pour lire cela—Amour toujours—*" Carla's English was equally breezy and misspelled. Her handwriting was a super-legible series of girlish loops. Chester had inherited her along with other remnants of his younger experience. He rested in Carla's sympathy. I imagined she knew the secret of the yellow wig.

Because of Tatyana—the mustard glow on Carla's mother's carpet—Chester was undistractible. When Carla tried to get his attention, he threw out some mockery, but it was to Tatyana. He was a man in a trance of adoration; he was illuminated. Tatyana stretched her catlike flanks and laughed her mermaid's laughter. She was woman, cat, fish—silvery, slithery, mustard-colored. She spread her hair and whirled it. She teased, turned, played, parried, flirted. The room swam with jealousy—not simply Carla's, or mine, or the other girls'. Call it the jealousy of the gods: Tatyana, a mortal young woman, was in the seizure of an unearthly instant. The engines of her eyeballs moved all around with the holy power of their femaleness.

The second and last time Chester came to Pelham Bay, it was in the company of Ben Solomons. Ben had become Chester's unlikely sidekick. Together they were Mutt and Jeff, squat pepperpot and tall broom, Humpty Dumpty and Arthur's handsomest knight. Ben was nicely dressed and not very talkative (taciturn!). He was a little older than I (even weeks counted), and had the well-polished shoes of a serious pre-med student. (When I heard, decades later, that he was Dr. Solomons, the psychiatrist, I was surprised. Not urology? Not gastroenterology?) Since he did not say much, it was hard to assess his intelligence. What mattered to me, though, was his breath, his tallness, his nearness. I had been sickened, that afternoon, by infatuation: out of the blue I was in love with Ben. The lunch my mother had left us had been mysteriously unsatisfactory; it lacked some bourgeois quality I was growing aware of—the plates, the tablecloth, the dining room chairs. It was only food. All my tries at entertainment were a nervous failure. At three o'clock we walked, in the eternal rain (Chester's jacket up over his head), to the next el station to see a movie at the Pilgrim Theater— called, in the neighborhood, the Pillbox, because it was so cramped. In the middle of the day the theater was desolate. I was self-conscious, guilty, embarrassed. It was as if I had dragged us to a pointless moonscape. We settled into the center of the house—myself, Ben, and Chester, in that order, along the row of vacant seats. The movie came on: I suffered. Next to me Ben was bored. Chester tossed out cracks about the dialogue; I laughed, miserably; Ben was silent. Then I shut my eyes, and kept them shut. It was a wall against tears. It was to fabricate boredom and flatter Ben's judgment. It was to get Ben to notice. His big hand on his left knee, with his gold high school graduation ring pressed against the knuckle, drew me into teary desire. I unsealed an eye to be sure that they were still there—the hand, the ring, the knuckle. Ben was sedate, waiting out the hours.

At the time it seemed a long friendship—Chester's with Ben—and, except for that single aching afternoon in Pelham Bay, which came like a fever and passed like a fever, I was as wary of Ben as I was of Carla, as I was of Chester's entrance into Tatyana's apotheosis. Like Byron's sister, I wanted Chester for myself. I soon understood that it was useless: he was a public magnet. Everyone was his straight man and acolyte. To be with Chester was to join his gang at the edge of bohemia, or what was imagined to be bohemia, since all the would-be bohemians went home every night, by subway, to their fathers and mothers in their Bronx and Brooklyn apartments. In our little house in Pelham Bay, I had my own tiny room, flowery with the do-it-yourself yellow wallpaper my mother had put up as a surprise. Onto this surface I pasted, with Scotch tape, a disjointed Picasso woman, cut out from *Life* magazine. She was all bright whorls and stripes and misplaced eyes and ears. She had whirligig breasts. She gave me pride but no pleasure. She stood for eccentricity, for the Unconventional—she was an inkling of what Chester was more consciously heading for. There was nothing of any of this in Ben—no scrambled testing-grounds, no pugnacity, no recklessness, no longing for the inchoate, no unconventionality. No intimations of unknown realms. He was a solid student, with inconspicuous notions; he was conspicuously good-looking, in the style of the familiar hero of a 1940's B movie: broad-shouldered, square-chinned, long-lashed. His chief attraction was the velvety plenitude of his deeply black hair: one wavy lock dropped in a scallop on his forehead, like Superman's. Ben was rarely seen in the Commons. He was not one of Chester's cosmopolitan hangers-on; he was too businesslike, too intent on propriety. But he represented for Chester what my Picasso woman represented for me: the thing closed off, the thing I could not become. I could not become one of the bohemians: I was diffident and too earnest, too "inhibited." I was considered "naive," I was not daring enough. When Chester's gang began to meet in Village bars after classes, I envied but could not follow.

Yellowing on the yellow walls, my cut-out Picasso lingered for years. Chester's attachment to Ben was, by contrast, brief, though while it lasted it was a stretched-out, slow-motion sequence—the stages of a laboratory experiment requiring watchful patience. Ben had the glamorous long torso Chester would have liked to have. He had, especially, the hair. Ben was a surrogate body, a surrogate head of hair. Girls were smitten by him. He was an ambassador from the nation of the normal and the ordinary. When Chester cast off Ben, it was his farewell to the normal and the ordinary. It was the beginning of the voyage out. In the Commons one day, not long after Ben was jettisoned, coming on Chester surrounded by his gang and dangling, between third finger and thumb, a single hair, I asked (the innocent candor of an assistant clown) what it was. "A pubic hair," he retorted.

He was never again not outrageous; he was never again soft. He had determined to shut down the dreamy boy who mooned over girls. Either they rebuffed him, or, worse, embraced him as a friendly pet, good for banter or hilarity. He was nobody's serious boyfriend. Tatyana, after Carla's party, had gone on cosseting him as a plaything to tantalize. Diana, always empathic, withheld the recesses of her heart. I was a literary rival, a puritan and a bluestocking. Carla was an old shoe. (Yet afterward she made herself new: she married into a family of Protestant clergymen and acquired a Scottish surname.) What, after having been so much crushed, was left for Chester's moist sensibility? It dried into celebrity. It dried into insolence and caprice. Chester's college fame depended—was founded—on the acid riposte, the quick sting; on anything implausible. He flung out the unexpected, the grotesque, the abnormal. Truman Capote's short stories were in vogue then, miniature Gothic concoctions specializing in weird little girls, in clairvoyance, in the uncanny. Chester began modeling his own stories on these. He committed to memory long passages from an eerie narrative called "Miriam"; he was bewitched by Truman Capote's lushness, mystery, baroque style. In his own writing he was gradually melting into Truman Capote. He opened his wallet and pulled out an address book: that number there, he bragged, was Truman Capote's unlisted telephone, set down by the polished little master himself.

All this while Chester was wearing the yellow wig. He wore it more and more carelessly. It was as curly as a sheep's belly, and now took on a ragged, neglected look, grimy. It hardly mattered to him if it went askew, lifting from his ears or pressing too far down over where the absent eyebrows should have been.

In 1966 he published a portion of *The Foot*, an abandoned novel that is more diary and memoir than fiction. By then his style was entering its last phase, disjointed, arbitrary, surreal—deliberately beautiful for a phrase or two, then deliberately unbeautiful, then dissolved into sloth. The characters are mercurial fragments or shadowless ghosts, wrested out of exhaustion by a drugged and disintegrating will: Mary Monday and her double, also named Mary Monday, a play on Susan Sontag; Peter Plate, standing for Paul Bowles, whom Chester knew in Morocco: Larbi ("the Arab"), Chester's cook, servant, and sexual companion. All changing themes and short takes, *The Foot* is part travelogue (portraits of Morocco and of New York), part writhing confession ("my long idle life, always occupied with my suffering," "I am afraid of who I am behind my own impersonations"), and part portentous pointless fantasy. The effect is of a home slide-show in a blackened room: the slides click by, mainly of gargoyles, and then, without warning, a series of recognizable family shots flashes out—but even these responsible, ordinary people are engaging in gargoylish activity. In this way one impressionist sketch after another jumps into the light, interrupted by satiric riffs—satiric even when mildly pornographic—until five heartbreaking pages of suffering recollected without tranquility all at once break out of their frames of dread, cry their child's cry, and fall back into the blackness. "Do you let a book like this, this book, go back into the world just as it is—with its wounds and blemishes, its bald head and lashless eyes, exposed to the light?" the section starts off, and darkens into a melancholy unburdening:

> I was fourteen when I put on my first wig. It was, I believe, my sister's idea. So she and my mother and I went—I forget where . . . Simmons & Co?—some elegantish salon with gold lamé drapes where they did not do such splendid work.
>
> I sat and accepted the wig. It was like having an ax driven straight down the middle of my body. Beginning at the head. Whack! Hacked in two with one blow like a dry little tree. Like a sad little New York tree.
>
> I wore it to school only. Every morning my mother put it on for me in front of the mirror in the kitchen and carefully combed it and puffed it and fluffed it and pasted it down. Then, before going out of the house, I

would jam a hat on top of it, a brown fedora, and flatten the wig into a kind of matting. I hated it and was ashamed of it, and it made me feel guilty.

And so to school. The Abraham Lincoln High School.

Up until then I'd gone to a Yeshiva where all the boys wore hats, little black yarmulkas. I too wore a hat, though not a yarmulka, which only covered the tip of the head. I wore a variety of caps. I'd wear a cap to shreds before getting a new one, since I felt any change at all focused more attention on my head . . .

Coming home from school was a problem. As once the world had been divided for me into Jews and Italians, it was now divided between those who could see me with the wig [and hat] and those who could see me [only] with a hat. Only my most immediate family—mother, father, sister, brother—could see me with both, and only they could see me bald.

Hat people and wig people. Wig people at school. Hat people at home. The wig people could see me with both wig *and* hat (hat-on-top-of-wig, that is). But the hat people must never see me with wig, or even with wig and hat.

This went on for years, decades.

The terror of encountering one side in the camp of the other. Of the wig people catching me without the wig. Of the hat people catching me with it. Terror . . .

And then, there from the corner where the trolley stopped, if it was a fair day, I would see my mother and maybe an aunt or two or a neighbor sitting on our porch in the sun.

Hat people.

Horrible, unbearable, the thought of walking past those ladies to get into the house . . . Sometimes I would go around corners, down alleys, through other people's gardens to reach our back fence. I'd climb over the back fence so I could get into the house via the back door which was usually open.

A thief! Just like a thief I'd have to sneak through the side lanes, unseen across backyards . . .

I could bear no references to the wig. If I had to wear it, all right. But I wasn't going to talk about it. It was like some obscenity, some desperate crime on my head. It was hot coals in my mouth, steel claws gripping my heart, etc. I didn't want to recognize the wig . . . or even my baldness. It just wasn't there. Nothing was there. It was just something that didn't exist, like a third arm, so how could you talk about it? But it hurt, it hurt . . .

My second wig was a much fancier job than the first. An old Alsatian couple made it; I think they were anti-Semitic, she out of tradition, he out of fidelity to her.

When the wig was ready, my father and mother and I went to collect it. Evening. I wish I could remember my father's reaction. Mama probably fussed and complained. I imagine Papa, though, like me, simply pretending that the whole thing didn't exist, wasn't even happening . . .

Anyway, most likely, he said something polite like— how nice it looks! . . .

But the evening of the new wig we went to a restaurant, me wearing the wig. A white-tiled Jewish restaurant. Vegetarian . . . With fluorescent lights . . .

I just want you to see the three of us—even at home we never ate together—at that white-linened, white-tiled, blue-white-lighted restaurant . . .

I wonder what we ate that night or why the evening took place at all. It is such a strange thing for Papa to have done. Gone to the wigmakers at all. Met me and Mama in the city. Taken us out to supper.

Perhaps there were a lot of mirrors in that restaurant. Catching a glimpse of myself, wig or no, is dreadful for me. I have to approach a mirror fully prepared, with all my armor on.

But I have a turn-off mechanism for mirrors as well. The glimpse-mirrors, I mean. I simply go blind.

When Chester set down these afflicted paragraphs, he was thirty-seven years old. He had long ago discarded the wig. He had long ago discarded our friendship. He had ascended into the hanging gardens of literary celebrity: *Esquire* included him in its annual Red Hot Center of American writing, and he was a prolific and provocative reviewer in periodicals such as *Partisan Review* and *Commentary*. He had lived in Paris, close to the founding circle of *Paris Review*: at parties he drank with Jimmy Baldwin and George Plimpton. He had been drawn to Morocco by Paul Bowles, the novelist and composer who, according to legend, ruled in Tangier like a foreign mandarin, ringed by respectful disciples and vaguely literary satellites devoted to smoking hemp. In Tangier Chester finally took off the wig for good; I, who had known him only when he was still at home with his family in Brooklyn, never saw him without it. His anguish was an undisclosable secret. The wig could not be mentioned, neither by wig-wearer nor by wig-watcher. No one dared any kind of comment or gesture. Yet there were hints—protective inklings—that Ben Solomons had somehow passed through this taboo: on the rainy day Chester brought him to Pelham Bay, it was Ben who, with a sheltering sweep around Chester's shoulders, made the first move to raise Chester's jacket up over his matted crown.

Gore Vidal, in his introduction to a posthumous collection, including *The Foot*, of Chester's fiction (*Head of A Sad Angel: Stories 1953–1966*, edited by Edward Field and published by Black Sparrow Press in 1990), speaks of Chester's life as "a fascinating black comedy." "Drink and drugs, paranoia and sinister pieces of trade did him in early," he concludes. I suppose he is not wrong. Yet "sinister pieces of trade" is an odious locution and a hard judgment, even if one lacks, as I confess I do, the wherewithal—i.e., the plain data—to see into its unreachable recesses. Vidal calls Chester "Genet with a brain." But if Vidal is alluding to the bleaker side of homosexual mores, Chester himself can be neither his source nor his guide; Chester's breezy erotic spirit has more in common with the goat-god Pan at play than with Genet in prison, digging a recording pencil into brown paper bags. (Genet's portraits of homosexuals were anyhow tantamount to heartbreak for Chester. "The naked truth of Genet's writing," he remarked in a 1964 review of *Our Lady of the Flowers*, "continues to be unbearable." And he noted that even "the ecstatic whole of [a] masterpiece" is "cold comfort to a man in agony.")

Except for that single passage in *The Foot*, nothing in Chester's mind was not literary. His life, nearly all of it, was a lyrical, satirical, or theatrical mirage. In the end the mirage hardened into a looking glass. But what was not strained through literary affectation or imitation or dreamscape, what it would be crueler than cruel to think of as black comedy, is the child's shame, the child's naked truth, that hits out like a blast of lightning in the middle of *The Foot*. The child is set apart as a freak. And then the bald boy grows into a bold man: but inside the unfinished man—unfinished because the boy has still not been exorcised—the hairless child goes on suffering, the harried boy runs. "I did have the great good luck never to have so much as glimpsed Alfred Chester." Vidal admits; nevertheless he does not hesitate to name him "a genuine monster." It may require a worldly imagination of a certain toughened particularity—i.e., a temperament familiar with kinkiness and hospitable to it—to follow Vidal into his conjectures concerning Chester's sexual practices ("sinister pieces of trade"), but one must leave all heartlessness behind in order to enter the terrors of the man, or the child, who believes he is a monster.

And it was only baldness. Or it was not so much baldness as wig. From any common-sense point of view, baldness is not a significant abnormality, and in the adult male is no anomaly at all. But the child felt himself to be abnormal, monstrous: the child was stricken, the child saw himself a frenzied freak tearing down lane after lane in search of a path of escape.

That path of escape (I was sure of this four decades ago, and am partly persuaded of it even now) was homosexuality—implying an alternative community, an alternative ethos, an alternative system of getting and receiving attention. Chester loved women; women would not love him back; Q.E.D. They would not love him back because, by his own reckoning, he was abnormal, monstrous, freakish. He was too horrifically ugly. With this gruesome impetus, he turned his hairless, beardless, lashless countenance to the alternative world, a world without women, where no woman could wound him because no woman belonged.

All this—folded invisibly, or not so invisibly, into notions of "the nature of love"—I wrote to Chester, in a letter sent to Paris. I had heard that he had "become homosexual." (A term learned at Washington Square College—not from Mr Emerson—at eighteen. "Gay" had not yet come into general use.) We had been corresponding, not without acrimony, about Thomas Mann. Chester was contemptuous. "Middle-brow," he growled from across the sea, 'Somerset Maugham in German," though he had so far not approached a word of anything by Mann. I urged him to read *Death in Venice*. He wrote back, exalted. It was, he said, among the great works of literature; he declared himself converted. By then we had been separated for two or three years. He had gone off to be an expatriate in the second Parisian wave—modeled on Hemingway and Gertrude Stein in the first—and I, return-ing from graduate school in the Midwest, had settled back into my tiny yellow bedroom in Pelham Bay to become a writer. My idea was to produce a long philosophical novel that would combine the attributes of André Gide, Henry James, George Eliot, Graham Greene, and Santayana's *The Last Puritan*; it was an awkward and juvenile sort of thing, and kept me in the dark for years. Chester, meanwhile, was writing and actually publishing short stories in newly estab-lished postwar periodicals—*Merlin, Botteghe Oscure, Paris Review, Proefscrift*. It was the era of the little magazines: these, springing up in Europe, had a luster beyond the merely contemporary. They smacked of old literary capitals, of Americans abroad (Scott and Zelda), of bistros, of Sartre and Simone de Beauvoir, of existentialist ennui. They were as intellectually distant from my little desk in Pelham Bay as it was possible to be. The Scotch tape that held my Picasso woman on the wall turned brittle; superannuated, she fell to pieces and was put in the trash. Chester in Paris was well into the beginnings of an international reputation—he was brilliantly in the world—while I, stuck in the same room where I had fussed over Mr. Emerson's assignments, was only another tormented inky cipher. I had nothing of the literary life but my trips on the bus to the Westchester Square Public Library, and the changing heaps of books these occasioned.

The letters from Paris crowed. Chester made it plain that he had arrived, and that I had been left behind. He condescended, I smarted. *Death in Venice* brought him up short. Literature—its beauty and humanity—had nothing to do with the literary barometer, with ambition and rivalry and the red-hot center. Only the comely sentence mattered. The sentence!

> With astonishment Aschenbach noted that the boy was absolutely beautiful. His face, pale and reserved, framed with honey-colored hair, the straight sloping nose, the lovely mouth, the expression of sweet and godlike seriousness, recalled Greek sculpture of the noblest periods; and the complete purity of the form was accompanied by such a rare personal charm that, as he watched, he felt that he had never met with anything equally felicitous in nature or the plastic arts.

We began to talk, as we never had before, of the varieties of human attraction. He was not "naturally" homosexual, I insisted; I *knew* he was not; he knew it himself. I reminded him of his old stirrings and infatuations. I made no mention of the old rebuffs. I felt a large, earnest, and intimate freedom to say what I thought—we had between us, after all, a history of undisguised tenderness. And had he not yearned after Diana? He was not obliged, or destined, to be homosexual; he had chosen dramatic adaptation over honest appetite.

His reply was a savage bellow. The French stamps running helter-skelter on the envelope had been licked into displacement by a wild tongue, and pounded down by a furious fist. He roared back at me, in capital letters, "YOU KNOW NOTHING ABOUT LOVE!"

He broke with me then, and I saw how I had transgressed. Privately I took virulence to be confirmation. He was protesting too much. His rage was an admission that he had followed the path of escape rather than the promptings of his own nature. He was not what he seemed; he was an injured boy absurdly compelled to wear a yellow wig. Shame gave him the power of sham—an outrageously idiosyncratic, if illusional, negation of his heart's truth. He could, as it were, hallucinate in life as vividly as on a page of fiction; he had license now for anything.

Chester is long dead, and though I speak retrospectively about the letter that exasperated him and put an end to our friendship, there are living voices much like his own, and probably just as exasperated. They will claim I am simple-minded in theorizing that Chester's self-revulsion (sad little New York tree grown into blindness before mirrors) was the true engine of his turning from women. Gay men will know better than I, bisexual men will know better, psychologists and psychoanalysts will know better. And yes, I know nothing about it. Or, rather, I know that no one knows anything about it: about the real sources of homosexuality. Besides, not every boy who supposes himself unattractive to girls will become a man who courts men. No doubt hundreds, if not thousands, of young men unhappy with their looks and their lives have moved on to conventionally heterosexual arrangements, including marriage. A wig is above all super-ficial: its site is on top of the head, not inside it. Proclivities are likely innate, not pasted on to accommodate circum-stance. The homoerotic matrix may inhabit the neural system.

These are fair objections. But how can I surrender what I genuinely saw? I saw that Chester had once loved. and had wanted to be loved by, women. Believing himself radically unfit, he sought an anodyne. Homosexuality was, at least initially, a kind of literary elixir. It brought him apparitions. Who does not recall, on the dust jacket of *Other Voices, Other Rooms*, the photograph of the beautiful young Truman Capote in a tattersall vest, reclining on a sofa, indolent as an obalisque, with lucent galactic eyes? And what of those luring draughts of Paris and North Africa—brilliant Proustian scenes, Durrellian sweeps of albino light? Anodyne; elixir; apparition. Beyond this, my understanding dims. I cannot pursue Chester into his future; I was not witness to it.

After our last exchange, I never expected to hear from him

again. I recognized that I had inflicted a violent hurt—though I had no accurate measure of that violence, or violation, until long afterward, when I came on *The Foot* and the "ax driven straight down the middle of my body."

But Chester had his revenge; he repaid me wound for wound. If I had intruded on his erotic turf, he, it developed, would tread on ground equally unnameable—our rivalry, or what was left of it. Nothing, in fact, was left of it. Chester was publishing, and being talked of, in Paris and New York. I was still futilely mired in my "ambitious first novel," which reached three hundred thousand words before I had the sense to give up on it. Mr Emerson had pushed us into a race, and Chester had indisputably won.

About two years after I had lectured him on love, I took the bus to the post office and mailed a short story to Italy— to *Botteghe Oscure*, at an address in Rome. It had already been submitted to *The New Yorker*, for which I had hungrily but mistakenly designed it, relying on some imitative notion of what "a *New Yorker* story" was in those days reputed to be. The story was a failure—the characters were artificial and brittle, the theme absurd. When it was rejected, instead of disposing of my folly, with the recklessness of envy I thought of Chester's dazzlements in *Botteghe Oscure*. He had matured quickly. Whereas I was still writing what I would eventually classify as juvenilia, Chester's Paris stories were exquisite, and more—focused and given over to high diction, they seemed the work of an old hand. They had the tone and weight of translations from this or that renowned classical European author whose name you could not quite put your finger on: Colette, or Lampedusa, or the author of *Death in Venice*. Their worked and burnished openings were redolent of delectable old library books: "Once, in autumn, I sat all night beside the immense stone wall that surrounds the ancient cemetery of Père Lachaise." Or: "Our appointment was for after lunch, down the street from my house in a little formal park full of trees and flowers called the Garden of the Frog." When I reread these early stories now, they some- times have, here and there, a poison drop of archaism—as if the 1950s had all collapsed into the very, very long ago. And

I am startled to notice that we were writing then—both of us—in what from this distance begins to look like the same style, possessed, in the manner of the young, by the ravishments of other voices.

Several months went by. A letter from Paris! But Chester and I had stopped corresponding. He had cut me off and thrown me out. It was a period, I discovered later, when he was writing hundreds of letters, a number of them to new friends made at Columbia University, where, after college, he was briefly enrolled as a graduate student. When his father died and left him a little money, he escaped courses and schedules and headed for Mexico, and then on to Paris. With no constraints now, he was fashioning a nonconformist life for himself—partly out of books, but mainly inspired by the self-proclaimed expatriate nonconformists who were doing exactly the same. He had made it plain that there was no place in that life for me. Impossible, after our rupture, that I would hear from him; yet I knew no one else in Paris. I looked again at the letter. In the upper left-hand corner, in faint green rubber-stamped print, were two intoxicating words: *Botteghe Oscure*. The big manila envelope with my story in it, containing another big manila envelope for its return, had been addressed to Rome. This was not a big manila envelope; no manuscript was being returned; it was a thin small letter. Why from Paris, why not from Rome? *Botteghe Oscure* had its headquarters, whatever they might be (a row of dark shops), in Rome. Princess Marguerite Caetani, the founder, sponsor, and deep pockets of *Botteghe Oscure*, was a princess of Italy; but ah, nobility travels glitteringly from capital to capital. Princess Caetani—it must be she—was writing not from Rome, where the season had ended, but from a grand apartment in Paris, in the grandest *arrondissement* of all, not far from a little formal park full of trees and flowers. She had put aside her gold-embossed lorgnette to pick up a silver-nibbed pen. A thin green sheet peeped from the thin small envelope. I drew the paper out in a strange kind of jubilation, half-regretful—it was late, nearly too late, for this glimmer of good fortune. It was years after Chester's success, though we had set out together. I had been writing seriously since the age of twenty-two, and had never yet been published—all my literary eggs, so far, were in that dubious basket of an unfinished, unfinishable novel.

I recognized the handwriting in an instant. The letter was not from the Princess. Chester was reading for the Princess, he explained, winnowing, going through the pile of awful things the mail habitually brought—the Princess sent everything over from Rome. You wouldn't believe what awful things he was obliged to slog through. Well, here was my story. It wasn't all that good, he liked a few things in it, they weren't completely awful—he would make sure the Princess got his recommendation anyhow.

Chester on Mount Olympus, tossing crumbs. Humiliation: my story was published in *Botteghe Oscure*. He had won, he had won.

What happened afterward I gathered from rumor and report. Chester left Paris in 1959. Between 1959 and 1963 he lived in New York, and so did I. We never met, spoke, or wrote. As always, he was noisily surrounded, prodding to get a rise out of people, on the lookout for adventures, upheavals, darkening mischiefs. His reviews, of books and theater, were as ubiquitous as sky-writing: you looked up, and there he was. For a while he abandoned the wig, then put it on again. Edmund Wilson, notorious for crusty reclusiveness, sent him a fan letter. But he was restless and ambitious for more, especially for fame of the right sort. He wanted to be writing stories and novels. In 1960 he went off to the perilously companionable isolation of the MacDowell Colony—a retreat in rural New Hampshire for writers, artists, and composers—and stumbled into a private loneliness so absolute that he was beginning to populate it with phantom voices. Unable to sustain his own company, he took on the more engaging job of busybody and troublemaker, begging for attention by riling everyone in sight. In letters that have since been published (how this would have delighted him: he did nothing not for dissemination), he complained to a pair of friends back in New York:

They all have cars and seem rich. Except some of the painters. They see me walking into town and wave to me as they fly by in their convertibles on their way to lakes and cookouts. They are mainly dumb. They are very square. Nobody's queer, not even me anymore. Besides I hate myself too. I can't stand it anymore not having any stable I. It is too much. Thrust into a totally new situation, here, I don't know who I am. My neighbor Hortense Powdermaker walks by and I feel some creature in me rise. I just want to scream fuck I am alfred chester who? But no one will believe me, not even me, who is writing this now? . . . And the voices in my head go on and on. As there is no me except situationally, I have to have mental conversation in order to be . . . Ugh. It's to die . . . WRITE TO ME WRITE TO ME WRITE TO ME AS I FADE AWAY WITH LONELINESS.

I have had a blowout with Mme. Powdermaker at breakfast this morning and am still quivering. I come to the table, at which she, Ernst Bacon, Leon Hartl (a French painter I adore), and Panos, a Greek, sit. Morning, Powdie, say I, for I have been shaking since last night, aching to give it to her. Aching to give it to most of them in fact, this rude, ungenerous, terrified, ungiving teaparty group who preserve nothing but the surface, so illmannered and illbred, so lacking in spirit . . . Last night I decided I was no longer going to submit, but to rebel against every act of unkindness. The colony is in an uproar . . . First of all I have been persona non grata since last Saturday night when I danced with Gus the cook at the MacDowell version of wild party in Savidge Library . . . Gus wanted to fuck me but I wouldn't let him because of his wife. There has been a party every day since, sometimes twice a day, to which I have been cordially uninvited by the wild young set. I don't mind. It is all like a tea party with the people made of china. But what I do mind is their hypocrisy, the extreme courtesy toward someone they can't bear: me. I also mind their bad manners, like leaving me to put away the pieces in the scrabble board, or Powdie saying yes, very snidely, yes she'd guessed I was a Russian Jew.

There followed a dustup over Chester's having requested Hortense Powdermaker for a lift in her car, which, according to Chester's account, she refused, deliberately allowing him to stand futilely in the road in the dark of a summer's night.

It got pretty hysterical after this and the other tables as well as the kitchen staff were hysterical . . .

She: (to Ernst Bacon) As head of the house committee, I wish you would take the matter up with this young man. I'm not obliged to be anyone's chauffeur. It is customary to wait to be offered something. Not to ask for it. You're a brash young man. You don't know anything about communal living. You have no place in this colony.

After an official dressing-down, he was asked to leave MacDowell. He was, as he put it in a telegram, "flung out." He announced that Gus, the cook, and Gus's wife, were departing with him, along with Chester's two rambunctious dogs, Columbine and Skoura, who had sunk their teeth into assorted mattresses and the body parts of other residents. (He had been given special permission to bring the dogs with him to MacDowell. He was also supplied with a new typewriter and "a full-length mirror for my yoga.") "And he is lovely," he said of himself. "I love him. He is sweet and cute . . . O I'm so much gladder to be me than all these pathetic silly other people."

Half a decade later, he was similarly flung out of Morocco, where he had been living since 1963, invited there by Paul Bowles. A young Arab fisherman named Dris, who practiced sympathetic witchcraft and genial conning, became his lover, factotum, and dependent. "It is traditional in Morocco," Chester remarks in a story ("Glory Hole," subtitled "Nickel Views of the Infidel in Tangier"), "to pay for sex. There are nicer, but not truer, ways of putting it. The lover gives a gift to the beloved: food, clothing, cash. The older pays the younger." It was not because of his sexual conduct that Chester was expelled from Morocco. Tangier was, one might say, a mecca for "Nazarene" homosexuals from the States, who were as officially welcome as any other dollar-bearing visitors. As far as anyone can make out, Chester's landlord complained to the authorities about the savagery of Chester's dogs, and of Chester's own furies, his fits of quarreling with the neighbors over the racket their numerous children made. At MacDowell he had brought in booze to supplement the bland fare in the dining room. In Tangier he turned to pills and *kif*, a local hallucinogen, and fell into spells of madness. Bounced out of Morocco, he fled to New York and then to London, where he was deranged enough to be tended by a psychiatric social worker. He repeatedly attempted to be allowed back into Morocco, enlisting Paul Bowles to intervene for him. Tangier remained obdurate.

In 1970 I was in Jerusalem for the first time, to read a literary paper at a conference. I had published, four years earlier, a very long "first" novel that was really a third novel. It was sparsely reviewed, and dropped, as first novels are wont to do, into a ready oblivion. In Jerusalem, though, I was surprised by a fleeting celebrity: my essay—many thousands of words, which had taken nearly two hours to deliver—was reprinted almost in its entirety, along with my picture, in the weekend book section of the English-language *Jerusalem Post*. All this I saw as fortuitous and lucky bait.

Chester was now living in Jerusalem. The moment I arrived in Israel I tried to find him. I had been given the address of a poet who might know how to reach him, but the poet was himself inaccessible—he was sick and in the hospital. I waited for Chester to come to me. I felt hugely *there*; you couldn't miss me. The *Post* had published, gratuitously, the biggest "personals" ad imaginable. Every day I expected Chester's telephone call. It had now been fourteen years since he had winnowed on behalf of the Princess, and more than two decades since I had looked into his bleached and lashless eyes. I longed for a reunion; I thought of him with all the old baby tenderness. I wanted to be forgiven, and to forgive. In contemplating the journey to Israel, my secret, nearly single-minded, hope had been to track him down. In New York his reputation had dwindled: his name was no longer scrawled across the sky. An episodic "experimental" novel, *The Exquisite Corpse* (horrific phantasmagoria bathed in picture-book prose that Chester himself called "delicious"), appearing three years before, had left no mark. Even rumors of Chester's travels had eluded me: I had heard nothing about the life in Morocco, or of his meanderings in Spain and Greece and Sicily; I had no idea of any of it. Jealousy, of Chester or anyone, had long ago burned itself out. It was an emotion I could not recognize in myself. I was clear of it—cured. The ember deposited on the cold hearth of Mr Emerson's ancient conflagration was of a different nature altogether: call it love's cinder. It lay there, black and gray, of a certain remembered configuration, not yet disintegrated. Chester did not turn up to collect it.

He did not turn up. He was already dead, or dying, or close to dying—perhaps even while I was walking the curved and flowering streets of Jerusalem, searching for the ailing poet's house, the poet who was to supply the clue to Chester's whereabouts.

Why had Chester come to Jerusalem? In 1967, back in Paris again, he put on a new English fedora over his now exposed and glossy scalp, and plunged into the byways of the Marais to seek out a synagogue. Not since his boyhood in the yeshiva had he approached the Hebrew liturgy. Despite this singular visit, his habits continued unrestrained and impenitent. He drank vodka and bourbon and cognac by the quart, smoked *kif* and hashish, took barbiturates and tranquilizers, and was unrelentingly, profoundly, mercilessly unhappy.

In Jerusalem he set to work on a travel report, never published, called "Letter from the Wandering Jew"—a record, really, of personal affronts, most of them provoked by loneliness in quest of sensationalism. In it he purports to explain why he had left Europe for Israel. "No reads lead to Israel," the manuscript begins. A parenthesis about the opening of a "sex-aids" shop in Tel Aviv follows. And then:

Why I came is a very long story, a couple of thousand years long, I suppose. I'd been living unhappily in France since May, I and my two dogs Momzer [Hebrew for "bastard"] and Towzer who are Arabs, having been born in Morocco. The idea of Israel had been with me for some time, a kind of latent half-hearted hope that there was a place on this planet where people who had suffered had come together to shelter each other from pain and persecution: a place of lovingkindness. Besides, does a Jew ever stop being a Jew? Especially one like me whose parents had fled the Russian pogroms for the subtler barbarisms of New York? Yiddish was as much my first language as English, and Hebrew came soon after, for, [since I was his] a youngest and belated child, my father was determined that at least one of his sons would be a good Jew.

This faintly sentimental opening (not counting the parenthesis) misrepresents. The rest is bitter stuff, bitter against father and mother, against going to school, against childhood and children, against teachers and rabbis and restaurants and waiters, against God ("that pig called Jehovah"), against France and the French, against Arab hotels and Jewish hotels, against Arabs, against Jews, against traffic noise, even against the scenery. Once again there are the rows over the dogs, flocks of urchins teasing, exasperated neighbors, bewildered policemen. There are forays after eccentric houses to rent; unreasonable landlords; opportunistic taxi drivers. There are rages and aggression and digression and jokes in the mode of sarcasm and jokes in the mode of nihilism. Satire wears out and reverts to snideness, and snideness to open fury. Eventually vodka and Nembutal and little blue Israeli transquilizers take charge of the language—now gripping, now banal, now thrilling, now deteriorated, now manic, now shocking. At moments it is no more than pretty, a make-do remnant of what was once a literary style:

The neighborhood was quiet, the house pleasant and sunny; the dogs had a great garden to run around in

54

and there was a pack of ferocious Airedales next door to bark at all the time. Flowers grew all through the winter—roses, narcissi, pansies, and lots of others whose names I don't know—and when spring came, virtually on the heels of [winter], the roof of the house went absolutely crazy with those gorgeous Mediterranean lilacs that have hardly any smell but almost make up for it by the tidal madness of their bloom.

"Letter from the Wandering Jew" was Chester's last performance. A paranoid document, it is not without self-understanding. The Promised Land is always over the crest of the hill, and then, when you have surmounted the hill and stepped into the lovely garden on the other side, you look around and in ten minutes discover that everything has been corrupted. The truth is that the traveler himself, arriving, is the corrupter. Chester, in his last words, fathomed all this to the lees:

Aren't you tired of listening to me? I am. If I had any tears left, I would cry myself to sleep each night. But I haven't, so I don't. Besides, it is *morning* that comes twisting and torturing my spirit, not nights of dreamless sleep. Morning, another day. I open the shutters and am assailed by the long day unstretching itself like a hideous snake. Does hope spring eternal? Is there still within me the inane dream that somewhere, sometime, will be better?

A few wild poppies are blooming in my littered weedy garden. When I walk out with the dogs I see the poppies opening here and there among the weeds, and here and there a few sickly wilting narcissi. Surely death is no dream, and that being the case, there is then in truth a homeland, a nowhere, a notime, noiseless and peaceful, the ultimate utopia, the eternal freedom, the end to all hunting for goodness and home.

Chester wrote these sad cadences, I learned afterward, less than a block from my Jerusalem hotel. He never looked for me; I never found him. I never saw him alive again. (His dogs, I heard, were discovered locked in a closet, ravenous.)

He lives in my mind, a brilliant boy in a wig.

Very few are familiar with Chester's work or name nowadays, not even bookish people of his own generation. He counts, I suppose, as a "neglected" writer; or perhaps, more to the point, as a minor one. To be able to say what a minor writer is—if it could be done at all—would bring us a little nearer to defining a culture. The tone of a culture cannot depend only on the occasional genius, or the illusion of one; the prevailing temper of a society and a time is situated in its minor voices, in their variegated chorus, but above all in the certainty of their collective presence. There can be no major work, in fact, without the screen, or ground, of lesser artists against whom the major figure is illuminated. Or put it that minor writers are the armature onto which the clay of greatness is thrown, pressed, prodded. If we looked to see who headed the best-seller list the year *The Golden Bowl* came out, the likelihood is that not a single name or title would be recognizable. Minor writers are mainly dead writers who do not rise again, who depend on research projects—often on behalf of this ideology or that movement—to dig up their forgotten influence. Minor writers are the objects of literary scholarship—who else, if not the scholars, will creep through archives in search of the most popular novelists of 1904?

Quantity is not irrelevant. A minor writer may own an electrifying gift, but a trickle of work reduces power. In the absence of a surrounding forest of similar evidences, one book, no matter how striking, will diminish even an extraordinary pen to minor status. There are, to be sure, certain blazing exceptions—think, for example, of *Wuthering Heights*, a solo masterwork that descends to us unaccompanied but consummate. By and large, though, abundance counts. Balzac is Balzac because of the vast thick row of novel after novel, shelf upon shelf. Imagine Balzac as the author of *Lost Illusions,* say, a remarkable work in itself. Or imagine James as having written *The Golden Bowl* and nothing else. If *Lost Illusions* were to stand alone, if *The*

Golden Bowl were to stand alone, if there were no others, would Balzac be Balzac and James James?

Sectarianism also touches on minorness. There is nothing in the human predicament, of course, that is truly sectarian, parochial, narrow, foreign, of "special" or "limited" or "minority" interest; all subjects are universal. That is the convenience—for writers, anyhow—of monotheism, which, envisioning one Creator, posits the unity of humankind. Trollope, writing about nineteenth-century small-town parish politics, exactly describes my local synagogue, and, no doubt, an ashram along the Ganges. All "parochialisms" are inclusive. Sholem Aleichem's, Jane Austen's, Faulkner's, Garcia Marquez's villages have a census of millions. By sectarianism, for want of a better term, I intend something like monomania—which is different from obsessiveness. Geniuses are obsessive. Kafka is obsessive, Melville is obsessive. Obsessiveness belongs to ultimate meaning; it is a category of metaphysics. But a minor writer will show you a barroom, or a murder victim, or a sexual occasion, relentlessly, monomaniacally. Nothing displays minorness so much as the "genre" novel, however brilliantly turned out, whether it is a Western or a detective story or *The Story of O*, even when it is being deliberately parodied as a postmodernist conceit.

Yet minor status is not always the same as oblivion. A delectable preciousness (not inevitably a pejorative, if you consider Max Beerbohm), or a calculated smallness, or an unstoppable scheme of idiosyncrasy, comic or other—or simply the persnickety insistence on *being* minor—can claim permanence as easily as the more capacious qualities of a Proust or a Joyce. The names of such self-circumscribed indelibles rush in: Christina Rossetti, Edward Lear, and W. S. Gilbert out of the past, and, near our own period, Ronald Firbank, A. M. Klein, Ivy Compton-Burnett, Edward Dahlberg, S. J. Perelman, James Thurber. Perhaps Beerbohm above all. (There are a handful more among the living.) Minor art is incontrovertibly art, and minor artists, like major ones, can live on and on. Who can tell if Alfred Chester—whose fiction and essays are currently tunneling out into the world again via new editions—will carry on among the minor who are designed to survive, or among those others who will be lost because, beyond their given moment, they speak to no one?

The question leads once more to sectarianism and its dooms. It may be that Chester is a sectarian writer in a mode far subtler than genre writing (he once published a pornographic novel under a pseudonym, but let that pass) or monomania. Homosexual life, insofar as he made it his subject, was never, for Chester, a one-note monody: what moved him was the loneliness and the longing, not the mechanics. His sectarianism, if I am on the right track, took the form of what is sometimes called, unkindly and imprecisely, ventriloquism. It is a romantic, even a sentimental, vice that only unusually talented writers can excel at—the vice, to say it quickly, of excessive love of literature; of the *sound* of certain literatures. Ventriloquist writers reject what they have in common with their time and place, including its ordinary talk, and are so permeated with the redolence of Elsewhere that their work, even if it is naturally robust, is plagued by wistfulness. I am not speaking of nostalgia alone, the desire to revisit old scenes and old moods. Nor am I speaking of the concerns of "mandarin" writers, those who are pointedly out of tune with the vernacular, who heighten and burnish language in order to pry out of it judgments and ironies beyond the imagination of the colloquial. Ventriloquist writers may or may not be nostalgic, they may or may not be drawn to the mandarin voice. What ventriloquist writers want is to live inside *other literatures*.

Chester, I believe, was one of these. It made him seem a poseur to some, a madman to others; and he was probably a little of both. He drove himself from continent to continent, trying out the Moroccan sunlight as he had read of it, Malcolm Cowley's Paris as the garden of liberating "exile," the isles of Greece for the poetry of the words, Jerusalem for the eternal dream. Literature was a costume, or at any rate a garment: he hardly ever went naked. He saw landscapes and cities through a veil of bookish imaginings. Inexorably, they failed him. The Greek island had unworkable plumbing. Jerusalem had traffic noise. Paris turned out to be exile in earnest. The Moroccan sunlight came through as promised, but so did human nature. Wherever he ran, the nimbus grew tattered, there were quotidian holes in the literary gauze.

This is not to say that Chester was not an original, or that he had a secondhand imagination. Who is more original than a man who fears he is not there? "And I would watch myself, mistrustful of my presence ... I want to be *real*," he wrote in an early story. (Its title, "As I Was Going Up the Stair," echoes the nursery chant: "I met a man who wasn't there.") For the tormented who blind themselves before mirrors, a wash of hallucination will fill the screen of sight. Woody Allen's Zelig falls into old newsreels, his Kugelmass into a chapter of *Madame Bovary*. Chester allowed himself to become, or to struggle to become, if not a character in fiction, then someone who tilted at life in order to transmogrify it into fiction. He is remembered now less as the vividly endowed writer he was born to be than as an eccentric ruin in the comical or sorrowing anecdotes of a tiny circle of aging scribblers.

Most of the writers who on occasion reminisce about Chester have by now lived long enough to confirm their own minor status. If he was in a gladiatorial contest, and not only from the perspective of Mr Emerson's adolescent amphitheater, but with all of his literary generation, then it is clear that Chester has lost. In 1962, commenting on a first collection of short stories by John Updike, he was caustic and flashy: "A God who has allowed a writer to lavish such craft upon these worthless tales is capable of anything." A reviewer's callow mistake, yes. Updike has gone from augmentation to augmentation, and nobody can so much as recognize Chester's name. It is common enough that immediately after writers die, their reputations plummet into ferocious eclipse: all at once, and unaccountably, a formerly zealous constituency will stop reading and teaching and talking about the books that only a short while before were objects of excitement and gossip. It is as if, for writers, vengeful mortality erases not only the woman or the man but the page, the paragraph, the sentence—pages, paragraphs, and sentences that were pressed out precisely in order to spite mortality. Writers, major or minor, may covet fame, but what they really *work* for is that transient little daily illusion—phrase by phrase, comma after comma—of the stay against erasure.

I sometimes try to imagine Chester alive, my own age (a few months younger, actually), still ambitiously turning out novels, stories, essays. No white hair for Chester; he would be perfectly bald, and, given his seniority, perfectly undistinguished by it. I see him as tamed though not restrained, a practiced intellectual by now, industrious; all craziness spent. Instead of those barbaric dogs, he owns a pair of civilized cats. If I cannot untangle the sex life of his later years, I also know that it is none of my business. (In *The Foot* he speaks glancingly of having had sexual relations with a woman for the first time, at thirty-seven.) His ambition, industry, and cantankerous wit have brought him a quizzical new celebrity; he is often on television. In degree of attention-getting he is somewhere between Norman Mailer and Allen Ginsberg, though less political than either. He avoids old friends, or, if not, he anyhow avoids me; my visits with him take place in front of the television set. There he is, talking speedy Brooklynese, on a literary panel together with Joyce Carol Oates and E. L. Doctorow.

I look into the bright tube at those small, suffering, dangerous eyes under the shining scalp and think: *You've won, Chester, you've won.*

CYRIL CONNOLLY AND THE GROANS OF SUCCESS

I FIRST CAME ON a paperback reprint of Cyril Connolly's *Enemies of Promise* when I was already in my despairing middle thirties. Though I had been writing steadily and obsessively since the age of twenty-two, I was still mainly unpublished: a handful of poems, a couple of short stories, a single essay, and all in quirky little magazines printed, it seemed, in invisible ink. Connolly's stringent dissertation on the anatomy of failure had a morbid attraction for me: it was like looking up one's disease in the *Merck Manual*—I knew the symptoms, and it was a wound I was interested in. One day I urgently pressed my copy of Connolly on another failed writer a whole decade younger than myself; we were both teaching freshman composition at the time. He promised to read it; instead he hurried off into analysis and gay pride. I never saw the book again. My ex-colleague has, so far, never published. *Enemies of Promise* went out of print.

After that, I remembered it chiefly as a dictionary of low spirits; even as a secret autobiography. Over the years one of its interior titles—"The Charlock's Shade"—stayed with me, a mysterious phrase giving off old mournful fumes: the marsh gas writers inhale when they are not getting published, when they begin to accept themselves as having been passed by, when envy's pinch is constant and certain, when the lurch of humiliation learns to precede the predictable rebuff. Writers who publish early and regularly not only are spared these hollow desolations, but acquire habits of strength and self-confidence. Henry James, George Sand, Balzac, Mann: these amazingly prolific presences achieved as much as they did not simply because they began young, but because they were permitted to begin young. James in America started off with book reviews; so, in London, did Virginia Woolf.

But in my despairing thirties it was hardly these colossi of literary history I was fixed on. All around me writers five years older and five years younger were having their second and third novels published, establishing their idiosyncratic and intractable voices, and flourishing, sometimes with the left hand, this and that indomitable essay: Mailer's "The White Negro," Sontag's "Notes on Camp," Roth's "Writing American Fiction," Baldwin's "The Fire Next Time," Styron's reply to the critics of *Nat Turner*, and so on. John Updike, the paramount American instance of early publication, conquered *The New Yorker* in his twenties, undertaking even then the body of reviewing that nowadays rivals the amplitude and weight and attentiveness of Edmund Wilson's. At about the same time, in the New Rochelle Public Library, I pulled down from a high shelf of the New Books section a first volume of stories called *By the North Gate*. The author was an unknown writer ten years my junior; not long afterward, the name Joyce Carol Oates accelerated into a ubiquitous force. A good while before that, in college, I had known someone who knew Truman Capote; and Capote had published in magazines before he was twenty.

In short, these were the Famous of my generation, and could be read, and read about, and mulled over, and discussed. They were—or anyhow they embodied, they were shot through with—the Issues; and meanwhile I was a suffering onlooker, shut out. I could not even say that I was being ignored—to be ignored you have first to be published. A hundred periodicals, both renowned and "little," sent me packing. An editor who later went to Hollywood to write *Superman* led me into his *Esquire* cubicle to turn back a piece of fiction with the hard-hearted charm of indifference; he looked like someone's baby brother. Another day I stood on the threshold of the office of the *New York Review of Books*, a diffident inquirer of thirty-five, and was shooed away by a word thrown out from a distant desk; I had come to ask for a review to write. *Partisan, Kenyon, Sewanee, American Scholar, Quarterly Review, Furioso*, dozens of others, declined my submissions. An editor of a small Michigan periodical, a poet, wrote to remark that I "had yet to find a voice." In New York, a respected reader at a well-known publishing house, having in hand three-quarters of my novel, said it wouldn't do, and rocked me into a paralysis of hopelessness lasting nearly a year. And all the while I was getting older and older. Envy of the published ate at me; so did the shame of so much nibbling defeat. Twenty years of print-lust, muscular ambition, driving inquisitiveness, and all the rest, were lost in the hurt crawl away from the locked door. I wrote, and read, and filled volumes of Woolworth diaries with the outcry of failure—the failure to enter the gates of one's own literary generation, the anguish of exclusion from its argument and tone, its experience and evolution. It wasn't that I altogether doubted my "powers" (though often enough I did, profoundly, stung by disgrace); I saw them, whatever they were, scorned, disparaged, set outside the pale of welcome. I was ashamed of my life, and I lived only to read and write. I lived for nothing else; I had no other "goals," "motivations," "interests"—these shallownesses pointing to what the babblers of the hour call psychological health. Nor was it raw Fame I was after; I was not deluded that publishing a first novel at twenty-five, as Mann had done, would guarantee a *Buddenbrooks*.

What I wanted was access to the narrowest possibilities of my own time and prime; I wanted to bore a chink. I wanted a sliver of the apron of a literary platform. I wanted to use what I was, to be what I was born to be—not to have a "career," but to be that straightforward obvious unmistakable animal, a writer. I was a haunted punctuator, possessed stylist, sorter of ideas, burrower into history, philosophy, criticism; I wrote midnight poetry into the morning light; I burnished the sentences of my prose so that each might stand, I said (with the arrogance of the desperately humiliated), for twenty years. And no one would publish me.

For this predicament, it was clear, I needed not an anodyne, but salt—merciless salt. Connolly not only supplied the salt, he opened the wounds, gave names to their mouths, and rubbed in the salt. He analyzed—or so it appeared—all the venoms of failure. He spoke, in a kind of metaphoric delirium borrowed from Crabbe, of "the blighted rye," "the slimy mallow," "the wither'd ears"—all those hideous signs of poison and decomposition from which the suffocated writer, kept from the oxygen of the age, deprived of print, slowly dies. There was no victory crow to be had from reading Connolly. If he provoked any sound at all, it was the dry cough that comes with panic at the dawn's early light.

This, at least, is how, all these years, I have kept *Enemies of Promise* in my head: as a mop and sop for the long, long bleeding, the intellectual slights, the disgraced imagination, the locked doors, the enervating growths of the literary swamp, the dry cough of abandonment. The rest I seem to have forgotten, or never to have noticed at all, and now that the book is once again on the scene, and again in paperback, I observe that it is a tripartite volume, and that, distracted by what I believed to be its diagnostic powers, I missed two thirds of its substance. What I once saw as a pillar of salt turns out to be, in fact, a puff of spun sugar. And this is not because I have "gotten over" the pounding of denigration and rejection; I have never properly recuperated from them, and on their account resent the white hairs of middle age with a spitefulness and absurdity appropriate only to the hungry young.

"*Enemies of Promise* was first published in 1938," Cyril Connolly's 1948 Introduction begins, "as a didactic enquiry into the problem of how to write a book which lasts ten years." Yet the question of literary longevity is raised and almost instantly dropped; that this particular book has now "lasted" more than four decades is hardly the answer. And I am not sure it *has* lasted, at least in the form it claims, i.e., as an essay about certain ideas. It hangs on instead as a curiosity, which does not mean it is wholly obsolete; it is only peculiar. Even in organization there is peculiarity: a trinity that does not immediately cohere. The first section divides prose style into Mandarin (a term Connolly takes credit for coining in this context) and vernacular; surely this issue is with us as bemusedly as ever. The second section— "The Charlock's Shade," which so fed my gripes and twinges—now looks to be not so much about failure as about success and its distractions. The third part, finally, is a memoir of Connolly's childhood in a boarding school for the rich called St. Wulfric's, and afterward at Eton. In my zealously partial reading long ago, though I was attracted by Connolly's definitions of Mandarin and vernacular diction, it appears I never took in the autobiographical segment at all; and what drew me to "The Charlock's Shade" (or so it now strikes me) was three lone sentences, as follows:

> Promise is like the mediaeval hangman who after settling the noose, pushed his victim off the platform and jumped on his back, his weight acting as a drop while his jockeying arms prevented the unfortunate from loosening the rope.

> Sloth in writers is always a symptom of an acute inner conflict, especially that laziness which renders them incapable of doing the thing which they are most looking forward to.

> Perfectionists are notoriously lazy and all true artistic indolence is deeply neurotic; a pain not a pleasure.

Here, and only here, was the poisonous wisdom that served my travail. All the rest supposed a sophistication and advancement that meant nothing to a writer who had barely begun, and Connolly's classifications of dangers hardly applied. To succeed as a writer, he admonished, beware of journalism, politics, "escapism," sex, and success itself. Journalism: never write "a review that cannot be printed, i.e. that is not of some length and on a subject of permanent value." Politics: once the writer "has a moment of conviction that his future is bound up with the working classes ... his behaviour will inevitably alter"—in other words, he will be much improved. "Escapism": drink, drugs, talk, daydreaming, religion, sloth. Sex: hazards of homosexuality, domesticity, babies, wives. And, aha, success: here the peril lies in getting taken up by the upper crust, according to E. M. Forster's dictum as cited by Connolly: "To be aristocratic in Art one must avoid polite society." But how could any of these cautionary alarms have mattered to a writer who had for years gone altogether unnoticed? Speaking for myself: I never thought about politics. Journalism was something less than a snare, since no one would offer me so much as a five-hundred-word review. I was in no danger of becoming a fad or a celebrity. I didn't drink or shoot up. I confined religion to philosophical reading, and daydreaming to a diary. I had no baby and no wife. (Connolly, though he mentions Virginia Woolf among the Mandarins, has an ineradicable difficulty in positing a writer who is not male. This is a pity, because the writer's husband is a worthy, perplexing, and often tragic subject.) Even talk was no drain; what went up into air for others, I mainly put down in letters to literary friends— letters, those vessels of calculated permanence. Then what in Connolly could possibly appeal to the untried and the buried? In his infinite catalogues of "promise" and its risks, only the terrors of perfectionism and the pain of sure decline had the least psychological concurrence. For the sake of this pins-in-the-ribs pair, Connolly stuck.

He begins now to unstick. "It was Edmund Wilson who remarked that [*Enemies of Promise*] was not a very well-written book," Connolly confesses. Wilson was right. Connolly is a ragged writer, unraveling his rags behind him as he goes, and capable of awful sentences. If Wilson recoiled from some of them, it might have been in part on account of Connolly's description of Wilson's own *Axel's Castle*, which, we are reminded, "includes essays on Yeats, Valéry, Eliot, Proust, Joyce and Gertrude Stein. His summing up," Connolly continues in a typically unpunctuated long breath, "is against them, in so far as it is against their cult of the individual which he feels they have carried to such lengths as to exhaust it for a long time to come but it is a summing up which also states everything that can be said in their favour when allowance for what I have termed 'inflation' is made."

(Observe that the style is neither Mandarin nor vernacular, but Rattling Boxcars.)

Patches of this sort might unglue any essayist, but there is something beyond mere prose at stake. Did Connolly notice that his so-called enemies of promise were in reality the appurtenances of certain already-achieved successes? The warning that journalism threatens art applies, after all, only to fairly established writers long familiar with the practice of getting paid for writing. "He is apt to have a private income, he renews himself by travel," Connolly says of the homosexual writer, assuming long-standing privilege and money. A successful wife, he remarks, not only is "intelligent and unselfish enough to understand and respect the working of the unfriendly cycle of the creative imagination," but "will recognize that there is no more sombre enemy of good art than the pram in the hall." And of course: "Of all the enemies of literature, success is the most insidious."

Does failure ever appear at all in *Enemies of Promise*—the word or the idea? Once. "Failure is a poison like success. Where a choice is offered, prefer the alkaline," and that is all. Such sentiments burn rather than salve. And even while cautioning against the "especial intimacies" of the fashionable, Connolly has a good word for them: "It must be remembered that in fashionable society can be found warmhearted people of delicate sensibility who form permanent friendships with artists which afford them ease and encouragement for the rest of their lives and provide them with sanctuary." And in defense of the seductions of wealth not one's own: "It is because we envy [social success] more than other success that we denounce it so often," Connolly explains. He himself does not denounce the ingratiation of writers with the rich so much as their ingratiation with one another:

> There is a kind of behaviour which is particularly dangerous on the moving staircase—the attempt to ascend it in groups of four or five who lend a hand to each other and dislodge other climbers from the steps. It is natural that writers should make friends with their contemporaries of talent and express a mutual admir-

ation but it leads inevitably to a succession of services rendered and however much the writers who help each other may deserve it, if they too frequently proclaim their gratitude they will arouse the envy of those who stand on their own feet, who succeed without collaboration. Words like "log-rolling" and "back-scratching" are soon whispered and the death-watch ticks the louder.

The death-watch? If there is any warning being rattled in all this, surely it must compete with the complicit wink of the sound counselor. A denunciation, one might say, that has the look of a paragraph in a handbook on the wherewithal of success. And a wherewithal that, at a particular rung of society, is affable enough: the comfortable network of class and school associations.

It is the moment for bluntness. *Enemies of Promise* is an essay—according to the usual English conventions of the early part of the twentieth century—about class and modishness. It has almost no other subject important to Connolly. There are disgressions on, say, age, that are nearly worthwhile—more worthwhile when the aperçu is not Connolly's own (though the syntax is): "Butler said an author should write only for people between twenty and thirty as nobody read or changed their opinions after that." There is much recognizable humanity in this, whereas Connolly, attempting to generalize in his own voice, manages mainly a self-indulgent turn: "The shock, for an intelligent writer, of discovering for the first time that there are people younger than himself who think him stupid is severe." Or: "It would seem that genius is of two kinds, one of which blazes up in youth and dies down, while the other matures, like Milton's or Goethe's. . . . The artist has to decide on the nature of his own or he may find himself exhausted by the sprint of youth and unfitted for the marathon of middle age." As if one could choose to be Milton or Goethe merely by deciding, as Connolly advises, to "become a stayer." Modishness dominates: the notion of likely styles in will, the short-length will and the longer-range.

Modishness rules especially in the politics. Writing in 1948 (the famous year of Orwell's *Nineteen Eighty-Four*), Connolly suggests that he has 'retained all the engagingly simple left-wing militancy [of 1938] since it breathes the air of the period." True enough: ten years after its composition, Connolly is offering us *Enemies of Promise* frankly as a period piece. But the point of the exercise, we are bound to remember, is that ten years after its composition he is also offering it as a successful instance of "how to write a book which lasts ten years." Are we to conclude, then, that the more a book is dated, the longer its chances of survival? A remarkable hypothesis. No, it won't wash, this period-piece candor: Connolly had no wish to revise or update or tone down the "left-wing militancy" (less "engaging," forty-five years later, and in an age of left-linked terrorism, than he might have supposed); perhaps it was only "artistic indolence." Or perhaps it was because of an intuition about his own character and its style: a certain seamlessness, the absence of self-contradiction. Connolly is always on the side of his own class, never more so than in his expression of "left-wing militancy." It is not that Connolly, in 1938, is mistaken when he declares that "today the forces of life and progress are ranging on one side, those of reaction and death on the other," or that "fascism is the enemy of art," or that "we are not dealing with an Augustus who will discover his Horace and his Virgil, but with Attila or Hulaku, destroyers of European culture whose poets can contribute only battle-cries and sentimental drinking songs." He means Hitler: but the very next year, in 1939, the year of the Hitler-Stalin pact, would he have been willing to mean Stalin too? "The poet is a chemist and there is more pure revolutionary propaganda in a line of Blake than in all *The Rights of Man*," he asserts: a sophistry that can only be the flower of an elitist education. In 1938 what literary intellectual was not moved by the word "revolutionary"?

Nothing, in fact, is less dated than the combination of Connolly's elitism and his attraction to revolutionary militancy. Any superficial excursion into universities in Western Europe and the United States currently bears this out, nowhere more vividly than in American elitist departments, history, literature and political science especially. All this is a cliché of our predicament as it was of Connolly's. "The atmosphere of orthodoxy is always damaging to prose," Orwell wrote in *Inside the Whale*, and here is Connolly as prooftext: "Often [solidarity with the working classes] will be recognized only by external symptoms, a disinclination to wear a hat or a stiff collar, an inability to be rude to waiters or taxi-drivers or to be polite to young men of his own age with rolled umbrellas, bowler hats and 'Mayfair men' moustaches or to tolerate the repressive measures of his class." This wizened sentence may be worth the belly laugh due anachronism, but its undigested spirit lingers on. For "disinclination to wear a hat" substitute an earnest inclination to wear Che boots. And "the repressive measures of his class" is as bruisingly trite and vacuous as any bright young Ivy graduate's assault on the American bourgeoisie, of which he or she is the consummate product.

The consummate product of his class. Should Connolly be blamed for this? Probably. Orwell went to the same schools at the same time, Eton preceded by St. Cyprian's (St. Wulfric's in Connolly's genial account, Crossgates in Orwell's lugubrious one), and saw straight through what Connolly thrived on. Orwell despised the tyrant-goddess who ruled over St. Cyprian's; Connolly maneuvred to get on her good side. And of Eton Connolly writes (in the ardently arrested parochial tone of one of the "bloody-minded people at the top"), "My last two years of Eton . . . were among the most interesting and rewarding of my whole life and I do not believe they could have been so at any other public school or in any other house than College." The allusion is to school elections; Connolly was, we learn, an ecstatic member of the exclusive "Pop," which he counts, along with romantic homoerotic adolescence, among those "experiences undergone by boys at the great public schools . . . so intense as to dominate their lives." Orwell, reviewing *Enemies of Promise* soon after its appearance, hoots: "He means it!" And sums up the politics of those cosseted few who, between 1910 and 1920, after "five years in a lukewarm bath of snobbery," have fabricated sympathies they have no way of feeling: "Hunger, hardship, solitude, exile, war, prison, persecution, manual labor—hardly even words. No wonder," Orwell charges, "that the huge tribe known as 'the right left people' found it so easy to condone the purge-and-Ogpu side of the Russian régime and the horrors of the First Five Year Plan. They were so gloriously incapable of understanding what it all meant."

Nothing in his brief 1948 introductory note to *Enemies of Promise* tells us whether Connolly did or did not remain one of the right left people a decade later. "We grow up among theories and illusions common to our class, our race, our time," Connolly opens his schooldays memoir, but only as a frame for the apology that follows: "I have to refer to something which I find intolerable, the early aura of large houses, fallen fortunes and country families common to so many English autobiographies." He ends by fretting over whether "the reader can stomach this." What is even harder to stomach is a self-repudiation that is indistinguishable from self-congratulation. The memoir itself, with its luxuriant pleasure in "our class, our race, our time," its prideful delight in British Platonism, "popping up in sermons and Sunday questions . . . at the headmaster's dinner-parties or in my tutor's pupil-room," its insurmountable glorying in the stringent achievements of an English classical education—the memoir itself repudiates nothing, least of all the narrator's background, character, or capacities. To preface such an account of high social and intellectual privilege with the hope that it can be "stomached," and then to proceed with so much lip-smacking delectation, is, as Orwell saw, to understand nothing, and to stop at words.

Words, it turns out, are what deserve to last in *Enemies of Promise*—not Connolly's own sentences, which puff and gasp and occasionally strangle themselves, but the subject of his observations about styles of prose. Critical currencies have altered in the extreme since Connolly first set down his categories of Mandarin and vernacular, and unless one reminds oneself that these terms once had some originality of perspective (they are not so facile as they sound), they drop into the hackneyed posture they now permanently evoke. It is true that the New Criticism, which had the assurance of looking both omnipotent and immortal, has come and gone, and that the universal semiotics shock even now hints at softening, if not receding (though only slightly, and then out of factionalism). And other volumes of this kind, siblings or perhaps descendants of *Enemies of Promise*, have ventured to record the politics and history of the writer's predicament— among them critical summaries by Malcolm Cowley, Van Wyck Brooks, John Aldridge, Alfred Kazin, Tony Tanner, Tillie Olsen. The post-Connolly landscape is cluttered with new literary structures of every variety. All the same, Connolly's report on the increasing ascendancy of journalistic style over the life of contemporary fiction—language stripped of interpretive complexity, language stripped even of "language," i.e., of the resources of the lyrical or intellectual imagination—remains urgent. The Mandarin "dialect," as Connolly intelligently calls it (and he is wary in his praise of it, especially when it decays into dandyism, "the ability to spin cocoons of language out of nothing"), has now given way to a sort of telegraphic data-prose, mainly in the present tense, in which sympathies and deductive acuities are altogether eliminated. In poetry, the minimalists (whether in all their determined phalanxes they know it or not) are by now played out, moribund, ready for a turning; only the other day I heard a leading subjectivist, a lineal heir of William Carlos Williams, yearn aloud to sink into a long Miltonic sequence. But among fiction writers, the fossilized Hemingway legacy hangs on, after all this time, strangely and uselessly prestigious. (I attribute this not to the devoted reading of Hemingway, but to the decline of reading in general.)

Connolly's distinctions and his exposition of them, however, address the adherents of both "dialects." "From the Mandarins," he exhorts, the writer

> must borrow art and patience, the striving for perfection, the horror of clichés, the creative delight in the material [a phrase that itself arouses horror], in the possibilities of the long sentence and the splendour and subtlety of the composed phrase. From the Mandarins, on the other hand, the new writer will take warning not to burden a

sober and delicate language with exhibitionism. There will be no false hesitation and woolly profundities, no mystifying, no Proustian onanism.

From the "talkie-novelists," he continues—i.e., from the laconic anti-stylists influenced by film—the new writer can acquire the "cursive style, the agreeable manners, the precise and poetical impact of Forster's diction, the lucidity of Maugham, last of the great professional writers, the timing of Hemingway, the smooth cutting edge of Isherwood, the indignation of Lawrence, the honesty of Orwell," as well as the gift of construction. (It is notable that in nearly fifty years not one of these names, not excluding Maugham and Isherwood, has lost its high familiarity, and Orwell, in fact, has increased in prestige.) The defects of realist or colloquial style Connolly lists as the consequence of "flatness"—"the homogeneity of outlook, the fear of eccentricity, the reporter's horror of distinction, the distrust of beauty, the cult of violence and starkness that is masochistic." Nowadays we might add the conviction of existential nihilism. "It is no more a question of taking sides about one way or another of writing, but a question of timing," Connolly sensibly concludes. All these are good and salubrious particulars—though it is worth recalling that, in prose at least, and wherever we find ourselves in the cycle of reaction, there are no stripped-down Conrads or Joyces; and that modernism never turned its back on plenitude.

As for my own disappointment in encountering *Enemies of Promise* after so long a hiatus: it was never Connolly's fault that I made up a book that wasn't there. I wanted to brood over failure. Connolly presides over the groans of success. He knows no real enemies—unless you count the threat to revolution ambushed in Mayfair moustaches.

THE LESSON OF THE MASTER

THERE WAS A period in my life—to purloin a famous Jamesian title, "The Middle Years"—when I used to say, with as much ferocity as I could muster, "I hate Henry James and I wish he was dead."

I was not to have my disgruntled way. The dislike did not last and turned once again to adoration, ecstasy, and awe; and no one is more alive than Henry James, or more likely to sustain literary immortality. He is among the angels, as he meant to be.

But in earlier days I felt I had been betrayed by Henry James. I was like the youthful writer in "The Lesson of the Master" who believed in the Master's call to live immaculately, unspoiled by what we mean when we say "life"— relationship, family mess, distraction, exhaustion, anxiety, above all disappointment. Here is the Master, St. George, speaking to his young disciple, Paul Overt:

> "One has no business to have any children," St. George placidly declared. "I mean, of course, if one wants to do anything good."
> "But aren't they an inspiration—an incentive?"
> "An incentive to damnation, artistically speaking."

And later Paul inquires:

> "Is it deceptive that I find you living with every appearance of domestic felicity—blest with a devoted, accomplished wife, with children whose acquaintance I haven't yet had the pleasure of making, but who *must*

be delightful young people, from what I know of their parents?"

St. George smiled as for the candour of his question. "It's all excellent, my dear fellow—heaven forbid I should deny it. . . . I've got a loaf on the shelf; I've got everything in fact but the great thing."

"And the great thing?" Paul kept echoing.

"The sense of having done the best—the sense which is the real life of the artist and the absence of which is his death, of having drawn from his intellectual instrument the finest music that nature had hidden in it, of having played it as it should be played. He either does that or he doesn't—and if he doesn't he isn't worth speaking of."

Paul pursues:

"Then what did you mean . . . by saying that children are a curse?"

"My dear youth, on what basis are we talking?" and St. George dropped upon the sofa at a short distance from him. . . . "On the supposition that a certain perfection's possible and even desirable—isn't it so? Well, all I say is that one's children interfere with perfection. One's wife interferes. Marriage interferes."

"You think, then, the artist shouldn't marry?"

"He does so at his peril—he does so at his cost."

Yet the Master who declares all this is himself profoundly, inextricably, married; and when his wife dies, he hastens to marry again, choosing Life over Art. Very properly James sees marriage as symbol and summary of the passion for ordinary human entanglement, as experience of the most commonplace, most fated kind.

But we are also given to understand, in the desolation of this comic tale, that the young artist, the Master's trusting disciple, is left both perplexed and bereft: the Master's second wife is the young artist's first love, and the Master has stolen away his disciple's chance for ordinary human entanglement.

So the Lesson of the Master is a double one: choose

ordinary human entanglement, and live; or choose Art, and give up the vitality of life's passions and panics and endurances. What I am going to tell now is a stupidity, a misunderstanding, a great Jamesian life-mistake: an embarrassment and a life-shame. (Imagine that we are in one of those lavishly adorned Jamesian chambers where intimate confessions not accidentally but suspensefully take place.) As I have said, I felt myself betrayed by a Jamesian trickery. Trusting in James, believing, like Paul Overt, in the overtness of the Jamesian lesson, I chose Art, and ended by blaming Henry James. It seemed to me James had left out the one important thing I ought to have known, even though he was saying it again and again. The trouble was that I was listening to the Lesson of the Master at the wrong time, paying powerful and excessive attention at the wrong time; and this cost me my youth.

I suppose a case can be made that it is certainly inappropriate for anyone to moan about the loss of youth and how it is all Henry James's fault. All of us will lose our youth, and some of us, alas, have lost it already; but not all of us will pin the loss on Henry James.

I, however, do. I blame Henry James.

Never mind the sublime position of Henry James in American letters. Never mind the Jamesian prose style—never mind that it too is sublime, nuanced, imbricated with a thousand distinctions and observations (the reason H. G. Wells mocked it), and as idiosyncratically and ecstatically redolent of the spirals of past and future as a garlic clove. Set aside also the Jamesian impatience with idols, the moral seriousness active in both the work and the life. (I am thinking, for example, of Edith Wharton's compliance in the face of their mutual friend Paul Bourget's anti-Semitism, and James's noble and definitive dissent.) Neglect all this, including every other beam that flies out from the stupendous Jamesian lantern to keep generations reading in rapture (which is all right), or else scribbling away at dissertation after dissertation (which is not so good). I myself, after all, committed a Master's thesis, long ago, called "Parable in Henry James," in which I tried to catch up all of James in the net of a single idea. Before that, I lived many months in the black hole of a microfilm cell, transcribing every letter James ever wrote to Mr. Pinker, his London agent, for a professorial book; but the professor drank, and died, and after thirty years the letters still lie in the dark.

All that while I sat cramped in that black bleak microfilm cell, and all that while I was writing that thesis, James was sinking me and despoiling my youth, and I did not know it.

I want, parenthetically, to recommend to the Henry James Society—there is such an assemblage—that membership be limited: no one under age forty-two and three-quarters need apply. Proof of age via birth certificate should be mandatory; otherwise the consequences may be harsh and horrible. I offer myself as an Extreme and Hideous Example of Premature Exposure to Henry James. I was about seventeen, I recall, when my brother brought home from the public library a science-fiction anthology, which, through an odd perspective that perplexes me still, included "The Beast in the Jungle." It was in this anthology, and at that age, that I first read James—fell, I should say, into the jaws of James. I had never heard of him before. I read "The Beast in the Jungle" and creepily thought: Here, here is my autobiography.

From that time forward, gradually but compellingly—and now I yield my scary confession—I became Henry James. Leaving graduate school at the age of twenty-two, disdaining the Ph.D. as an acquisition surely beneath the concerns of literary seriousness, I was already Henry James. When I say I "became" Henry James, you must understand this: though I was a near-sighted twenty-two-year-old young woman infected with the commonplace intention of writing a novel, I was *also* the elderly bald-headed Henry James. Even without close examination, you could see the light glancing off my pate; you could see my heavy chin, my watch chain, my walking stick, my tender paunch.

I had become Henry James, and for years and years I remained Henry James. There was no doubt about it: it was my own clear and faithful truth. Of course, there were some small differences: for one thing, I was not a genius. For another, even in my own insignificant scribbler class, I was not prolific. But I carried the Jamesian idea, I was of his cult,

I was a worshiper of literature, literature was my single altar; I was, like the elderly bald-headed James, a priest at that altar; and that altar was all of my life. Like John Marcher in "The Beast in the Jungle," I let everything pass me by for the sake of waiting for the Beast to spring—but unlike John Marcher, I knew what the Beast was, I knew exactly, I even knew the Beast's name: the Beast was literature itself, the sinewy grand undulations of some unraveling fiction, meticulously dreamed out in a language of masterly resplendence, which was to pounce on me and turn me into an enchanted and glorious Being, as enchanted and glorious as the elderly bald-headed Henry James himself.

But though the years spent themselves extravagantly, that ambush never occurred: the ambush of Sacred and Sublime Literature. The great shining Beast of Sacred and Sublime Literature did not pounce. Instead, other beasts, lesser ones, unseemly and misshapen, sprang out—all the beasts of ordinary life: sorrow, disease, death, guilt, responsibility, envy, grievance, grief, disillusionment—the beasts that are chained to human experience, and have nothing to do with Art except to interrupt and impede it, exactly according to the Lesson of the Master.

It was not until I read a certain vast and subtle book that I understood what had happened to me. The book was not by Henry James, but about him. Nowadays we give this sort of work a special name: we call it a nonfiction novel. I am referring, of course, to Leon Edel's ingenious and beautiful biography of Henry James, which is as much the possession of Edel's imagination as it is of the exhilaratingly reported facts of James's life. In Edel's rendering, I learned what I had never before taken in—but the knowledge came, in the Jamesian way, too late. What I learned was that Henry James himself had not always been the elderly bald-headed Henry James!—that he too had once been twenty-two years old.

This terrible and secret knowledge instantly set me against James. From that point forward I was determined to eradicate him. And for a long while I succeeded.

What had happened was this: in early young-womanhood I believed, with all the rigor and force and stunned ardor of religious belief, in the old Henry James, in his scepter and his authority. I believed that what *he* knew at sixty I was to encompass at twenty-two; at twenty-two I lived like the elderly bald-headed Henry James. I thought it was necessary—it was imperative, there was no other path!—to be, all at once, with no progression or evolution, the author of the equivalent of *The Ambassadors* or *The Wings of the Dove*, just as if "A Bundle of Letters," or "Four Meetings," or the golden little "The Europeans" had never preceded the great late Master.

For me, the Lesson of the Master was a horror, a Jamesian tale of a life of mishap and mistake and misconceiving. Though the Master himself was saying, in *The Ambassadors*, in Gloriani's garden, to Little Bilham, through the urgent cry of Strether, "Live, live!"—and though the Master himself was saying, in "The Beast in the Jungle," through May Bartram, how ghastly, how ghostly, it is to eschew, to evade, to turn from, to miss absolutely and irrevocably what is all the time there for you to seize—I mistook him, I misheard him, I missed, absolutely and irrevocably, his essential note. What I heard instead was: *Become a Master.*

Now the truth is it could not have been done, even by a writer of genius; and what a pitiful flicker of the flame of high ambition for a writer who is no more than the ordinary article! No one—not even James himself—springs all at once in early youth into full Mastery, and no writer, whether robustly gifted, or only little and pale, should hope for this implausible fate.

All this, I suppose, is not at all a "secret" knowledge, as I have characterized it, but is, rather, as James named it in the very person of his naïve young artist, most emphatically *overt*—so obvious that it is a mere access of foolishness even to talk about it. Still, I offer the implausible and preposterous model of myself to demonstrate the proposition that the Lesson of the Master is not a lesson about genius, or even about immense ambition; it is a lesson about misreading—about what happens when we misread the great voices of Art, and suppose that, because they speak of Art, they *mean* Art. The great voices of Art never mean *only* Art;

they also mean Life, they always mean Life, and Henry James, when he evolved into the Master we revere, finally meant nothing else.

The true Lesson of the Master, then, is, simply, never to venerate what is complete, burnished, whole, in its grand organic flowering or finish—never to look toward the admirable and dazzling end; never to be ravished by the goal; never to worship ripe Art or the ripened artist; but instead to seek to be young while young, primitive while primitive, ungainly when ungainly—to look for crudeness and rudeness, to husband one's own stupidity or ungenius.

There *is* this mix-up most of us have between ourselves and what we admire or triumphantly cherish. We see this mix-up, this mishap, this mishmash, most often in writers: the writer of a new generation ravished by the genius writer of a classical generation, who begins to dream herself, or himself, as powerful, vigorous and original—as if being filled up by the genius writer's images, scenes, and stratagems were the same as having the capacity to pull off the identical magic. To be any sort of competent writer one must keep one's psychological distance from the supreme artists.

If I were twenty-two now, I would not undertake a cannibalistically ambitious Jamesian novel to begin with; I would look into the eyes of Henry James at twenty-two, and see the diffident hope, the uncertainty, the marveling tentativeness, the dream that is still only a dream; the young man still learning to fashion the Scene. Or I would go back still further, to the boy of seventeen, misplaced in a Swiss Polytechnic School, who recalled in old age that "I so feared and abhorred mathematics that the simplest arithmetical operation had always found and kept me helpless and blank." It is not to the Master in his fullness I would give my awed, stricken, desperate fealty, but to the faltering, imperfect, dreaming youth.

If these words should happen to reach the ears of any young writer dumbstruck by the elderly bald-headed Henry James, one who has hungrily heard and ambitiously assimilated the voluptuous cathedral-tones of the developed organ-master, I would say to her or him: put out your lean and clumsy forefinger and strike your paltry, oafish, feeble, simple, skeletal, single note. Try for what Henry James at sixty would scorn—just as he scorned the work of his own earliness, and revised it and revised it in the manner of his later pen in that grand chastisement of youth known as the New York Edition. Trying, in youth, for what the Master in his mastery would condemn—that is the only road to modest mastery. Rapture and homage are not the way. Influence is perdition.

ON PERMISSION TO WRITE

> I hate everything that does not relate to literature, conversations bore me (even when they relate to literature), to visit people bores me, the joys and sorrows of my relatives bore me to my soul. Conversation takes the importance, the seriousness, the truth, out of everything I think.
>
> FRANZ KAFKA, from his diary, 1918

IN A SMALL and depressing city in a nearby state there lives a young man (I will call him David) whom I have never met and with whom I sometimes correspond. David's letters are voluminous, vehemently bookish, and—in obedience to literary modernism—without capitals. When David says "I," he writes "i." This does not mean that he is insecure in his identity or that he suffers from a weakness of confidence— David cannot be characterized by thumbnail psychologizing. He is like no one else (except maybe Jane Austen). He describes himself mostly as poor and provincial, as in Balzac, and occasionally as poor and black. He lives alone with his forbearing and bewildered mother in a flat "with imaginary paintings on the walls in barren rooms," writes stories and novels, has not yet published, and appears to spend his days hauling heaps of books back and forth from the public library.

He has read, it seems, everything. His pages are masses of flashy literary allusions—nevertheless entirely lucid, witty, learned, and sane. David is not *exactly* a crank who writes to writers, although he is probably a bit of that too. I don't know how he gets his living, or whether his letters romanticize either his poverty (he reports only a hunger for books) or his passion (ditto); still, David is a free intellect, a free imagination. It is possible that he hides his manuscripts under a blotter, Jane-Austenly, when his mother creeps mutely in to collect his discarded socks. (A week's worth, perhaps, curled on the floor next to Faulkner and Updike and Cummings and *Tristram Shandy*. Of the latter he remarks: "a worthy book. Dare any man get offspring on less?")

On the other hand, David wants to be noticed. He wants to be paid attention to. Otherwise, why would he address charming letters to writers (I am not the only one) he has never met? Like Joyce in "dirty provincial Dublin," he says, he means to announce his "inevitable arrival on the mainland." A stranger's eye, even for a letter, is a kind of publication. David, far from insisting on privacy, is a would-be public man. It may be that he pants after fame. And yet in his immediate position—his secret literary life, whether or not he intends it to remain secret—there is something delectable. He thirsts to read, so he reads; he thirsts to write, so he writes. He is in the private cave of his freedom, an eremite, a solitary; he orders his mind as he pleases. In this condition he is prolific. He writes and writes. Ah, he is poor and provincial, in a dim lost corner of the world. But his lonely place (a bare cubicle joyfully tumbling with library books) and his lonely situation (the liberty to be zealous) have given him the permission to write. To be, in fact, prolific.

I am not like David. I am not poor, or provincial (except in the New York way), or unpublished, or black. (David, the sovereign of his life, invents an aloofness from social disabilities, at least in his letters, and I have not heard him mythologize "negritude"; he admires poets for their words and cadences.) But all this is not the essential reason I am not like David. I am not like him because I do not own his permission to write freely, and zealously, and at will, and however I damn please; and abundantly; and always.

There is this difference between the prolific and the non-prolific: the prolific have arrogated to themselves the permission to write.

By permission I suppose I ought to mean *inner* permission.

Now "inner permission" is a phrase requiring high caution: it was handed to me by a Freudian dogmatist, a writer whose energy and confidence depend on regular visits to his psychoanalyst. In a useful essay called "Art and Neurosis," Lionel Trilling warns against the misapplication of Freud's dictum that "we are all ill, i.e., neurotic," and insists that a writer's productivity derives from "the one part of him that is healthy, by any conceivable definition of health . . . that which gives him the power to conceive, to plan, to work, and to bring his work to a conclusion." The capacity to write, in short, comes from an uncharted space over which even all-prevailing neurosis can have no jurisdiction or dominion. "The use to which [the artist] puts his power . . . may be discussed with reference to his particular neurosis," Trilling concedes; yet Trilling's verdict is finally steel: "But its essence is irreducible. It is, as we say, a gift."

If permission to write (and for a writer this is exactly equal to the power to write) is a gift, then what of the lack of permission? Does the missing "Go ahead" mean neurosis? I am at heart one of those hapless pre-moderns who believe that the light bulb is the head of a demon called forth by the light switch, and that Freud is a German word for pleasure; so I am not equipped to speak about principles of electricity or psychoanalysis. All the same, it seems to me that the electrifying idea of inward obstacle—neurosis—is not nearly so often responsible for low productivity as we are told. Writer's permission is not something that is switched off by helpless forces inside the writer, but by social currents— human beings and their ordinary predilections and prejudices—outside. If David writes freely and others don't, the reason might be that, at least for a while, David has kidnapped himself beyond the pinch of society. He is Jane Austen with her hidden manuscript momentarily slipped out from under the blotter; he is Thoreau in his cabin. He is a free man alone in a room with imaginary pictures on the walls, reading and writing in a private rapture.

There are some writers who think of themselves as shamans, dervishes of inspiration, divinely possessed ecstatics— writers who believe with Emerson that the artist "has cast off the common motives of humanity and has ventured to trust himself for a task-master": himself above everyone. Emerson it is who advises writers to aspire, through isolation, to "a simple purpose ... as strong as iron necessity is to others," and who—in reply to every contingency—exhorts, "O father, O mother, O wife, O brother, O friend, I have lived with you after appearances hitherto. Henceforward I am the truth's." These shaman-writers, with their cult of individual genius and romantic egoism, may be self-glamorizing holy madmen, but they are not maniacs; they know what is good for them, and what is good for them is fences. You cannot get near them, whatever your need or demand. O father, O mother, O wife, O brother, O friend, they will tell you—*beat it*. They call themselves caviar, and for the general their caviar is a caveat.

Most writers are more modest than this, and more reasonable, and don't style themselves as unbridled creatures celestially privileged and driven. They know that they are citizens like other citizens, and have simply chosen a profession, as others have. These are the writers who go docilely to gatherings where they are required to marvel at every baby; who yield slavishly to the ukase that sends them out for days at a time to scout a samovar for the birthday of an elderly great-uncle; who pretend to overnight guests that they are capable of sitting at the breakfast table without being consumed by print; who craftily let on to in-laws that they are diligent cooks and sheltering wives, though they would sacrifice a husband to a hurricane to fetch them a typewriter ribbon; and so on. In short, they work at appearances, trust others for task-masters, and do not insist too rigorously on whose truth they will live after. And they are honorable enough. In company, they do their best to dress like everyone else: if they are women they will tolerate panty hose and high-heeled shoes, if they are men they will show up in a three-piece suit; but in either case they will be concealing the fact that during any ordinary row of days they sleep in their clothes. In the same company they lend themselves, decade after decade, to the expectation that they will not lay claim to unusual passions, that they will believe the average belief, that they will take pleasure in the average pleasure. Dickens, foreseeing the pain of relinquishing his pen at a time not of his choosing, reportedly would not accept an invitation. "Thank God for books," Auden said, "as an alternative to conversation." Good-citizen writers, by contrast, year after year decline no summons, refuse no banquet, turn away from no tedium, willingly enter into every anecdote and brook the assault of any amplified band. They will put down their pens for a noodle pudding.

And with all this sterling obedience, this strenuous courtliness and congeniality, this anxious flattery of unspoken coercion down to the third generation, something goes wrong. One dinner in twenty years is missed. Or no dinner at all is missed, but an "attitude" is somehow detected. No one is fooled; the cordiality is pronounced insincere, the smile a fake, the goodwill a dud, the talk a fib, the cosseting a cozening. These sweating citizen-writers are in the end always found out and accused. They are accused of elitism. They are accused of snobbery. They are accused of loving books and bookishness more feelingly than flesh and blood.

Edith Wharton, in her cool and bitter way, remarked of the literary life that "in my own family it created a kind of restraint that grew with the years. None of my relations ever spoke to me of my books, either to praise or to blame— they simply ignored them; . . . the subject was avoided as if it were a kind of family disgrace, which might be condoned but could not be forgotten."

Good-citizen writers are not read by their accusers; perhaps they cannot be. "If I succeed," said Conrad, "you shall find there according to your deserts: encouragement, consolation, fear, charm—all you demand—and, perhaps, also that glimpse of truth for which you have forgotten to ask." But some never demand, or demand less. "If you simplified your style," a strict but kindly aunt will advise, "you might come up to par," and her standard does not exempt Conrad.

The muse-inspired shaman-writers are never called snobs, for the plain reason that no strict but kindly aunt will ever get within a foot of any of them. But the good-citizen writers—by virtue of their very try at citizenship—are suspect and resented. Their work will not be taken for work. They will always be condemned for not being interchangeable with nurses or salesmen or schoolteachers or accountants or brokers. They will always be found out. They will always be seen to turn longingly after a torn peacock's tail left over from a fugitive sighting of paradise. They will always have hanging from a back pocket a telltale shred of idealism, or a cache of a few grains of noble importuning, or, if nothing so grandly quizzical, then a single beautiful word, in Latin or Hebrew; or else they will tip their hand at the wedding feast by complaining meekly of the raging horn that obliterates the human voice; or else they will forget not to fall into Montaigne over the morning toast; or else they will embarrass everyone by oafishly banging on the kettle of history; or else, while the room fills up with small talk, they will glaze over and inwardly chant "This Lime-Tree Bower My Prison"; or else—but never mind. What is not understood is not allowed. These citizen-pretenders will never be respectable. They will never come up to par. They will always be blamed for their airs. They will always be charged with superiority, disloyalty, coldness, want of family feeling. They will always be charged with estranging their wives, husbands, children. They will always be called snob.

They will never be granted the permission to write as serious writers are obliged to write: fanatically, obsessively, consumingly, torrentially, above all comically—and for life.

And therefore: enviable blissful provincial prolific lonesome David!

THE SEAM OF THE SNAIL

IN MY DEPRESSION childhood, whenever I had a new dress, my cousin Sarah would get suspicious. The nicer the dress was, and especially the more expensive it looked, the more suspicious she would get. Finally she would lift the hem and check the seams. This was to see if the dress had been bought or if my mother had sewed it. Sarah could always tell. My mother's sewing had elegant outsides, but there was something catch-as-catch-can about the insides. Sarah's sewing, by contrast, was as impeccably finished inside as out; not one stray thread dangled.

My uncle Jake built meticulous grandfather clocks out of rosewood; he was a perfectionist, and sent to England for the clockworks. My mother built serviceable radiator covers and a serviceable cabinet, with hinged doors, for the pantry. She built a pair of bookcases for the living room. Once, after I was grown and in a house of my own, she fixed the sewer pipe. She painted ceilings, and also landscapes; she reupholstered chairs. One summer she planted a whole yard of tall corn. She thought herself capable of doing anything, and did everything she imagined. But nothing was perfect. There were always some clear flaw, never visible head-on. You had to look underneath, where the seams were. The corn thrived, though not in rows. The stalks elbowed one another like gossips in a dense little village.

"Miss Brrrroooobaker," my mother used to mock, rolling her Russian *r*'s, whenever I crossed a *t* she had left uncrossed, or corrected a word she had misspelled, or became impatient with a *v* that had tangled itself up with a *w* in her speech. ("*Vvv*entriloquist," I would say. "*Vvv*entriloquist," she would obediently repeat. And the next time it would come out "wiolinist.") Miss Brubaker was my high school English teacher, and my mother invoked her name as an emblem of raging finical obsession. "Miss Brrrroooobaker," my mother's voice hoots at me down the years, as I go on casting and recasting sentences in a tiny handwriting on monomaniacally uniform paper. The loops of my mother's handwriting—it was the Palmer Method—were as big as soup bowls, spilling generous splashy ebullience. She could pull off, at five minutes' notice, a satisfying dinner for ten concocted out of nothing more than originality and panache. But the napkin would be folded a little off center, and the spoon might be on the wrong side of the knife. She was an optimist who ignored trifles; for her, God was not in the details but in the intent. And all these culinary and agricultural efflorescences were extracurricular, accomplished in the crevices and niches of a fourteen-hour business day. When she scribbled out her family memoirs, in heaps of dog-eared notebooks, or on the backs of old bills, or on the margins of last year's calendar, I would resist typing them; in the speed of the chase she often omitted words like "the," "and," "will." The same flashing and bountiful hand fashioned and fired ceramic pots, and painted brilliant autumn views and vases of imaginary flowers and ferns, and decorated ordinary Woolworth platters with lavish enameled gardens. But bits of the painted petals would chip away.

Lavish: my mother was as lavish as nature. She woke early and saturated the hours with work and inventiveness, and read late into the night. She was all profusion, abundance, fabrication. Angry at her children, she would run after us whirling the cord of the electric iron, like a lasso or a whip; but she never caught us. When, in seventh grade, I was afraid of failing the Music Appreciation final exam because I could not tell the difference between "To a Wild Rose" and "Barcarole," she got the idea of sending me to school with a gauze sling rigged up on my writing arm, and an explanatory note that was purest fiction. But the sling kept slipping off. My mother gave advice like mad—she boiled over with so much passion for the predicaments of strangers that they turned into permanent cronies. She told intimate stories about people I had never heard of.

Despite the gargantuan Palmer loops (or possibly because of them), I have always known that my mother's was a life of—intricately abashing word!—excellence: insofar as excellence means ripe generosity. She burgeoned, she proliferated; she was endlessly leafy and flowering. She wore red hats, and called herself a gypsy. In her girlhood she marched with the suffragettes and for Margaret Sanger and called herself a Red. She made me laugh, she was so varied: like a tree on which lemons, pomegranates, and prickly pears absurdly all hang together. She had the comedy of prodigality.

My own way is a thousand times more confined. I am a pinched perfectionist, the ultimate fruition of Miss Brubaker; I attend to crabbed minutiae and am self-trammeled through taking pains. I am a kind of human snail, locked in and condemned by my own nature. The ancients believed that the moist track left by the snail as it crept was the snail's own essence, depleting its body little by little; the farther the snail toiled, the smaller it became, until it finally rubbed itself out. That is how perfectionists are. Say to us Excellence, and we will show you how we use up our substance and wear ourselves away, while making scarcely any progress at all. The fact that I am an exacting perfectionist in a narrow strait only, and nowhere else, is hardly to the point, since nothing matters to me so much as a comely and muscular sentence. It is my narrow strait, this snail's road; the track of the sentence I am writing now; and when I have eked out the wet substance, ink or blood, that is its mark, I will begin the next sentence. Only in treading out sentences am I perfectionist; but then there is nothing else I know how to do, or take much interest in. I miter every pair of abutting sentences as scrupulously as Uncle Jake fitted one strip of rosewood against another. My mother's worldly and bountiful hand has escaped me. The sentence I am writing is my cabin and my shell, compact, self-sufficient. It is the burnished horizon—a merciless planet where flawlessness is the single standard, where even the inmost seams, however hidden from a laxer eye, must meet perfection. Here "excellence" is not strewn casually from a tipped cornucopia, here disorder does not account for charm, here trifles rule like tyrants.

I measure my life in sentences pressed out, line by line, like the lustrous ooze on the underside of the snail, the snail's secret open seam, its wound, leaking attar. My mother was too mettlesome to feel the force of a comma. She scorned minutiae. She measured her life according to what poured from the horn of plenty, which was her own seamless, ample, cascading, elastic, susceptible, inexact heart. My narrower heart rides between the tiny twin horns of the snail, dwindling as it goes.

And out of this thinnest thread, this ink-wet line of words, must rise a visionary fog, a mist, a smoke, forging cities, histories, sorrows, quagmires, entanglements, lives of sinners, even the life of my furnace-hearted mother: so much wilderness, waywardness, plenitude on the head of the precise and impeccable snail, between the horns. (Ah, if this could be!)

Portrait of the Artist as a Bad Character

FINALLY THERE IS something new to say about Mona Lisa's smile. A current theory holds that La Gioconda is a self-portrait—Leonardo without his beard—and that the smile is, in fact, a trickster's derisive glimmer, a transvestite joke: five centuries of pulling the wool over everyone's eyes.

Well, all right, suppose it's really so: a da Vinci witticism unmasked at last. What would that mean for all those duped dead generations who marveled at Mona Lisa for her harmonious specificity as a woman, or, more romantically, as Woman? If they believed in the innocence they saw, was it a lie they were seeing? Or, because he fooled the ages, ought we to send the hangman after Leonardo's ghost? And what of us—we who are advantaged, or, conceivably, deprived—in the wake of this putative discovery? In recognizing the artist's ruse, are we seeing Mona Lisa plain for the first time in the history of her unflagging secret laughter? Or do we tamper with intention when we superimpose what we may now know on that unaccoutered loveliness? Mona Lisa mustached! The graffiti vandal's dream.

Moonings like these may be of little use to da Vinci scholars, but they are charged with a certain literary irritation. They prod us to recall that the work of art is in its nature figment and fraud—but figment and fraud we have pointedly agreed to surrender to. If the fraud ends up a screw-twist more fraudulent than bargained for, that is what happens when you strike a bargain with someone dressed up in cap and bells. The Mona Lisa is made out of five-hundred-year-old paint, no matter who the model was, and it's the viewer who assents to the game of her being there at all. A portrait, like a novel, is a fiction, and what we call fiction is rightly named. In the compact between novelist and reader, the novelist promises to lie, and the reader promises to allow it.

These are notations so conspicuous and so stale that they are inscribed, no doubt, among the sacred antlers on neolithic cave walls; but they raise somewhat less obvious questions about the writer's potential for decent citizenship—the writer, that is, of fiction. Literary essayists, critical and social thinkers, historians, journalists, and so forth, don't in general, or at least not ideally, set out to defraud. The essayist's contract is exactly contrary to the novelist's—a promise to deliver ideas and "issues," implicit in which is a promise to show character. Fiction writers may easily begin as persons of character—more easily, say, than political columnists who are tempted to put a finger lightly on the scale—but the likelihood is that in the long run fiction bruises character. Novelists invent, deceive, exaggerate, and impersonate for several hours every day, and frequently on the weekend. Through the creation of bad souls they enter the demonic as a matter of course. They usurp emotions and appropriate lives.

As to the latter: "We all like to pretend we don't use real people," E. M. Forster once confessed, "but one does actually. I used some of my family. Miss Bartlett was my Aunt Emily— they all read the book but none of them saw it. . . . Mrs. Honeychurch was my grandmother. The three Miss Dickinsons condensed into two Miss Schlegels. Philip Herriton I modeled on Professor Dent. He knew this, and took an interest in his own progress." That may sound benign, but more often Professor Dent turns out to be sour and litigious, eager to muzzle, maim, or brain the writer into whose inspirations he has been unfortunate enough to fall. Saul Bellow's ingenious Shawmut, the put-down expert of "Him with His Foot in His Mouth," a self-described vatic type who stands for the artist, deduces that "I don't have to say a word for people to be insulted by me . . . my existence itself insults them. I come to this conclusion unwillingly, for God knows that I consider myself a man of normal social instincts and am not conscious of any will to offend." Yet Shawmut acknowledges he is in the grip of a manic force—a frenzy—signifying "something that is inaccessible to revision."

Good citizens are good—the consequence of normal social instincts—because they are usually accessible to revision; they are interested in self-improvement. Fiction writers have a different program for ego: not to polish it up for public relations, but to make it serve rapture—the rapture of language and drama, and also the rapture of deceit. The drive to rapture is resistant to revision in a big way, and will nail grandmothers and condense ladies no matter what. Professor Dent is right to look sweetly to his progress; he never had a chance to escape it. A well-worked fable is nothing but outright manipulation of this sort, not simply because it is all theater—what seems to be happening never actually happened—but because readers of fiction are forcibly dispossessed of a will of their own, and are made to think and feel whatever the writer commands. The characters in a novel are ten thousand times freer than their readers. Characters are often known to mutiny against the writer by taking charge of their books; readers, never. Readers are docile in succumbing to the responses prescribed for them; or else the book uncompromisingly closes its gates and shuts them out. In either case the writer is master.

Letters and diaries are not necessarily less fraudulent than works of fiction. It might be worthwhile for a scholar of deception—some ambitious graduate student in American literature, say—to compare a writer's journal entry on a particular day with a letter sent that same day. "Dear W: Your new poems have just come. Supernal stuff! You surpass yourself," the letter will start off. And the journal entry: "This A.M. received bilgewater from W; wrote him some twaddle." But even journals may not be trustworthy; a journal is a self-portrait, after all, and can white out the wens. I once met a young novelist who admitted that he was ashamed to tell his private diary his real secrets. On the other hand, the absence of abashment in a writer's diary is not the same as truth: who will measure Thomas Mann by the record of his flatulence, or the bite of Edmund Wilson by his compulsive nature pastels ("Mountains stained by blue shade—and, later, the pale brown rungs of the eucalyptus screens all pink in the setting sun")?

Storytellers and novelists, when on the job, rely on a treacherous braid of observation and invention; or call it memory and insinuation. Invention despoils observation, insinuation invalidates memory. A stewpot of bad habits, all of it—so that imaginative writers wind up, by and large, a shifty crew, sunk in distortion, misrepresentation, illusion, imposture, fakery. Those who—temporarily—elude getting caught out as bad characters are the handful of mainly guileless writers who eat themselves alive, like Kafka or Bruno Schulz. Such creatures neither observe nor invent. They never impersonate. Instead, they use themselves up in their fables, sinew by sinew. They are not in the world at all, or, if for a time they seem to be, it is only a simulacrum of a social being, and another lie.

Who will blame Leonardo for fooling us? The work was a sham to begin with. Those granules of chemicals on canvas were never Mona Lisa. She comes to life only with our connivance. And if the artist shows no character at all, and piles a second trick on the first, isn't he exactly the rascal we know him for?

GEORGE STEINER'S EITHER/OR

IN AN ESSAY pointedly called "The Archives of Eden,"
George Steiner makes a case for America (a case against,
actually) as the great museum hall of Europe. Almost no
element of American cultural expression, he argues, is
indigenously American. Even American literature is compelled to come under the heading of fundamental parasitism:
"Strictly regarded," Steiner avers, "American English and the
literature it produces is one of the branches, if statistically
the most forceful, of the prodigal ramifications of the mother-
tongue." Among the latter he lists "the language and literature of Canada, Australia, New Zealand, of the Anglo-Indian
community of the West Indies [and] of the English-speaking
nations of Africa." These, along with American English, continue to depend on "the eroded but still canonic primacy of
the motherland." American letters are, in fact—and in spite
of "claims to classic occasion"—a manifestation of a "conti-
nentally regional literature."

"The [literary] summits," Steiner finds, "are *not* American:
they are Thomas Mann, Kafka, Joyce and Proust."

As for painting and music, "American museums and art
collections are brimful of classical and European art. . . .
American orchestras, chamber groups, opera companies, perform European music." In philosophy and social thought,
"American philosophers edit, translate, comment upon and
teach Heidegger, Wittgenstein or Sartre but do not put forth
a major metaphysics. . . . the pressure of presence throughout
the world of the mind and moral feeling exercised on civilization by a Marx, a Freud, even a Lévi-Strauss, is of a caliber
which American culture does not produce."

96

The reason, in a word, is democracy; or, rather, democracy's indifference to high culture. Genius of this kind, Steiner believes, cannot be nurtured in a society lacking an "elite model": "It does look, and this is a somewhat perplexing phenomenon, as if the number of human beings capable of responding intelligently, with any genuine commitment of sensibility, to, say, a Mozart sonata, a Gauss theorem, a sonnet by Dante, a drawing by Ingres or a Kantian proposition and deductive chain is, in any given time and community, very restricted." And he concludes: "The first thing a coherent culture will do, therefore, is to maximalize the chances for the quantum leap, for the positive mutation which is genius."

But American culture has chosen to concentrate on something else: democratic meliorism, the broad hope of social progress. Steiner hardly denies the value of such a choice: "The flowering of the humanities is not worth the circumstance of the inhuman. No play by Racine is worth a Bastille, no Mandelstam poem an hour of Stalinism." Nor does he deny the harsh cost of a Periclean age; for the sake of honesty, the cost is what he insists on. Willingly, Steiner summons up the dark landscape that is likely, he assures us, to surround the gold:

> . . . the fabric of high literacy in the Periclean and European vein offers little protection against political oppression and folly. Civilization, in the elevated and formal sense, does not guarantee civility, does not inhibit social violence and waste. No mob, no storm-troop has ever hesitated to come down the Rue Descartes.

And yet for a moment he opens a chink into a possibly different notion of what high literacy might command: "An authentic culture," he tells us, focuses

> on the understanding, the enjoyment, the transmission forward, of the best that reason and imagination have brought forth in the past and are producing now. An authentic culture is one which makes of this order of response a primary moral and political function. It

makes "response" "responsibility," it makes echo "answerable to" the high occasions of the mind.

This second glimpse, which for an instant demotes despair, offers a view of authentic high culture commensurate with, and even giving rise to, ideas of "moral function," of "responsibility," of "answerability"—in short, all those signposts of the kind of liberal society we usually call "democratic humanism."

It is the second glimpse that makes me wonder about Steiner's conclusion—his Kierkegaardian Either/Or. The choice of democratic humanism, he grants, is "thoroughly justifiable." But it is "puerile hypocrisy" to want it both ways. Either the democratic society or the Periclean: one or the other. Still, Steiner's second glimpse suggests that at least for the space of that glimpse, he too sees a hope for having it both ways: visualizes it as possible, in fact, to have an "authentic culture" with a "fabric of high literacy" not only flourishing in a context of morality, responsibility, and answerability, but actually determining and stimulating these. When Steiner ascends, however fleetingly, to this vision (or maybe, in his view, is distracted by it), the meliorist American in me wants to cheer.

He does not allow a meliorist American (which anyhow is not what I usually think I am) to cheer for long. It would indeed be puerile to imagine that Steiner supposes the interests of the KGB to be a validation of the worth of culture. He leads us into the profoundest thickets of irony when he writes: "They order these matters better in the world of the gulag. . . . The KGB and the serious writer are in total accord when both know, when both *act on the knowledge* that a sonnet . . . , a novel, a scene from a play can be the power-house of human affairs." And earlier, Steiner aptly quotes Borges: "Censorship is the mother of metaphor." That is a maxim to gasp at; but Aesopian responses to oppression, however brilliant, can have only a limited life. Finally oppression destroys literature because it eats away at words, so that eventually an abused language will be of no use to an artist, no matter how metaphorical and Aesopian his devices. These are lessons that, following Orwell, Steiner was among the first to teach us. In "The Hollow Miracle," an essay on post-Holocaust Germany, he warned: 'Something will happen to the words."* Namely: when the public language is hanged in the public square, it will ultimately put the noose around the interior language. The sublime Mandelstam, to take one of Steiner's own examples, was martyred and perished because of a poem in which he compared Stalin's mustache to an insect. Of course Steiner doesn't mean us to think that tyranny, in its acknowledgment of the power in the poem—in its ceding importance to the poem—is "good for" culture. All the same, he reminds us that even when the barbarians were upon him, Archimedes did not flee; he stuck to his meditations and kept working on his theorem. Here is Plutarch's account:

> Archimedes was then, as fate would have it, intent upon working out some problem by a diagram, and having fixed his mind alike and his eyes upon the subject of speculation, he never noticed the incursion of the Romans, nor that the city was taken. In this transport of study and contemplation, a soldier unexpectedly coming up to him, commanded him to follow; which he declined to do before he had worked out his problem to a demonstration; the soldier, enraged, drew his sword and ran him through.

Yet elsewhere in his own demonstration Steiner counts up all

---

* In response to this allusion, Steiner comments: "I was entirely mistaken, more than twenty years ago, when I conjectured that the German language and its literatures (there are, of course, several) would not recover from Nazi evisceration. Poetry, fiction, drama and philosophic argument are intensely alive in both Germanies." Among "writers of the first rank" he cites "Thomas Bernhard, Ingeborg Bachmann, Christa Wolf, Günter Grass." But if German culture has indeed wholly recovered, and is now to be judged by the usual standards of civilization, and if Steiner requires American writing to be measured against "Thomas Mann, Kafka, Joyce and Proust" (two of whom emerge from two of the German "literatures"), then why will he not demand the same measure of grandeur for a recovered Germany? And if the vitality of the new German democracy contributes to this lack—just as American democracy is seen to be responsible for American high-cultural barrenness—why should Steiner find himself so easily satisfied by a Bernhard, a Bachmann, a Wolf, a Grass, when he is not at all satisfied by their American equivalents?

those mathematical thinkers of foreign birth who flourished in America precisely because they *did* flee the barbarians.

But leaving all that aside, doesn't history grant us at least one miraculous age when the munificence of "high literacy" came to pass in a vigorously open society, sans barbarians or storm troopers? Steiner himself urges us to remember that "the passionate outpouring of popular interest in the often competitive, agonistic achievements of Renaissance artists and men of learning, of the complex manifold of adherence which made possible the Elizabethan theater audience, is not nostalgic fiction." Would it then be futuristic fiction—and not an instance of "puerile hypocrisy"—to imagine that absolute thought and absolute art might one day happen in America, despite the absence of popular interest and adherence? Despite all the horrendously recognizable descriptions Steiner has given us of America as a busy, vulgarized, well-stocked, but sterile warehouse for the fossils of European civilization?

I want to make a small quick—perhaps comical—case for such a futuristic fiction, based not on any idea of my own, but on Steiner's own portrait of the "matrix of creation"—of the genius. Here, culled at random, are some phrases and fragments that represent Steiner's depiction of genius:

"Privacy *in extremis*"
"A leprosy which seeks apartness"
"The inebriate of thought"
"The *cordon sanitaire* which a Wittgenstein could draw around himself in order to secure minimal physical survival and autonomy of spirit"
"Obsession"
"Contagion"
"Craziness"
"Ecstatic lives"
"Calling"
"Talisman of true clerisy"
"Transcendence"
"Ontological astonishment"
"Artistic absolutes of possession and self-possession"

The pursuit of art characterized as "pathological"

The use of the word "espouse" with its accompanying gloss: "a justly sacramental verb"

Obsession "that overrides the claims of social justice"

"A cultivation of solitude verging on the pathological"

"Absolute thought" as "antisocial, resistant to gregariousness, perhaps autistic"

"Personal apartness, self-exile"

It would be diminishing, and not to Steiner, to characterize these particles of portraiture as "romantic." He may seem momentarily romantic in that special sense when he speaks of "Montaigne's tower, Kierkegaard's room, Nietzsche's clandestine peregrinations." But Steiner himself warns us not to mistake his meaning for mere romanticism: "one need not mouth romantic platitudes on art and infirmity, on genius and madness, on creativity and suffering, in order to suppose that absolute thought, the commitment of one's life to a gamble on transcendence, the destruction of domestic and social relations in the name of art and 'useless' speculation, *are* part of the phenomenology which is, in respect of the utilitarian, social norm, pathological."

It would also be diminishing to make a joke about the extremely American tone of Steiner's ultimately anti-American, if I may use that term, essay. How would one buttress such a joke? As follows, with still more fragments on the necessary isolation and antisocial pathology of genius:

> . . . truly it demands something godlike in him who has cast off the common motives of humanity and has ventured to trust himself for a taskmaster. High be his heart, faithful his will, clear his sight, that he may in good earnest be doctrine, society, law, to himself, that a simple purpose may be to him as strong as iron necessity is to others! . . . Your isolation must not be mechanical, but spiritual, that is, must be elevation. . . . Be it known unto you that henceforward I will obey no law less than the eternal law. . . . I will so trust that what is deep is

101

holy, that I will do strongly before the sun and moon whatever inly rejoices me and the heart appoints.

Here again is Archimedes in concentration the moment before the barbarian sword runs him through. But you have already recognized the joke. These words are almost paraphrases of Steiner's "cultivation of solitude verging on the pathological," his "absolute thought" as "antisocial, resistant to gregariousness, perhaps autistic." You know that they are from Emerson's "Self-Reliance." The joke, if one were looking for a joke, would be to point out that Steiner's chord, with all its antipathy for the American culture-warehouse, carries nearly breath-for-breath the heartbeat of the quintessentially American essay.

But the reason I cannot accept Steiner's delineation of the absolute thinker and artist has nothing to do with any specious accusation of romanticism, and still less to do with Emersonian ironies and echoes. I cannot accept his portrait of the artist because I am willing to take his portrait as seriously as he himself takes it: the artist as a kind of shaman or holy figure, set apart from the tribe by special powers and magickings. Steiner alludes, at one point, to the sacramental valuation set on epileptics, who in some societies are automatically regarded as shamans. "There *is* a strategy of chosen illness in Archimedes' decision to die rather than relinquish a geometric deduction (this gesture being the talisman of a true clerisy)." These last three words—"talisman," "true," "clerisy"—are a trinity testifying to the priestly position Steiner accords the absolute artist, the absolute thinker. He endows his genius with godlike concentration; he agrees that "common sense, civics, and political humanity" can make no such espousal.

But consider another path. Believing as thoroughly and as passionately as he does in the artist as thaumaturge, in the nearly autistic, obsessive, privacy-seeking autonomy of the creative genius, perhaps Steiner may be genuinely led not to decry American philistinism, but to see it as a wry opportunity. Unlike the KGB, Steiner notes, American culture is totally indifferent to the claims of high art. "What text,"

Steiner asks, "what painting, what symphony, could shake the edifice of American politics? What act of abstract thought really matters at all? Who *cares*?"

If it is true that the answer is *nobody cares*—and *nobody cares* is the answer Steiner certainly gives us—then American society ought to be the ideal seedbed, the perfect fertilization dish, for the genius for whom isolation is the *sine qua non*. What is more isolating than our philistinism? What offers a deeper privacy? I am afraid that what I am saying now will come to you with a touch of the sardonic: a joke, you may think, like Emerson. But it is not a joke and I am not aiming for the merely sardonic. If high culture is really a matter, as Steiner has it, of *nascitur non fit*, born-not-made (the philosopher, say, in whom complex and arduous thought is latent, and who cannot be trained into his idiosyncratic calling); if high culture is really a matter of obsessive privacy, originality, autonomy, then the surrounding indifference makes everything possible. What is missing, of course, is that "competitive, agonistic" Elizabethan responsiveness; but does a shaman need that? Isn't a shaman complete in himself, a circle of fire, torch and conflagration both, the dancer and the dance? Isn't the theorem its own reward, the living note of music its own delight, the line of a poem its own rapture? Everything Steiner reports to us about his conception of the requirements of absolute (and absolutely elitist) art would have us believe this. Why then should he deplore the absence of an animate and responsive culture as a context for his godlike creator?* Isn't it more than enough for the thinker

---

* To this Steiner has replied: "There is a great difference between an isolation which remains so because the surrounding community could not care less and one which is instrumental toward work which the community waits for and regards as central (the isolation of a Webern, of a Heidegger, of a Wittgenstein, of a Borges)." But if this is so, then Steiner must surrender his admiration for the death of Archimedes; or at least surrender it as an emblem of the original thinker's isolated obsessiveness. Archimedes keeps up his concentration, sticks to his work, even when the "surrounding community" is no more welcoming than a single murderous barbarian soldier. The point of the story for Steiner, if I properly understand his use of it, is precisely the absolute thinker's consummate indifference to the idea of a community that waits for his work and regards it as central. Who will care less for Archimedes' demonstration than that barbarian?

to say, Let there be light, and to see for himself that the light is good?

But if Steiner asserts—and he has magnificently asserted it—that a society must be more than a storehouse for the culture of another continent, that a society must answer back the claims of art and science with appropriate understanding and joy, gratitude and gratification—then should he not require for this responsiveness, this seizing and answering, a different definition of the artist, the thinker, the "matrix of creation," the genius? A definition less dependent on holy pathology?

OF BASILISKS AND BAROMETZES

IS REALITY NECESSARY?

Light-hearted, light-footed reader, do not flee! Our subject is no tough ontological rind. (Philosophers, go home.) It is, rather, the mazy gossamer of make-believe; the desire to be invisible; the longing for strange histories that never were; the urge to slip loose from one's own life. In short, the overcrowded precinct of non-existence.

To wit: A celebrated American novelist recently sought to vanish—or, if not precisely to vanish, then to be transformed, as in any tale of magic, from true and accessible being to the arcane grottoes of subterranean fancy. Joyce Carol Oates, casting a spell over her husband's name—Raymond Smith— became Rosamond Smith, who doesn't exist. ("I wanted to escape from my own identity," Rosamond Smith's inventor explained.) The imaginary Smith instantly signed a contract with a publisher for a first novel. Almost as instantly, the ruse was aborted—it may be that the literary famous are forbidden clandestine play, and too bad. It is easy to find Joyce Carol Oates in any bookshop; but Rosamond Smith has yet to be read, and now never will be. To protest that it makes no difference, that the very same novel will be published anyhow, is not to the point. A book by Rosamond Smith is in no way a book by Joyce Carol Oates, even if the words are identical. We know, after all, what to expect of Joyce Carol Oates, however unexpected her devisings: the imprint of reputation inheres in every phrase. But what kind of writer might Rosamond Smith have turned out to be?

The brief materialization and speedy vaporization of the phantom Smith will leave a melancholy mark in literary

105

history, yet hardly an anomalous one. There are whole phalanxes of non-existent writers who have written real books—
among them Lewis Carroll, Mark Twain, George Orwell;
and some would even dare to charge Homer, Shakespeare,
and David the Psalmist with the scam of attaching phony
names to popular hits. Still, the assurance of corporeal authenticity—half a dozen writers more or less in the world—
will scarcely shake society. Far more significant are the vast
libraries, corridors stretching into infinity, of books that have
never been written. We ought to declare our gratitude for
these non-existent works on two counts: first, writing that is
confined to mere potentiality is in almost all instances reliably
superior to words actually on a page. What drudging novelist
has not been alarmed by the corruption of a visionary text
the moment it begins to creep from the satanically forked
nib of a fountain pen, or to solidify on a gelid green screen?
And second, if every volume dreamed of were committed to
paper ("I could write a book!" cry landlady, doorman, and
cabby), our crammed and diminutive planet would have to
choose, ecologically speaking, between new publishing
houses and new generations.

Non-existent books offer relief in other ways. For example,
a disappointed writer whose own novels have sunk into nul-
lity (without the advantage of prior non-existence) can satu-
rate himself in the putative bliss of fame simply by tossing
off a romance about an illustrious author of genius. All that
is required in such a scheme is to *name* the glorious works
in question; toiling at a facsimile of, say, *The Magic Mountain*
will be superfluous, since the delectable emoluments of
acclaim rush in to be relished as early as Chapter Two.
Compensation for the ache of mediocrity, no doubt—a
notion swiped, I admit, not from the immortal Emerson but
from the indispensable Max Beerbohm. Beerbohm deserves
to be kept on the kitchen counter along with other household
helps; he is as valuable for appeasing the consciences of
people who hate giving dinner parties (see his "Hosts and
Guests") as for having produced an actual *list* of non-existent
books. The handful of volumes that he regards as first-rate
(there are many more judged inferior though seductive) seems

to have sprung mainly from the heads of non-existent writers who have sprung from the head of Henry James; we are provocatively reminded that the ectoplasmic passions promised in "The Middle Years," "Shadowmere," and "The Major Key," not to mention the magisterial "Beltraffio," are all grievously beyond our reach.

But if it is a sad thing to know there are books we will never be allowed to read for no better reason than that they do not exist, this does not imply we are to learn nothing of the careers of other spectral authors. Jorge Luis Borges, the century's most flagrant, ingenious, and industrious compiler of manuscripts that fall short of reality (including their plots, footnotes, and commentaries), is even more intent on fathoming the curious minds of his imaginary scribes. One of these, Jaromir Hladík, author of an unfinished tragedy in verse, is about to be shot by a firing squad; in the final seconds of consciousness his electrified brain is able to revise and complete his play—a full year's labor—down to its last turn and syllable. Pierre Menard—whose definitive if counterfeit bibliography Borges meticulously catalogues—attempts, in 1934, to rewrite Cervantes's *Don Quixote*, though in language painstakingly unaltered from the sixteenth-century original. ("The archaic style of Menard," Borges pedantically notes, "suffers from a certain affectation. Not so that of his precursor, who handles easily the ordinary Spanish of his time.") Borges also introduces a novel by a non-existent Bombay lawyer named Mir Bahadur Ali, along with an analysis of its publishing history, theology, and mythological derivations. Similarly, he describes the astounding erudition of the non-existent author of "The God of the Labyrinth," Herbert Quain, who unfortunately died "totally used to failure" at the age of forty. All these writers have in common not only their commanding non-existence, but also their confidence in the power of the insubstantial. As the courageous Hladík puts it, "unreality . . . is the necessary condition of art."

It should not be assumed, however, that it is solely authors and books that are eligible for non-existence. Not at all; such a claim would be parochial. One has only to consult Borges's own *Book of Imaginary Beings* to encounter chimeras, phoe-nixes, basilisks, barometzes (the last a kind of vegetable lamb), and the like. As for the geography of non-being—here the terrain is very wide indeed—every sleepless tourist is familiar with the Land of Cockaigne; but for directions to such sites as Icaria, Limanora, Amneran Heath, the Waq Archipelago, or Wastepaperland, one must go to the exhaus-tive *Dictionary of Imaginary Places*, an encyclopaedic work admirably edited by Alberto Manguel and Gianni Guadalupi. The objection may be raised that make-believe creatures and make-believe localities are themselves a branch of the library of non-existence, and will inevitably be classified as book-ish—but that is a tedious and literal-minded quibble. Pope-figs' Island is currently without a single bookshop, and hippogriffs are notorious for fearing librarians.

Of course, it must be conceded that the non-existent—while admittedly necessary—is not always more inviting, original, interesting, or praiseworthy than what is stocked in the more limited warehouse of reality. To be persuaded of this truth, merely recall, from *Middlemarch*, the desiccated Mr. Casaubon's huge manuscript volumes: those deadly notes for his appalling "Key to All Mythologies." Though we may regret that we will never get the chance to read the exquisite "Beltraffio," or Pierre Menard's punctilious "Don Quixote," there are some non-existent books we can well do without.

THE MUSE, POSTMODERN AND
HOMELESS

If you're a writer and if you're by nature Sublime and
   Magisterial,
but you need cash—lots and lots—
don't try to change your literary spots.
Spot-changing won't get you any dough or even any cereal.
You'll only end up feeling gypped, not to mention funereal.
So if you're a hifaluting ineffable Artist of noble intent,
   you might as well stick to your last,
since nobody who reads for fun will read *you* for fun
   because it's impossible to read you fast.

THESE ARE LINES Ogden Nash did not write. Henry James
did, sort of, in the form of a melancholy comic tale called
"The Next Time." Its hero is a genius novelist who, in the
hope of making his fortune, attempts to become a popular
hack. Again and again he feels sure he has finally gotten the
hang of it—grinding out a best-selling quick read—but each
time, to his disappointment, what emerges is only another
masterpiece.

James himself once contrived to write a letter of Paris chat
for the New York *Tribune*. He managed to keep it going for
months, but the column was a failure. He could not "enter-
tain." When the editor complained that James's themes were
"too remote from popular interests," James snapped back:
"If my letters have been 'too good' I am honestly afraid that
they are the poorest I can do, especially for the money!" "I

thought in all conscience," he said privately, "they had been flimsy enough."

"The Next Time" appeared in 1895; modernism was not yet born. But in his portrait (however teasing) of the artist as a sovereign and unbetrayable focus of authenticity, James had put his finger on what modernism was going to be mainly about.

"Things fall apart; the center cannot hold." That, we used to think, was the whole of modernism—Yeats mourning the irrecoverable old assurances while the surprising new shapes of things, symbols and fragments, flashed by in all their usurping alterations. Now we know better, and also, in a way, worse. Yeats hardly foresaw how our dissolutions would surpass his own—but where we are now is, after all, what he was describing.

And where we are now is the no-man's-land that more and more begins to inherit the name postmodern—atomized, leveled, thoroughly democratic turf where anything goes, everything counts, significance is what I say it is, literature is what's there for the exegetes: comic strips, 1950s sitcoms, fast-food hamburger ads. The elitism of High Art was vanquished long ago, and not only by the Marxists. The divide between Bob Dylan and Dylan Thomas is plugged by critical egalitarianism; so is the difference between poet and critic. *Allee samee*, as Allen Ginsberg once remarked of the great religions—as if wanting to repair the world and wanting to get out of it were indistinguishable. History is whatever selection most favors your cultural thesis. Movements move so rapidly that their direct ancestors are on to something else before they can be undermined and undone as rival precursors. Whether in painting or in literary theory, there is the glee of plenitude and proliferation along these postmodern boulevards, and a dogged pluralism, and individualism splintering off into idiosyncratic fits of unconventionality desperate to pass for original. With so much originality at hand (originality without an origin), and no center (or any number of centers, one to a customer), what's left to be called eccentric?

Modernism had its own widening gyres and ruptures—ruptures enough, hollow men and waste lands, the smashing of every rooted assumption and literary guaranty—but one center did hold, one pledge stuck. This was the artist's pledge to the self. Joyce, Mann, Eliot, Proust, Conrad (even with his furies): they *knew*. And what they knew was that—though things fall apart—the artist is whole, consummate. At bottom, in the deepest brain, rested the supreme serenity and masterly confidence of the sovereign maker.

Prior to modernism, genius scarcely needed to be centered—self-centered, "magisterial"—in this way. Jane Austen and Trollope had their village certainties to keep the balance, to pull toward the center: society, tradition, "realism," the solid verity of the vicar's wife. Even the Romantics, haunting the lonely periphery, deserting the matrix, still had a matrix to desert. The moderns looked all around, saw that nothing held, and began to make themselves up as law, and sometimes as religion. James, preparing in his Notebooks for a new piece of work, secretly crooned down at his pen: *mon bon, caro mio*. His dearest good angel, his faithful Muse, was housed in himself.

Almost no writer, not even the most accomplished, is like that now. Postmodernism, for writers, means fear and flux, unsureness, inward chaos, self-surprise. Virginia Woolf's *Common Reader* in full sail may suggest she is among the moderns, but her diaries show her trembling. Of contemporaries we read in English, only Nadine Gordimer, Joseph Brodsky, and V. S. Naipaul seem to own that central stillness, pride, and genuinely autocratic play of the humors that the moderns had; all three have been embattled by dislocations (Naipaul aggressively, by choice), and it is hard to tell whether it is the seizures of history we feel in these writers, or a true residue of modernist authority.

Those born into American indulgences are less flinty. John Updike in an interview last year spoke of the writer's work as "a little like handwriting. It comes out to be you no matter what you do. That is, it's recognizably Updike." A tendril of astonishment in that, as if there might reasonably have been an alternative. The moderns were unsurprised by their consistencies, and expected to come out what they were: inviolable. The characters in Philip Roth's *The Counterlife* are so wilily infiltrated by postmodernist inconstancy that they keep revising their speeches and their fates: you can't trust them even to stay dead. It goes without saying that we are forbidden to speculate whether the writer who imagined them is as anxiously protean, as cleft by doubt, as they.

Literary modernism, despite clangor and disjunction, was gilded by a certain voluptuousness: it came of the writer's self-knowledge—or call it self-anointment, a thing that properly embarrasses us today. But there was mettle in it; and also prowess, and defiance, and accountability. If the raggedy improvisations of postmodernism have killed off the idea of the Sublime and Magisterial Artist, it suits and gratifies our democratic temperament; the Sublime and the Magisterial were too long on their deathbeds anyhow.

Still, without modernism to give her shelter in the supernal confidence of genius, where can the Muse lodge now?

CROCODILED MOATS IN THE KINGDOM OF LETTERS

For constantly I felt I was moving among two groups—comparable in intelligence, identical in race, not grossly different in social origin, earning about the same incomes, who had almost ceased to communicate at all, who in intellectual, moral and psychological climate had so little in common that . . . one might have crossed an ocean.

C. P. SNOW, *The Two Cultures
and the Scientific Revolution*

DISRAELI IN HIS novel *Sybil* spoke of "two nations," the rich and the poor. After the progress of more than a century, the phrase (and the reality) remains regrettably apt. But in the less than three decades since C. P. Snow proposed his "two cultures" thesis—the gap of incomprehension between the scientific and literary elites—the conditions of what we still like to call culture have altered so drastically that Snow's arguments are mostly dissolved into pointlessness. His compatriot and foremost needler, the Cambridge critic F. R. Leavis, had in any case set out to flog Snow's hypothesis from the start. Snow, he said, "rides on an advancing swell of cliché," "doesn't know what literature is," and hasn't "had the advantage of an intellectual discipline of any kind." And besides—here Leavis emitted his final boom—"there is only one culture."

In the long run both were destined to be mistaken—Leavis perhaps more than Snow. In 1959, when Snow published *The Two Cultures*, we had already had well over a hundred years to get used to the idea of science as a multi-divergent venture—dozens and dozens of disciplines, each one nearly a separate nation with its own governance, psychology, entelechy. It might have been possible to posit, say, a unitary medical culture in the days when barbers were surgeons; but in recent generations we don't expect our dentist to repair a broken kneecap, or our orthopedist to practice cardiology. And nowadays we are learning that an ophthalmologist with an understanding of the cornea is likely to be a bit shaky on the subject of the retina. Engineers are light-years from astrophysicists. Topology is distinct from topography, paleobotany from paleogeology. In reiterating that scientific culture is specialist culture—who doesn't know this?—one risks riding an advancing swell of cliché. Yet science, multiplying, fragmented, in hot pursuit of split ends, is in a way a species of polytheism, or, rather, animism: every grain of matter, every path of conceptualization, has its own ruling spirit, its differentiated lawgiver and traffic director. Investigative diversity and particularizing empiricism have been characteristic of science since—well, since alchemy turned into physical chemistry (and lately into superconductivity); since the tea-kettle inspired the locomotive; since Icarus took off his wax wings to become Pan Am; since Archimedes stepped out of his tub into Einstein's sea.

Snow was in command of all this, of course—he was pleased to identify himself as an exceptional scientist who wrote novels—and still he chose to make a monolith out of splinters. Why did he do it? In order to have one unanimity confront another. While it may have been a polemical contrivance to present a diversiform scientific culture as unitary, it was patently not wrong, thirty years ago, to speak of literary culture as a single force or presence. That was what was meant by the peaceable word "humanities." And it was what Leavis meant, too, when he growled back at Snow that one culture was all there was worth having. "Don't mistake me," Leavis pressed, "I am not preaching that we should defy, or try to reverse, the accelerating movement of external civilization (the phrase sufficiently explains itself, I hope) that is determined by advancing technology.... What I *am* saying is that such a concern is not enough—disastrously not enough." Not enough, he argued, for "a human future . . . in full intelligent possession of its full humanity." For Leavis, technology was the mere outer rind of culture, and the job of literature (the hot core at the heart of culture) was not to oppose science but to humanize it. Only in Snow's wretchedly deprived mind did literature stand apart from science; Snow hardly understood what literature was *for*. And no wonder: Snow's ideas about literary intellectuals came, Leavis sneered, from "the reviewing in the Sunday papers."

It has never been easy to fashion a uniform image of science—which is why we tend to say "the sciences." But until not very long ago one could take it for granted (despite the headlong decline of serious high art) that there was, on the humanities side, a concordant language of sensibility, an embracing impulse toward integration, above all the conviction of human connectedness—even if that conviction occasionally partook of a certain crepuscular nostalgia we might better have done without. Snow pictured literature and science as two angry armies. Leavis announced that there was only one army, with literature as its commander-in-chief. Yet it was plain that both Leavis and Snow, for all their antagonisms, saw the kingdom of letters as an intact and enduring power.

This feeling for literary culture as a glowing wholeness—it *was* a feeling, a stirring, a flush of idealism—is now altogether dissipated. The fragrant term that encapsuled it—belles-lettres—is nearly archaic and surely effete: it smacks of leather tooling for the moneyed, of posturing. But it was once useful enough. "Belles-lettres" stood for a binding thread of observation and civilizing emotion. It signified not so much that letters are beautiful as that the house of letters is encompassingly humane and undivisive, no matter how severally its windows are shaped, or who looks out or in. Poets, scholars, journalists, librarians, novelists, playwrights, art critics, philosophers, writers for children, historians, political theorists, and all the rest, may have inhabited different rooms, differently furnished, but it was indisputably one house with a single roof and plenty of connecting doors and passageways. And sometimes—so elastic and compressive was the humanist principle—poet, scholar, essayist, philosopher, etc., all lived side by side in the same head. Seamlessness (even if only an illusion) never implied locked and separate cells.

And now? Look around. Now "letters" suggests a thousand enemy camps, "genres" like fortresses, professions isolated by crocodiled moats. The living tissue of intuition and inference that nurtured the commonalty of the humanities is ruptured by an abrupt invasion of specialists. In emulation of the sciences? But we don't often hear of astronomers despising molecular biologists; in science, it may be natural for knowledge to run, like quicksilver, into crannies.

In the ex-community of letters, factions are in fashion, and the business of factions is to despise. Matthew Arnold's mild and venerable dictum, an open-ended, open-armed definition of literature that clearly intends a nobility of inclusiveness— "the best that is known and thought in the world"—earns latter-day assaults and jeers. What can all that mean now but "canon," and what can a received canon mean but reactionary, racist, sexist, elitist closure? Politics presses against disinterestedness; what claims to be intrinsic is counted as no more than foregone conclusion. All categories are suspect, no category is allowed to display its wares without the charge of vested interest or ideological immanence. What Arnold called the play of mind is asked to show its credentials and prove its legitimacy. "Our organs of criticism," Arnold complained in 1864 (a period as uninnocent as our own), "are organs of men and parties having practical ends to serve, and with them those practical ends are the first thing and the play of mind the second."

And so it is with us. The culture of the humanities has split and split and split again, always for reasons of partisan ascendancy and scorn. Once it was not unusual for writers— Dreiser, Stephen Crane, Cather, Hemingway!—to turn to journalism for a taste of the workings of the world. Today novelists and journalists are alien breeds reared apart, as if imagination properly belonged only to the one and never to the other; as if society and instinct were designed for estrangement. The two crafts are contradictory even in method: journalists are urged to tell secrets in the top line; novelists insinuate suspensefully, and wait for the last line to spill the real beans. Dickens, saturated in journalism, excelled at shorthand; was a court reporter; edited topical magazines.

In the literary academy, Jacques Derrida has the authority that Duns Scotus had for medieval scholastics—and it is authority, not literature, that mainly engages faculties. In the guise of maverick or rebel, professors kowtow to dogma. English departments have set off after theory, and use culture as an instrument to illustrate doctrinal principles, whether Marxist or "French Freud." The play of mind gives way to signing up and lining up. College teachers were never so cut off from the heat of poets dead or alive as they are now; only think of the icy distances separating syllables by, say, Marianne Moore, A. R. Ammons, May Swenson, or Amy Clampitt from the papers read at last winter's Modern Language Association meeting—viz., "Written Discourse as Dialogic Interaction," "Abduction, Transference, and the Reading Stage," "The Politics of Feminism and the Discourse of Feminist Literary Criticism."

And more: poets trivialize novelists, novelists trivialize poets. Both trivialize critics. Critics trivialize reviewers. Reviewers retort that they *are* critics. Short-story writers assert transfigurations unavailable to novelists. Novelists declare the incomparable glories of the long pull. Novelizing aestheticians, admitting to literature no claims of moral intent, ban novelizing moralists. The moralists condemn the aestheticians as precious, barren, solipsist. Few essayists essay fiction. Few novelists hazard essays. Dense-language writers vilify minimalists. Writers of plain prose ridicule complex sentences. Professors look down on commercial publishers. Fiction writers dread university presses. The so-called provinces envy and despise the provinciality of New York. New York sees sour grapes in California and everywhere else. The so-called mainstream judges which writers are acceptably universal and which are to be exiled as "parochial." The so-called parochial, stung or cowardly or both, fear all particularity and attempt impersonation of the acceptable. "Star"

117

writers—recall the 1986 International PEN Congress in New York—treat lesser-knowns as invisible, negligible. The lesser-knowns, crushed, disparage the stars.

And even the public library, once the unchallenged repository of the best that is known and thought, begins to split itself off, abandons its mandate, and rents out Polaroid cameras and videotapes, like some semi-philanthropic electronics mart. My own local library, appearing to jettison the basic arguments of the age, flaunts shelf after shelf prominently marked Decorating, Consumer Power, How To, Cookery, Hooray for Hollywood, Accent on You, What Makes Us Laugh, and many more such chitchat categories. But there are no placards for Literature, History, Biography; and Snow and Leavis, whom I needed to moon over in order to get started on this essay, were neither one to be had. (I found them finally in the next town, in a much smaller if more traditionally bookish library.)

Though it goes against the grain of respected current belief to say so, literature is really *about* something. It is about us. That may be why we are drawn to think of the kingdom of letters as a unity, at least in potential. Science, teeming and multiform, is about how the earth and the heavens and the microbes and the insects and our mammalian bodies are constructed, but literature is about the meaning of the finished construction. Or, to set afloat a more transcendent vocabulary: science is about God's work; literature is about our work. If our work lies untended (and what is our work but aspiration?), if literary culture falls into a heap of adversarial splinters—into competing contemptuous clamorers for turf and mental dominance—then what will be left to tell us that we are one human presence?

To forward that strenuous telling, Matthew Arnold (himself now among the jettisoned) advised every reader and critic to "try and possess one great literature, at least, besides his own; and the more unlike his own, the better." Not to split off from but to add on to the kingdom of letters: so as to uncover its human face.

An idea that—in a time of ten thousand self-segregating literary technologies—may be unwanted, if not obsolete.

LITERATURE AND THE POLITICS OF SEX: A DISSENT

WOMEN WHO WRITE with an overriding consciousness that they write *as women* are engaged not in aspiration toward writing, but chiefly in a politics of sex. A new political term makes its appearance: *woman writer*, not used descriptively— as one would say "a lanky brown-haired writer"—but as part of the language of politics.

Now a politics of sex can be very much to the point. No one would deny that the movement for female suffrage was a politics of sex, and obviously any agitation for equality in employment, in the professions, and in government is a politics of sex.

But the language of politics is not writer's language. Politics begins with premises; imagination goes in search of them. The political term *woman writer* signals in advance a whole set of premises: that, for instance, there are "male" and "female" states of intellect and feeling, hence of prose; that individuality of condition and temperament do not apply, or at least not much, and that all writing women possess—not by virtue of being writers but by virtue of being women—an instantly perceived common ground; that writers who are women can best nourish other writers who are women.

"There is a human component to literature," according to Ellen Moers, "which a woman writer can more easily discuss with another woman writer, even across an ocean, than she can with the literary man next door."*

* *Literary Women.*

119

I deny this. There is a human component to literature that does not separate writers by sex, but that—on the contrary—engenders sympathies from sex to sex, from condition to condition, from experience to experience, from like to like, and from unlike to unlike. Literature universalizes. Without disparaging particularity or identity, it universalizes; it does not divide.

But what, with respect to particularity or identity, is a "woman writer"? Outside its political uses, "woman writer" has no meaning—not intellectually, not morally, not historically. A writer is a writer.

Does a "woman writer" have a separate psychology—by virtue of being a woman? Does a "woman writer" have a separate body of ideas—by virtue of being a woman? It was these misleading currencies that classical feminism was created to deny.

Does a "woman writer" have a body of separate experience—by virtue of being a woman? It was this myth-fed condition of segregation that classical feminism was created to bring an end to.

Insofar as some women, and some writers who are women, have separate bodies of experience or separate psychologies, to that degree has the feminism of these women not yet asserted itself. In art, feminism is that idea which opposes segregation; which means to abolish mythological divisions; which declares that the imagination cannot be "set" free, because it is already free.

To say "the imagination is free" is, in fact, a tautology. The imagination is by definition, by nature, freedom and autonomy. When I write, I am free. I am, as a writer, whatever I wish to become. I can think myself into a male, or a female, or a stone, or a raindrop, or a block of wood, or a Tibetan, or the spine of a cactus.

In life, I am not free. In life, female or male, no one is free. In life, female or male, I have tasks; I have obligations and responsibilities; I have a toothache, being contingent on nature; I am devoured by drudgery and fragmentation. My freedom is contingent on need. I am, in short, claimed. Female or male, I am subject to the disciplines of health or disease, of getting and spending, of being someone's child and being someone's parent. Society—which is not yet utopia—tells me to go stand there and do that, or else keep my distance and not do this. In life, I accept those dictums of Society which seem to me to be the same as Civilization, and quarrel with the rest.

But when I write, what do Society and its protocol mean to me? When I write, I am in command of a grand *As If*. I write *As If* I were truly free. And this *As If* is not a myth. As soon as I proclaim it, as soon as my conduct as a writer expresses it, it comes into being.

A writer—I mean now a fiction writer or a poet, an *imagining* writer—is not a sociologist, or a social historian, or a literary critic, or a journalist, or a politician. The newspeak term "woman writer" has the following sociological or political message: "Of course we believe in humanity-as-a-whole. Of course we believe that a writer is a writer, period. But let us for a little while gather together, as women, to become politically strong, strong in morale, a visible, viable social factor; as such, we will separate ourselves only temporarily, during this strengthening period, and then, when we can rejoin the world with power and dignity in our hands, we *will* rejoin it, and declare ourselves for the unity of the human species. This temporary status will be our strategy in our struggle with Society.'

That is the voice of the "woman writer." But it is a mistaken voice. Only consider: in intellectual life, a new generation comes of age every four or five years. For those who were not present at the inception of this strategy, it will not seem a strategy at all; it will be the only reality. Writers will very soon find themselves born into one of two categories, "woman writer" or "writer," and all the "writers" will be expected to be male—an uninspiring social and literary atmosphere the world has known before. "Literature cannot be the business of a woman's life, and it ought not to be," the Poet Laureate Robert Southey scolded Charlotte Brontë. But that was the early half of the nineteenth century. Only twenty years ago, an anthologist of Russian literature, speaking of a Russian writer's international influence, remarked

121

that "in the case of certain British lady-writers it may be said to have been nothing short of disastrous." He does not tell us about those British gentleman-writers who were also bad literary imitators. One could raise a mountain of such quotations, all specializing in the disparagement that inevitably emerges out of segregation. The success of feminism inhibited such views, but regression will be made easy once the pure, unqualified, unpolemical, unpoliticized word "writer" begins all over again to refer to only half the writers there are.

And not only this. The strategy is based on a temporary assumption of an untruth. When the strategy's utility passes, we are assured, the natural condition of unity will be resumed. But it is dangerous to accommodate to a falsehood even for a single minute. The so-called temporary has an ineluctable inclination to turn into long-range habit. All politicians know that every "temporary" political initiative promised as a short-term poultice stays on the books forever. *Strategies become institutions.* If writers promise themselves that they will organize as "women writers" only "temporarily," that they will yoke themselves to a misleading self-definition only for the sake of a short-term convenience, it is almost certain that the temporary will become the long-term status quo, and "convenience" will be transmogrified into a new truth.

But worse than that. Belief in a "new truth" nearly always brings authoritarianism in its wake. As the temporary-segregation strategy more and more loses its character both as to "temporary" and as to "strategy," it begins also to lay claim to a full, in fact to the only, definition of feminism, More and more, apartness is perceived as the dominant aim, even the chief quality, of feminism. More and more, women are urged to think of themselves in tribal terms, as if anatomy were the same as culture. More and more, artists who are women are made to feel obliged to deliver a "women's art," as if ten thousand other possibilities, preoccupations, obsessions, were inauthentic for women, or invalid, or, worse yet, lyingly evasive. We grow familiar, currently, with the presumption of a "woman's photography";* will there eventually arise a women's entomology, or a women's astrophysics? Or will only the sciences, in their objective universalism, retain the freedom of the individual mind, unfettered by *a priori* qualification?

Art formed or even touched by any inflexibility—any topical or social expectation, any extrinsic burden, any axiom or presumption or political nuance, any prior qualification at all—will always make for a debased culture. Sometimes history gives this inflexibility the name of "dogma"; sometimes "party line"; sometimes, alas, "truth."

Classical feminism—i.e., feminism at its origin, when it saw itself as justice and aspiration made universal, as mankind widened to humankind—rejected anatomy not only as destiny, but as any sort of governing force; it rejected the notion of "female sensibility" as a slander designed to shut women off from access to the delights, confusions, achievements, darknesses, and complexities of the great world. Classical feminism was conceived of as the end of false barriers and boundaries; as the end of segregationist fictions and restraints; as the end of the Great Multiple Lie.

What was the Great Multiple Lie? It applied to all women, and its premise was that there is a "female nature" which is made manifest in all art by women. For imaginative writers, its assertions were especially limiting and corrosive. For example:

1. It assumed a psychology and an emotional temper peculiar to women.

2. It assumed a prose or verse style endemic in, and characteristic of, women.

3. It assumed a set of preoccupations appropriate, by nature, to female poets and novelists—e.g., female friendship,

---

* Molly Haskell, *Ms.*, September 1977: "There is a tendency (and this is true of women's films as well) toward a novelistic rather than dramatic organization of material, meaning that character is conveyed evocatively through an accumulation of small gestures, half notes, and ordinary details rather than through the climactic scenes of confrontation and revelation." Since all this is also an excellent description of the short stories and plays of, say, Chekhov, the attempt to prove female "tendency" through illustration turns out to be just as unimpressive when performed by a female critic as by a male critic.

female madness, motherhood, love and romance, domestic conflict, duty, religiosity, etc.

4. It assumed a natural social community grounded in biology and reproductive characteristics ("sisters under the skin"), rather than in intellect or temperament or derivation or societal experience.

5. It took for granted the difference (from "male" writing) or "women's" poetry and "women's" novels by assuming a "woman's" separate sensibility.

6. It posited for intellect and imagination a purely sexual base. It assumed the writer's gender inherently circumscribed and defined and directed the writer's subject matter, perspective, and aspiration.

All this emits a certain melancholy familiarity: the old, old prejudices, after all. Their familiarity in voices hostile to women is melancholy, and usual, enough; but now, more and more, the voices that carry these convictions are women's voices. With some small modifications (for love and romance, substitute sex; for domestic conflict, substitute home-and-career clashes; for female madness, female rage; and omit duty and religiosity altogether), these ideas make up the literary credo of the new feminism. More and more, there are writers and artists and other masters of imagination who declare themselves freed by voluntary circumscription. "Up till now I was mistaken," they will testify; "I was trying to write like a man. Then I began to write about myself as a daughter, as a lover, as a wife, as a mother, as a woman in relation to other women; as a *self*. I learned to follow the countours of my emotional life. I began to write out of my femaleness."

Thurber once wrote a story about a bear who leaned so far backward that he ended up by falling on his face. Now we are enduring a feminism so far advanced into "new truths" that it has arrived at last at a set of notions indistinguishable from the most age-encrusted, unenlightened, and imprisoning antifeminist views.

Occasionally one hears of prisoners who decline parole, preferring fences and cells. Having returned, they still continue, sensibly and sanely, to call their comfortable old cages "prison." Artists who insist on defining themselves as "women" artists may, after a fashion, flourish under that designation, but they should not stumble into the misnomer of calling voluntary circumspection "feminism." Classical feminism, while not denying the body, while not precluding self-image and self-knowledge, never dreamed of engaging these as single-minded objectives. Feminism means, has always meant, access to possibilities beyond self-consciousness. Art, freed of restrictions, grows in any space, even the most confined. But polemical self-knowledge is restricted knowledge. Self-discovery is only partial discovery. Each human being is a particle of a generation, a mote among the revealing permutations of Society. When you know yourself, when you have toiled through "the contours of emotional life," where are you, what is it that you know, how far can it take you? Self-consciousness—narcissism, solipsism—is small nourishment for a writer. Literature is hungrier than that: a writer with an ambitious imagination needs an appetite beyond the self. For writers who are women, the "new truth" of self-regard, of biologically based self-confinement, is the Great Multiple Lie freshly got up in drag.

For writers there *are* no "new truths." There is only one very old truth, as old as Sappho, as old as Homer, as old as the Song of Deborah, as old as the Songs of David—that the imagination is free, that the gift of making literature is accessible to every kind and condition of human being, that when we write we are not women or men but blessed beings in possession of a Promethean art, an art encumbered by peril and hope and fire and, above all, freedom. What we ought to do, as writers, is not wait for freedom, meanwhile idling in self-analysis; the freedom one waits for, or builds strategies toward, will never come. What we ought to do, as writers, is seize freedom now, immediately, by recognizing that we already have it.

INNOVATION AND REDEMPTION: WHAT LITERATURE MEANS

I. INNOVATION

A WHILE AGO, freed by a bout of flu from all responsibility, I became one of those nineteenth-century leisured persons we hear about, for whom the great novels are said to have been written. In this condition I came, for the first time, to the novels of Thomas Hardy. I began with *Tess of the D'Urbervilles*, and discovered this: it is possible first to ask the question "What is this novel *about?*" and then to give an answer. Hardy writes about—well, *life* (nowadays we are made to hesitate before daring seriously to employ this word); life observed and understood as well as felt. A society with all its interminglings and complexities is set before us: in short, knowledge; knowledge of convention and continuity; also knowledge of something real, something *there*. *Tess*, for instance, is thick with knowledge of Cow. What is a cow, how does it feel to lean against, how do you milk, what is the milkshed like, what is the life of a milker, who is the milker's boss, where does the milk go? To touch any element of Cow intimately and concretely is to enter a land, a society, a people, and to penetrate into the whole lives of human beings.

The world of Cow, or its current equivalents, is now in the possession of writers like Leon Uris and Harold Robbins— shadows of shadows of Hardy. Post-Joyce, the "real" writers have gone somewhere else. And though we may not, cannot, turn back to the pre-Joycean "fundamentalist" novel,

126

it is about time it was recognized that too much "subjectivity" has led away from mastery (which so-called "experimental" novelist tells us about Cow?) and from seriousness (to which black-humorist or parodist would you entrust the whole lives of human beings?).

What is today called "experimental" writing is unreadable. It fails because it is neither intelligent nor interesting. Without seriousness it cannot be interesting, and without mastery it will never be intelligent.

The idea of the experimental derives from the notion of generations: a belief in replacement, substitution, discontinuity, above all repudiation. Who invented "generations, " and when did they come into being? John Hollander, reflecting on children's literature, notes that the idea of "children" as a classification of fresh innocence is itself a remarkably short-lived fancy, squeezed into that brief pre-Freudian bourgeois moment that made Lewis Carroll possible; before the nineteenth century there *were* no children, only smaller-sized working people; and then Freud arrived to take the charm, and the purity, out of Victorian childhood.

There are, in fact, no "generations," except in the biological sense. There are only categories and crises of temperament, and these crisscross and defy and deny chronology. The concept of generations, moreover, is peculiarly solipsistic: it declares that because I am new, then everything I make or do in the world is new.

When I was a quite young child, just beginning to write stories, I had an odd idea of time. It seemed to me that because writing signified permanence, it was necessary to address not only everyone who might live afterward, but also everyone who had ever lived before. This meant one had to keep one's eye on the ancient Greeks in particular, to write for *them* too; and, knowing no ancient Greek, I got around the difficulty by employing the most archaic language the Green, Yellow, Blue, Red and Violet Fairy Books had to offer.

Now if this belief that everything counts forever, both backward and forward, is a kind of paradisal foolishness, it is no more nonsensical than the belief that nothing counts for long—the credo that the newest generation displaces the

127

one before it. The problem with believing in generations is not only the most obvious one—that you excise history, that you cut off even the most immediately usable past—but the sense of narrow obligation it imposes on the young, a kind of prisoner's outlook no less burdensome than all the following dicta taken together:

1. That each new crop of mass 'births must reinvent culture.
2. That models are unthinkable.
3. That each succeeding generation is inherently brighter and more courageous than the one before.
4. That "establishments" are irreversibly closed.
5. That whatever has won success is by definition stale.
6. That "structurelessness"—i.e., incoherence—must be understood as a paradox, since incoherence is really coherence.
7. That "experiment" is endlessly possible, and endlessly positive, and that the more "unprecedented" a thing is, the better it is.
8. That "alternative forms" are salvational.
9. That irrational (or "psychedelic") states represent artistic newness.

I could make this list longer, but it is already long enough to demonstrate the critical point that more useful cultural news inhabits the Fifth Commandment than one might imagine at first glance.

The sources of these statements are of course everywhere—they are the bad breath of the times. At best, "experimental" fiction aims for parody: it turns the tables on the old voices, it consists of allusion built upon allusion, it is a choreography of ridicule and satire. It goes without saying that no literature can live without satire; satire nourishes and cleanses and resuscitates. The great satires that have survived are majestic indictments. Our attention now is assaulted by ephemeral asterisks claiming to be satire: when you follow the dim little star to its destination, what you find is another littleness—parody. Parody without seriousness, without, in the end, irony. If the writer does not know what to do with the remnants of high culture, he parodies them; if he does not

128

know what to do with kitsch, he simply invites it in. Twenty years hence, the American fiction of parody is going to require an addendum—complete citations of the work and tone and attitude it meant to do in. Whatever seems implicit now because of its currency as memory or tradition will have to be made explicit later, for the sake of comprehension, when tradition is forgotten and memory is dead. (Compare any annotated copy of "The Rape of the Lock. ") And meanwhile, the trouble with parody is that it is endlessly reflective, one parody building on a previous parody, and so on, until eventually the goal becomes ingenuity in the varieties of derivativeness, and one loses sight of any original objective notion of what literature can be about, of the real sources of literature. Redundance is all—and in the name of escape from the redundance of convention.

One of the great conventions—and also one of the virtues—of the old novel was its suspensefulness. Suspense *seems* to make us ask "What will happen to Tess next?," but really it emerges from the writer's conviction of social or cosmic principle. Suspense occurs when the reader is about to learn something, not simply about the relationship of fictional characters, but about the writer's relationship to a set of ideas, or to the universe. Suspense is the product of teaching, and teaching is the product of mastery, and mastery is the product of seriousness, and seriousness springs not from ego or ambition or the workings of the subjective self, but from the amazing permutations of the objective world.

Fiction will not be interesting or lasting unless it is again conceived in the art of the didactic. (Emphasis, however, on *art*.) The experimental is almost never the innovative. The innovative imagines something we have never experienced before: think of Tolstoy's imagining the moment of dying in "The Death of Ivan Ilych. " The experimental fiddles with what has gone before, precisely and exclusively with what has gone before; it is obsessed by precedent and predecessors. The innovative, by contrast, sets out to educate its readers in its views about what it means to be a human being— though it too can fiddle with this and that if it pleases, and is not averse to unexpected seizures and tricks, or to the

129

jarring gifts of vitality and cunning. Innovation cannot be defined through mere *method*; the experimental can be defined no other way. And innovation has a hidden subject: coherence.

An avatar of "alternative kinds of literary coherence"* asks us to note how

> the criteria for measuring literacy change in time, so that the body of information and ideas that seemed "literate" in the forties may, because of the sheer increase of knowledge, seem only semi-literate now. Moreover, unless older writers' minds are open enough to recognize that what a young poet learns today may be quite different from what his predecessors know, they may miss evidences of his learning . . . very rare is the literary gent over forty who can recognize, for instance, such recent-vintage ideas as say, feedback, information theory and related cybernetic concepts. This deficiency partially explains why, try as hard as we might, it is often so frustrating, if not impossible, to conduct an intelligent dialogue with older writers, the most dogmatic and semi-literate of whom are simply unable to transcend their closed and hardened ways of thought and learning. Not only do the best educated young minds seem much better educated than older intellectuals were at comparable ages, but also what a well-informed young writer knows is likely to be more relevant, not just to contemporary understanding, but also to the problems of creating literary art today.

(Surely the authors of "The Waste Land" and *Finnegans Wake*, literary and intellectual heroes of the forties, would count as "older writers"—instances, no doubt, of semi-literacy and hardened ways.)

---

* Richard Kostelanetz, "Young Writers in North America," *The American Pen*, Fall 1971. Mr. Kostelanetz illustrates what he means by "alternative kinds of coherence," and perhaps also by literacy, in part with the following:

> Errect, do it, do it again
> Errect, o take me, have me, let Yourself out
> Errect, o yes, o yess, yesss i'm Out

Mindful that youth alone may not altogether make his argument, and relying on the McLuhanite vocabulary current a decade ago, the same writer offers still another variant definition of "coherence":

A truth of contemporary avant-garde esthetics is that "formless art" is either a polemical paradox or an impossible contradiction in terms, for any work that can be defined—that can be characterized in any way—is by definition artistically coherent. It follows that just because a work fails to cohere in a linear fashion need not mean that it cannot be understood; rather, as recent literature accustoms us to its particular ways of organizing expression, so we learn to confront a new work with expectations wholly different from those honed on traditional literature.

Or, history is bunk.

And just here is the danger and the grief—those "wholly different" expectations. If apprentice writers are trained to define away plain contradictions, bringing us at last to a skilled refinement of Orwellian doublethink (incoherence is coherence), if standardized new "information"—though no one doubts that "feedback, information theory and related cybernetic concepts" are the Cow of our time—is to take the place of the idiosyncratic cadences of literary imagination and integration, if "the criteria for measuring literacy" lead to the dumping of both cognition and recognition, if focus and possession are to be dissipated into the pointless distractions and distractabilities of "multimedia" and other devices, if becoming "wholly different" means the tedium of mechanical enmity toward and mechanical overthrow of "older writers," and if all this is to be programmed through hope of instantaneous dissolutions, then not only literature but *the desire to have a literature* will be subverted.

Culture is the continuity of human aspiration—which signifies a continuity of expectations. Innovation in art is not rupture. Innovation in art is not the consequence of the implantation of "wholly different" expectations. Innovation in art means the continuity of expectations.

131

Every new sentence, every new fragment of imaginative literature born into the world, is a heart-in-the-mouth experiment, and for its writer a profound chanciness; but the point of the risk is the continuation of a recognizably human enterprise. "Wholly different" means unrecognizable; unrecognizable means the breaking-off of a culture, and its supplanting. It cannot be true that the end of a culture is the beginning of art. When cultural continuity is broken off—as in the Third Reich—what happens is first the debasement, then the extirpation, of any recognizable human goals. First the violation of art (Mozart at the gas chamber's door), then the end of art.

Innovation in art is not the same as innovation in the human psyche; just the opposite. Innovation in art has as its motivation the extension of humanity, not a flow of spite against it. The difference between barbarian and civilized expectations is the difference between the will to dominate and the will toward regeneration. To dominate you must throw the rascals out; to regenerate, you have to take them with you. Spite vandalizes. Innovation redeems.

As for who the rascals are: there is no predicament that cures itself so swiftly as that of belonging to "the young." Alice, nibbling at the mushroom, shrank so quickly that her chin crashed into her shoe: *that* fast is how we go from twenty-three to fifty-four, and from fifty-five to eighty-six. *Vita brevis!* If writers are to have a program, it ought not to be toward *ressentiment*, but toward achronology. Younger writers who resent older ones will, before they are nearly ready for it, find themselves hated by someone astonishingly recently out of the pram. Older writers who envy younger ones have a bottomless cornucopia to gorge on: the baby carriages are packed with novelists and poets. The will to fashion a literature asserts the obliteration of time. The obliteration of time makes "experiment" seem a puff of air, the faintest clamor of celestial horselaugh.

II. REDEMPTION

At a party once I heard a gifted and respected American writer—a writer whose prestigious name almost everyone would recognize—say, "For me, the Holocaust and a corncob are the same." The choice of "corncob"—outlandish, unexpected, askew—is a sign of the strong and daring charge of his imagination, and so is its juxtaposition with the darkest word of our century. What he intended by this extraordinary sentence was not to shock the moral sense, but to clarify the nature of art.

He meant that there is, for art, no such element as "subject matter"; for art, one sight or moment or event is as good as another—there is no "value" or "worth" or "meaning"—because all are equally made up of language, and language and its patterns are no different from tone for the composer or color for the painter. The artist as citizen, the writer explained, can be a highly moral man or woman—one who would, if the Nazis came, hide Jews. But the artist as artist is not a moral creature. Within literature, all art is dream, and whether or not the artist is or is not in citizenly possession of moral credentials is irrelevant to the form and the texture of the work of art, which claims only the territory of the imagination, and nothing else.

For that writer, a phrase such as "a morally responsible literature" would be an oxymoron, the earlier part of the phrase clashing to the death with the latter part. To be responsible as a writer is to be responsible solely to the seizures of language and dream.

I want to stand against this view. The writer who says "For me, the Holocaust and a corncob are the same" is putting aside the moral sense in art, equating the moral impulse only with the sociologically real, or perhaps with the theologically ideal. In literature he judges the moral sense to be an absurd intrusion. He is in the stream that comes to us from Greece, through Walter Pater and Emerson: art for its own sake, separated from the moral life. He is mainly Greek.

For me, with certain rapturous exceptions, literature *is* the moral life. The exceptions occur in lyric poetry, which bursts

133

shadowless like flowers at noon, with the eloquent bliss almost of nature itself, when nature is both benevolent and beautiful. For the rest—well, one discounts stories and novels that are really journalism; but of the stories and novels that mean to be literature, one expects a certain corona of moral purpose: not outright in the grain of the fiction itself, but in the form of a faintly incandescent envelope around it. The tales we care for lastingly are the ones that touch on the redemptive—not, it should be understood, on the guaranteed promise of redemption, and not on goodness, kindness, decency, all the usual virtues. Redemption has almost nothing to do with virtue, especially when the call to virtue is prescriptive or coercive; rather, it is the singular idea that is the opposite of the Greek belief in fate: the idea that insists on the freedom to change one's life.

Redemption means fluidity; the notion that people and things are subject to willed alteration; the sense of possibility; of turning away from, or turning toward; of deliverance; the sense that we act for ourselves rather than are acted upon; the sense that we are responsible, that there is no *deus ex machina* other than the character we have ourselves fashioned; above all, that we can surprise ourselves. Implicit in redemption is amazement, marveling, suspense—precisely that elation-bringing suspense of the didactic I noted earlier, wherein the next revelation is about to fall. Implicit in redemption is everything against the fated or the static: everything that hates death and harm and elevates the life-giving— if only through terror at its absence.

Now I know how hazardous these last phrases are, how they suggest philistinism, how they lend themselves to a vulgar advocacy of an "affirmative" literature in order to fulfill a moral mandate. I too recoil from all that: the so-called "affirmative" is simple-minded, single-minded, crudely explicit; it belongs either to journalism or to piety or to "uplift." It is the enemy of literature and the friend of coercion. It is, above all, a hater of the freedom inherent in storytelling and in the poetry side of life. But I mean something else: I mean the corona, the luminous envelope—perhaps what Henry James meant when he said "Art is nothing

134

more than the shadow of humanity." I think, for instance, of the literature of *midrash*, of parable, where there is no visible principle or moral imperative. The principle does not enter into, or appear in, the tale; it *is* the tale; it realizes the tale. To put it another way: the tale is its own interpretation. It is a world that decodes itself.

And that is what the "corona" is: interpretation, implicitness, the nimbus of *meaning* that envelops story. Only someone who has wholly dismissed meaning can boast that the Holocaust and a corncob are, for art, the same. The writers who claim that fiction is self-referential, that what a story is about is the language it is made out of, have snuffed the corona. They willingly sit in the dark, like the strict-constructionist Karaites who, wanting to observe the Sabbath exactly, sat in the lampless black and the fireless cold on the very day that is most meant to resemble paradise. The misuse of the significance of language by writers who most intend to celebrate the comeliness of language is like the misuse of the Sabbath by the fundamentalist Karaites: both annihilate the thing they hope to glorify.

What literature means is meaning.

But having said that, I come to something deeply perilous: and that is imagination. In Hebrew, just as there is *t'shuva*, the energy of creative renewal and turning, so there is the *yetzer ha-ra*, the Evil Impulse—so steeped in the dark brilliance of the visionary that it is said to be the source of the creative faculty. Imagination is more than make-believe, more than the power to invent. It is also the power to penetrate evil, to take on evil, to become evil, and in that guise it is the most frightening human faculty. Whoever writes a story that includes villainy enters into and becomes the villain. Imagination owns above all the facility of becoming: the writer can enter the leg of a mosquito, a sex not her own, a horizon he has never visited, a mind smaller or larger. But also the imagination seeks out the unsayable and the undoable, and says and does them. And still more dangerous: the imagination always has the lust to tear down meaning, to smash interpretation, to wear out the rational, to mock the surprise of redemption, to replace the fluid force of suspense

135

with an image of stasis; to transfix and stun rather than to urge; to spill out, with so much quicksilver wonder, idol after idol. An idol serves no one; it is served. The imagination, like Moloch, can take you nowhere except back to its own maw. And the writers who insist that literature is "about" the language it is made of are offering an idol: literature for its own sake, for its own maw: not for the sake of humanity.

Literature is for the sake of humanity.

My conclusion is strange, and takes place on a darkling plain. Literature, to come into being at all, must call on the imagination; imagination is in fact the flesh and blood of literature; but at the same time imagination is the very force that struggles to snuff the redemptive corona. So a redemptive literature, a literature that interprets and decodes the world, beaten out for the sake of humanity, must wrestle with its own body, with its own flesh and blood, with its own life. Cell battles cell. The corona flickers, brightens, flares, clouds, grows faint. The *yetzer ha-ra*, the Evil Impulse, fills its cheeks with a black wind, hoping to blow out the redemptive corona; but at the last moment steeples of light spurt up from the corona, and the world with its meaning is laid open to our astonished sight.

In that steady interpretive light we can make distinctions; we can see that one thing is not interchangeable with another thing; that not everything is the same; that the Holocaust is different, God knows, from a corncob. So we arrive, at last, at the pulse and purpose of literature: to reject the blur of the "universal"; to distinguish one life from another; to illumine diversity; to light up the least grain of being, to show how it is concretely individual, particularized from any other; to tell, in all the marvel of its singularity, the separate holiness of the least grain.

Literature is the recognition of the particular.

For that, one needs the corona.

LITERATURE AS IDOL:
HAROLD BLOOM

OVER THE LAST several years, little by little, progressively though gradually, it has come to me that the phrase "Jewish writer" may be what rhetoricians call an "oxymoron"—a pointed contradiction, in which one arm of the phrase clashes so profoundly with the other as to annihilate it. To say "Jewish writer," or "Jewish poet," or "Jewish artist" is—so it has begun to seem to me—to retell the tale of the Calico Cat and the Gingham Dog: when they have finished chewing each other over, there is nothing left.

Encountering the work of Harold Bloom tends to reinforce these still-shadowy views. Bloom, a professor at Yale (who in his own person is, in fact, the entire Department of Humanities), is a singular figure. Bred like the rest of his graduate-school generation on the New Criticism, he increasingly represents its antithesis—but no, not its antithesis after all, because a thesis can imagine its opposite, and Bloom is not so much opposite as other. Bloom represents instead a frame of mind and of reference, and a source of fantasying power, that the New Criticism could by no stretch of its position or fancy arrive at. At the age of forty-nine, he is already outside the recognizable categories of American historical, psychological,* or textual literary criticism. The New Criticism, though it is by now more than thirty years since it *was* new, remains the model of literary text-analysis. Even when "psychology"—i.e., the writer's biography—is permit-

* An instance of the Bloomian use of psychology: "I do not think that the psyche is a text, but I find it illuminating to discuss texts as though they were psyches, and in doing so I consciously follow the Kabbalists."

ted once again to surround *explication de texte*, the habit of belief in the power of the text to mean its own meaning, which the student must pry out through word-by-word scrutiny, persists.

The New Critical formulation of how to read a page of literature was carried out against a background of nineteenth-century impressionistic "appreciation," which included not only the words of the poem, but speculations about the "mood" of the poet, with appropriate allusions to the poet's life, and often enough an account of the state of mind of the reader while under the mood-influence of the poem. The New Criticism, puritan and stringent, aimed to throw out everything that was extravagant or extraneous, everything smacking of "sensibility" or susceptibility, every deviation from biographical or psychological allegation. The idea was to look at the poem itself, rather than to generate metaphors about the poem.

The ideal of "the poem itself" has been with us for so long now, and is so bracing, that it is difficult to dislodge. Nevertheless, it is true that biography and psychology have begun to seep back into academic reading of texts, and some belletrists—one thinks immediately of William Gass—have even dared to revive the subjective style of impressionism, wherein the criticism of the text vies as a literary display with the text itself, and on a competitive level of virtuosity, even of "beauty."

The vice of the New Criticism was its pretense that the poem was a finished, sealed unit, as if nothing outside of the text could ever have mattered in the making of the poem; and further, it regarded the poem as a presence not simply to be experienced in the reading, but as an oracle to be studied and interpreted: the poem's real end was hermeneutic, its ideal state hermetic. The virtue of the New Criticism was a consequence of its vice—not only did it deny the opportunity, at least in theory, for displays of rivalrous writing ("beautiful" essays about "beautiful" poems), but in keeping out too much of the world, it also perforce kept out what was largely irrelevant to the poem and might, like a bumptious lodger with too much baggage, wreck the poem's furniture.

Into this devotedly swept and sanctified arena strode Bloom. Lacking verbal fancifulness, he was plainly no kin to the Gass school (a contemporary school of one or two, perhaps, but larger if one includes an army of literary ancestors, Virginia Woolf among them). He had little in common with the Trilling school of meticulous social understanding. He was overwhelmingly dissimilar from the early pure New Critics with their strict self-denials. He was not like any of these, yet somehow suggestive of all of them, and again light-years beyond the imaginings of all of them. Like Trilling and his students, Bloom made connections well out of the provincial text itself; like the New Critics, he paid fanatic homage to the real presence of palpable stanzas, lines, and phrases; like the most subjective and susceptible of poetry-readers, he conceived of poetry-reading as a kind of poetry-writing, or rewriting. And still he resembled no one and nothing that had come before, because, though he stuck to *explication de texte* in the old way, he made connections outside of the text in a new way—and, besides, he raised the subjectivist mode of vying with the original to a higher pitch than ever before, while draining it of all self-indulgence. Meanwhile, the connections beyond "the poem itself" that he found were neither social nor psychobiographical; they were entirely new to American literary criticism; they were, in fact, theological.

The theology Bloom chose was obsessive, syncretic, but not at all random—Jewish Gnosticism (i.e., Kabbalah, or what Robert Alter has called "linguistic mysticism") strained through Freud, Nietzsche, Vico, and, of course, Gershom Scholem, whom Bloom sees as "a Miltonic figure." This theology-of-text became for Bloom a continuing invention through four books of prophetic evolution: *The Anxiety of Influence, A Map of Misreading, Kabbalah and Criticism, Poetry and Repression: Revisionism from Blake to Stevens*—volumes that reinforce one another even as they enlarge, through fresh illustrations, allusions, paradoxes, and widening sources, the arena of the Bloomian stride.

In a brief passage remarkable not only for its renewing the

issue of Hellenism-versus-Hebraism as the central quarrel of the West, but also for its implicit claim that paganism—i.e., anti-Judaism—is the ultimate ground for the making of poetry, Bloom writes: "Vico understood, as almost no one has since, that the link between poetry and pagan theology was as close as the war between poetry and Hebrew-Christian theology was perpetual." And again: "Vico says that 'the true God' founded the Jewish religion 'on the prohibition of the divination on which all the gentile nations arose' "—this after Bloom has already made it clear that he agrees with Vico in equating the earliest poetry-makers with pagan diviners.

Now the New Criticism, while keeping clear of theology proper, had always had a soft spot for the Gentile sacral, and was never known for philo-Judaism (given its heroes and seers, Pound and Eliot), so in itself this equation of the origins of poetry with anti-Judaism would not have been enough to shake the academy. It was not simply in their seeking out a theological connection that Bloom's four volumes, each coming with astonishing speed on the heels of the one before, outraged one department of English after another, including his own at Yale. The real shock of Bloom was that he overturned what the academy had taken for granted for a good number of graduate-school generations: that if you analyze a poem closely enough, and with enough dogged attention to the inherent world of accessible allusion locked into every phrase, you will at length find out what the poem truly means. This New Critical premise had so much become received doctrine that it had, by now, entirely escaped questioning, and for the most recent graduate students it was there in a nameless way, like air or money: a heritage urged and used without contemplation, presumed to be both natural and permanent.

Bloom, then, came on this scene of unalterable precedent as a shatterer,* to show that the very critical medium that

* Bloom, though the most provocative, is not the only successor-rebel in reaction against the New Critics. I here propose to leave the cupboard bare of the others, but for a discussion of Bloom in conjunction with Northrop Frye, Paul de Man, Stanley E. Fish, Geoffrey Hartman, J. Hillis Miller, Angus Fletcher, and—among influential foreigners—Jacques Derrida and Roland Barthes, see Irene H. Chayes, "Revisionist Literary Criticism," *Commentary*, April 1976.

had seemed to work so well, both for the assimilation of literature and for exchanging its terms, was incomplete and beside the point. "Few notions," Bloom observed,

> are more difficult to dispel than the "commonsensical" one that a poetic text is self-contained, that it has an ascertainable meaning or meanings without reference to other poetic texts. Something in nearly every reader wants to say: "*Here* is a poem and *there* is a meaning, and I am reasonably certain that the two can be brought together." Unfortunately, poems are not things but only words that refer to other words, and *those* words refer still to other words, and so on, into the deeply populated world of literary language. Any poem is an inter-poem, and any reading of a poem is an inter-reading. A poem is not writing, but *rewriting*, and though a strong poem is a fresh start, such a start is a starting-again.

"Such a start is a starting-again." This idea, original when applied to literature, is brilliantly borrowed from the history of religion. The "strong" poet is like Paul, or Mohammed, or the Buddha; as visionaries, these were all revisers, not innovators. All the varieties of Christianity and Islam are inconceivable without the God of the Jews, and all the varieties of Buddhism are inconceivable without their Hindu base of Atman and Brahma. Kabbalah, in turn, revises Scripture by making it up again through the expansion of its language. For Bloom, analogously, Milton becomes a kind of Moses, Wordsworth perhaps a Joshua, and Blake (in whom Bloom reads Milton) an Isaiah, or even the Psalmist. Bloom is interested both in Genesis, the Beginning, and in Beginning Again, to which Genesis is indispensable. He divides poets into "precursors" and "ephebes," or revisers; and he defines revision as purposeful misinterpretation, or "misprision." The "strong" poet, in Bloom's view, makes use of his precursor, and the "tropes" or telltale traces of the precursor can be detected in the latecomer-poet. Further, the underlying problem of poetry-making, according to Bloom, is that Milton and Wordsworth, Emerson and Whitman have already appeared and played their notes of grandeur; and the grandeur remains. Any poet born afterward is born into Miltonic and Emersonian shadows and illuminations; any poet born afterward is born into the condition of "belatedness," which he fights by wresting not the flame of the precursor, which cannot be taken, but the power to remake the flame. Invention is replaced by interpretation.

The meaning of a poem can only be another poem . . .

Every strong poem, at least since Petrarch, has known implicitly what Nietzsche taught us to know explicitly: that there is only interpretation, and that every interpretation answers an earlier interpretation, and then must yield to a later one . . .

Poets' misinterpretations or poems are more drastic than critics' misinterpretations or criticism, but this is only a difference in degree and not at all in kind. There are no interpretations but only misinterpretations, and so all criticism is prose poetry.

In the Bloomian scheme, interpretation is a process nearly analogous to a process in physics; to describe and summarize it, Bloom has developed a kind of physics of rhetoric, a terminology concisely and meticulously calculated to account for each stage in the conduct of "belatedness."

We are studying a kind of labor that has its own latent principles, principles that can be uncovered and taught systematically.

Poems are, Bloom says, "*acts of reading*" (the emphasis is Bloom's own), and the description of how a poem comes into being out of its reading of an earlier poem, i.e., out of its own "swerving" from the influence of a powerful precursor-poem, Bloom names a "dialectic of revisionism." It would be unfair to try to paraphrase or condense Bloom's exposition of his "principles"; each of his four theoretical books is, in his own sense, a retelling or reinterpretation or revision of his starting insight, and each of the later three is a starting-again, a reinvigoration of the earliest. *Kaballah and Criticism*, for instance, restates the Bloomian concern in still another dress, this time the dress of Cordovera and Luria. The ingenuity of the restatements themselves testifies to Bloom's artistic intelligence, his supernal—even infernal—erudition, his architectural powers, both massive and rococo, his quick appetite for telling and then telling again in fresh garb. The tapestry is always changing, the critical fabrication is always new; but the obsessive narrative of the Bloomian drama beats unflaggingly below—the drama of giants who once walked the earth, and turned "originality" into an acrobatic labor for those who came after. Through misreadings, evasions, defenses, repressions, all the canny devices of "misprision" under the pressure of "influence," the strong newcomer at last converts the materials of the precursor into substitute, sometimes antithetical, matter. It is a story of purgation and renewal. Above all, it is a story of a contest for power, in which the competitors struggle for the possession of context; in which context *is* contest. And finally, it is a mode of Gnosticism, wherein, through the toil of attaining knowledge of the Sublime Maker, the searcher himself *becomes* that Maker.

Through all of this, Bloom has invented, and continues to invent, a vocabulary of concision, which he begins now to call a "shorthand." Here, for instance, is his "mapping" of "the pattern of ratios" in Whitman's *Song of Myself*:

Sections: 1– 6 *Clinamen*, irony of presence and absence
                 7–27 *Tessera*, synecdoche of part for whole
             28–30 *Kenosis*, metonymy of emptying out
             31–38 *Daemonization*, hyperbole of high and low
             39–49 *Askesis*, metaphor of inside vs. outside
             50–52 *Apophrades*, metalepsis reversing early and late

These inventions are later augmented by Kabbalistic terminology, as well as by vocabulary borrowings taken from Freud—without, however, subscribing in any way seriously to the Freudian scheme. (In fact, he sees Freud as still another interesting datum of revisionist criticism.) Revisionism, Bloom explains, "as a word and as a notion contains the triad of re-seeing, re-esteeming, and re-aiming, which in Kabbalistic terms becomes the triad of contraction, breaking-of-the-vessels, and restitution, and in poetic terms the triad of limitation, substitution, and representation."

It is possible that this fabricated and borrowed terminology may put off a reader of poetry as easily as a medical textbook may put off a philosopher; and just as anatomical taxonomy seems far from philosophy (though the philosopher himself may be no more than a sausage filled with all those named parts), so does the vocabulary Bloom has devised seem far from "normal" criticism, and still farther from poetry itself. Listed nakedly, the Bloomian glossary has the ring of engineers' shoptalk. But this is to miss—because of the smoke it gives out—a chance of sighting the burning bush. The glossary is the girandole—the scaffolding out of which the Bloomian fireworks erupt. And what the fiery wheel writes on the sky is, after all, a single idea: discontinuity. What Bloom means by "revisionism" is a breaking off with the precursor; a violation of what has been transmitted; a deliberate offense against the given, against the hallowed; an unhallowing of the old great gods; the usurpation of an inheritance by the inheritor himself; displacement. Above all, the theft of power. These themes—or, rather, this chorus chanting a uniform theme—Bloom expresses through a nervy prowess accompanied by all the voices of inspiration that a capacious and daring mind, richly packed, can bring to bear on a ruling fascination. The jeweled diversity of Bloom's expanding and self-paraphrasing glossary is the consequence of an intoxication with the beauty and persuasiveness of the bewitchment it serves—a bewitchment by force, power, seizure, rupture; the dream of storming, looting, and renovating heaven.

Bloom's appropriation, in the third book of the series, not simply of Kabbalistic terminology, but, going beyond analogy and metaphor, of Kabbalahlike vaultings of imagination in applying that terminology, has begun, it would seem, to win him a "Jewish" reputation. Not that Bloom, with his celebrated command of the Romantics, is perceived as a Jewish critic; but his unprecedented incursions into Hebrew—what

other American critic is at home with *shevirat ha-kelim?*—
has at least suggested that Jewish sources imply Jewish
insights—or, if not that, then surely a Jewish "stance."

Professor Alvin Rosenfeld, for instance, in an essay in *The
Southern Review* called "Notes on the Antithetical Criticism
of Harold Bloom," points out that the "strain of revisionary
defiance" represented by Kabbalah "was greatly feared by
the rabbis, who correctly understood its antinomian
impulses. For to the Gnostic, knowledge is always knowledge or origins, ultimately *a rival claim* upon origins, which
in human terms inevitably means an attempt to transform
man into God"—and yet, having shown in two sentences
how Bloom jumps past Jewish claims, Rosenfeld ends by
asking Bloom to be more "balanced," to stress "preser-
vation" and "continuation" as much as "rebellion" and
"loss." Rosenfeld concludes: "If [Bloom] can now adjust his
critical stance in a way that will allow for restitution
[through "balance"], a new power may be his." But this
is to shout "Go West!" to a comet flying eastward. The
"equilibrium," the "vitalizing tension . . . between . . . tradition and innovation" that Rosenfeld calls for in Bloom, is
precisely what Bloom, all along the way, has schemed to
destroy. Rosenfeld notes:

> Bloom's devotion to the Hebrew Bible has often been
> expressed in his writings. For instance, in *A Map of
> Misreading*, he identifies himself "as a teacher of litera-
> ture who prefers the morality of the Hebrew Bible to
> that of Homer, indeed who prefers the Bible aesthetically
> to Homer . . ." If present signs hold, one expects to see
> more, not less, emphasis on biblical thinking and exegsis
> in his work.

This would appear to promise a stronger Jewish element to
come, stronger even, and possibly more central, than Bloom's
Kabbalistic concerns—but the fact is opposite. Kabbalah is
Gnosticism in Jewish dress; still, it is not the Jewish dress
that Bloom is more and more attracted by—it is the naked
Gnosticism. To "prefer the morality of the Hebrew Bible to

that of Homer" is not to make a choice at all—there is no morality, of the kind Bloom means, in Homer. And simply to speculate whether one might prefer the Bible "aesthetically" to Homer is itself, of course, already to have chosen the Greek way: the Jewish way, confronting Torah, does not offer such a choice.

If, then, one intends to reflect on Bloom's work from a Jewish point of view, it is necessary to take him at his Gnostic word when he utters it. ("In the beginning was the Word, and the Word was with God, and the Word was God.") And if one means to find in Bloom a Jewish utterance, it must be the utterance itself, not in the prospect or the hope of an utterance. The *fait accompli* of Bloom's work judges the Jewish Bloom. If Bloom, with Vico, equates the origins of poetry with pagan divination—i.e., with anti-Judaism—and is persuaded of the "perpetual war" between poetry and Judaism, then it is inescapable that Bloom, in choosing poetry, also chooses anti-Judaism. Bloom's gifts, and the structures that derive from them, yield a clue to what those awesome architectural masters who devised the cathedrals must have been like; but the cathedrals were wanting, one might say, in Jewish content.

For myself, I believe Bloom to be engaged in the erection of what can fairly be called an artistic anti-Judaism. This does not place him with Pound and Eliot, who are simply anti-Semitic in the commonplace sense, nor yet with the New Critics, whose austere faculty for "tradition" was confined to Christianity. Bloom is neither anti-Jewish nor, as his incursions into Kabbalah prove, parochial in the usual way of English-speaking literary intellectuals. Bloom is no ordinary literary intellectual. Within the bowels of the Bloomian structure there lives, below all, the religious imagination: sibylline, vatic, divinatory—in short, everything that the Sinaitic force, bent on turning away from god-proliferation, denies. Bloom's four theorizing volumes vault beyond criticism toward their destination—which is a long theophanous prose-poem, a rationalized version of Blake's heroic Prophetic Books. Not unlike Blake, Bloom means to stand as a vast and subtle system-maker, an interrupter of expectations, a subverter of predictability—the writer, via misprision, of a new Scripture based on discontinuity of tradition. In this he is pure Kabbalist. Contrary to Jesus, whom the Gospels report to have declared, "Till heaven and earth pass, one jot or one tittle shall in no wise pass from the law" (a statement vividly anti-misprision, and one that those less stiff-necked interpreters, the rabbis of the Talmud who were Jesus's contemporaries, never made), Bloom invents subversion after subversion, until he comes at last to the job of idol-making.

Idol-making: I posit this not figuratively, not metaphorically, not what Bloom might call "metaleptically," but literally. And I choose for Bloom the more drastic term "idol-maker" over "idolater" because the idolater, having no self-consciousness, is a kind of innocent conformist. The idol-maker, by contrast, has the highest self-consciousness of all, and should be prepared philosophically, conscientiously, for the consequences of the pervasive idolatry in which he has, in effect, a vested interest.

Here, lifted out of the astonishing little volume called *Kabbalah and Criticism*, is a severe (a favorite adjective of Bloom's) representation of an idol:

> What then does an idol create? Alas, an idol *has* nothing, and *creates* nothing. Its presence is a promise, part of the substance of things hoped for, the evidence of things not seen. Its unity is in the good will of its worshipper.

Now a confession. Following one of Bloom's techniques in his reading of Nietzsche and Freud, I have substituted one word for another. Bloom wrote "poem," not "idol"; "reader," not "worshiper." What turns out to be an adeptly expressive description of an idol is also, for Bloom, a useful description of a poem.

The single most useful, and possibly the most usefully succinct, description of a Jew—as defined "theologically"—can best be rendered negatively: a Jew is someone who shuns idols, who least of all would wish to become like Terach, the maker of idols. A Jew—so Jews are taught to think—is like Abraham, who sees through idols. But Bloom is both: he is both Terach and Abraham.* He is a system-builder who is aware that a closed, internalized system is an idol, and that an idol, without power in itself, is nevertheless a perilous, indeed a sinister, taint in the world.

Before I offer the necessary explanations for these views, we should, I think, reach a sophisticated understanding of idols. An idol can be, and usually is, remarkably made, wonderfully persuasive in its parts, and in its parts often enough wonderfully true. An idol can have, above all, a psychological realism that is especially persuasive and seductive. And beyond this, an idol can be seen to *work*. (To illustrate most reductively: the Egyptian cat god tells us a great deal about cats, and something also about the mind of the Egyptian who worshiped it, and even more about the ingeniously imaginative mind that created it. Furthermore, it did its job in its time as a working divinity: it demanded awe and accommodation.)

The chief characteristic of any idol is that it is a system sufficient in itself. It leads back only to itself. It is indifferent to the world and to humanity. Like a toy or like a doll— which, in fact, is what an idol is—it lures human beings to copy it, to become like it. It dehumanizes. When we see a little girl who is dressed up too carefully in starched flounces and ribbons and is admonished not to run in the dirt, we often say, "She looks like a little doll." And that is what she has been made into: the inert doll has become the model for the human child, dead matter rules the quick. That dead matter will rule the quick is the single law of idolatry.†

---

* According to a *midrash*, Terach was a maker and seller of idols. One day he left the boy Abraham to watch the shop. After remonstrating with one customer after another, Abraham picked up an ax and smashed all the idols but one— the biggest. When Terach returned, he angrily asked for an explanation. Abraham replied: "Father, the idols were hungry, and I brought them food. But the big god seized your ax, killed the other gods, and ate all the food himself." "Abram," said Terach, "you are mocking me. You know well that idols can neither move, nor eat, nor perform any act." Abraham said: "Father, let your ears hear what your tongue speaks." *The Rabbis' Bible* (Behrman House, 1966).
† This law of idolatry is again and again expressed with great precision by Bloom. Writing on the "revisionary ration" he names "*Apophrades*, or The Return of the Dead," Bloom reflects, "But the strong dead return, in poems as in our lives, and they do not come back without darkening the living. . . . The precursors flood us, and our imaginations can die by drowning in them, but no imaginative life is possible if such inundation is wholly evaded."

Scripture tells us that the human being is made in the image of God, and since we do not know how to adumbrate God, we remain as free, as unpredictable, as unfated in our aspirations as quicksilver. But when we make ourselves into the image of an image, no matter how flexible the imagination of aspiration, we are bound, limited, determined, constrained; we cannot escape the given lineaments, and no matter how multitudinous are the avenues open to us, they all come, as in a maze, to a single exit.

A second important characteristic of any idol is that it is always assumed to pre-exist the worshiper.* An idol always has the authority of an ancestor or a precursor, even if it has just come fresh from the maker's carpentry bench or brainshop. In Rome, a just-hacked-out model of Venus has all the authority of a seven-hundred-year-old shrine to Astarte, because both rest on the precursor-goddess, the moon, which rules the tides of both sea and menstruation. Every idol is by nature an ideal, an image-known-before. Every idol is a precursor, and every idolater is a Johnny-come-lately, absorbing old news to refurbish for his instant needs.

A third characteristic of any idol is that, because it is inert, it cannot imagine history. It is always the same, no matter how multiform its appearances. It cannot create or alter history. When the God of the Jews said to Abraham, *lech l'cha*, Go forth, history was profoundly made, and continues to be made; the words *lech l'cha*, first heard five thousand years ago, at this moment agitate presidents, prime ministers, oil sheikhs, hawks and doves. But an idol, which cannot generate history, can be altered by it: from-the-sublime-to-the-ridiculous is the rule of every idol. Hadrian was a ferocious oppressor of Jews, and declared himself a god to be worshiped in statuary of mammoth beauty. Digging in the sand for old coins a few years ago, an American tourist in

---

* The *midrash* mentioned earlier also has Abraham asking the age of a man who has come to buy an idol to protect his house. "I am fifty years old," says the customer, "and have been a soldier for more than thirty years." "You are fifty," Abraham scoffs, "whereas this idol was carved by my father only last week. And though you are a seasoned warrior, you ask protection from it!"

Israel drew up the great curly bronze head of the Emperor. He, the god, is reduced to curio.

A fourth characteristic of any idol is perhaps the most universally repugnant, because it demonstrates how the power of the (powerless) idol—i.e., the powerful imaginations of its devotees—can root out human pity. From this uniquely Jewish observation flows the Second Commandment. The Commandment against idols is above all a Commandment against victimization, and in behalf of pity. Pity, after all, is not "felt," as if by instinct or reflex. Pity is taught; and what teaches it is the stricture against idols. Every idol is a shadow of Moloch, demanding human flesh to feed on. The deeper the devotion to the idol, the more pitiless in tossing it its meal will be the devotee. Moloch springs up wherever the Second Commandment is silenced. In the absence of the Second Commandment, the hunt for victims begins. The Second Commandment is more explicit than the Sixth, which tells us simply that we must not kill; the Second Commandment tells us we must resist especially that killing which serves our belief. In this sense, there are no innocent idols. Every idol suppresses human pity; that is what it is made for. When art is put in competition, like a god, with the Creator, it too is turned into an idol; one has only to recall the playing of Mozart at the gates of Auschwitz to see how the muses can serve Moloch—the muses, like the idols they are, have no moral substance or tradition. What the Second Commandment, in its teaching against victimization and in behalf of pity, also teaches, is the fear of godhood. And the "fear of godhood," Bloom unequivocally writes, "is a fear of poetic strength, for what the ephebe enters upon, when he begins his life cycle as a poet, is in every sense a process of divination." The strivings of divination—i.e., of God-competition—lead away from the Second Commandment, ultimately contradict it, and crush the capacity for pity.

These four essential characteristics of idolatry—that an idol can lead only to itself and has no meaning other than itself; that an idol always has an ideal precursor on which to model its form; that an idol can have no connection to human deed and human history-making; that an idol crushes pity—

these are also the characteristics that, in Bloom's scheme, mark the way of poems. Bloom tells us that every poem born into the world is, so to speak, the consequence of an idolatry, and has been made in the image of an older poem, a precursor-poem at whose feet the new poem has worshiped. And just as an idolator takes away from his contemplation of the idol whatever his psychological hunger requires, so does the new poem take from the older poem whatever *it* needs for its life. Moreover, even when Bloom's structures, unlike the actual Molochs of ancient, recent, and current history, appear to be socially harmless and gossamer, they nevertheless dream of a great swallowing and devouring. Even Bloom's superficially bloodless "interpretation" turns out to be annihilation. (Cf., once again, *kenosis* and *shevirat ha-kelim*.) The sacrificial victim is endemic to the Bloomian system, and links it ineluctably with the pagan sacral.

So far I have been describing Bloom as Terach, the maker of idols. But I said earlier that he is also Abraham, who sees through the hollowness and human uselessness of idols. Like Abraham, Bloom recognizes that Terach is courting perversity, that Terach in his busy shop has put himself in competition with the Creator, luring away customers by means of loss leaders, that Terach refuses to accept Creation as given, and has set up counter-realities in the form of instant though illusory gratifications—namely, immediate answers to riddles. The answers may or may not be lies. Often enough the answer an idol gives is a workable answer. Doubtless fertility goddesses have been as responsible for as many births as any current fertility drug manufactured by Upjohn or Lederle. But they are exceptionally poor at urging the moral life, because to understand the moral life, one must know how to pay attention to, and judge, history—and at this idols are no good at all.

In a brief passage in his breathtaking albeit iconolatrous book *The Anxiety of Influence*, Bloom acknowledges how idols and icons—i.e., poems—are no good at all in urging the moral life. It seems to me this passage is the most significant commentary on Bloom's system; in it he becomes Abraham and chases all the customers out of Terach's shop. Above all, it is a statement that calls into question the entire volume that surrounds it, and all the subsequent volumes:

> If the imagination's gift comes necessarily from the perversity of the spirit, then the living labyrinth of literature is built upon the ruin of every impulse most generous in us. So apparently it is and must be—we were wrong to have founded a humanism directly upon literature itself, and the phrase "humane letters" is an oxymoron.... The strong imagination comes to its painful birth through savagery and misrepresentation. The only humane virtue we can hope to teach through a more advanced study of literature than we have now is the social virtue of detachment from one's own imagination, recognizing always that such detachment made absolute destroys any individual imagination.

"The social virtue of detachment from one's own imagination"—this splendidly humane sequence, set in a paragraph of clarified self-comprehension, expressed precisely the meaning of the Second Commandment. The "strong imagination," born out of a "savagery and misrepresentation" neither yoked nor undone by the Second Commandment, created the earliest Moloch, the furnace-god, and encouraged mothers to throw their babies into the fire. The savagery is plain; the misrepresentation is the general conviction that throwing children into furnaces is a social good. Since, as we have seen, idols always imitate their precursor-ideals, it can be no surprise that the post-Enlightenment Moloch of the Nazis reproduced the very Moloch recounted in the Bible—not simply in the furnace (here "misprision" was introduced in the form of technological substitutions, perhaps), but also in the ideal of a service to society.

Based on Bloomian premises, it comes down to this: no Jew may be idolator or idol-maker; poems are the products of "strong imaginations," and poets are dangerously strong imaginers, vampirishly living on the blood of earlier imaginers, from Moloch to Moloch; no Jew ought to be a poet.

One might want to intervene here with the reasonable

reflection that "Tintern Abbey" is not yet Moloch. Quite. But push, push "Tintern Abbey" a little farther, and then a little farther, and one arrives finally at Moloch. "Tintern Abbey" assumes that the poet, in contemplating his own mind and seeking his own mood, inspired by a benign landscape, will be "well pleased to recognise / In nature and the language of the sense / . . . [the] soul / Of all my moral being." But the ecstatic capacity, unreined, breeds a license to uncover not only joy, love, and virtue, but a demon. The soul's license to express everything upon the bosom of a Nature perceived as holy can beget the unholy expression of savagery. It is not a new observation that the precursors of the Hitler Youth movement were the *Wandervögel*, young madcap bands and bards who wandered the German landscape looking for a brooding moodiness to inspire original feelings.

Still another passage from *The Anxiety of Influence* (this one on Terach's side) introduces in detail one of the ingenious terms of Bloom's special analytic vocabulary:

> *Kenosis*, or "emptying," at once an "undoing" and an "isolating" movement of the imagination. I take *kenosis* from St. Paul's account of Christ "humbling" himself from God to man. In strong poets, the *kenosis* is a revisionary act in which an "emptying" or "ebbing" takes place *in relation to the precursor*. This "emptying" is a liberating discontinuity, and makes possible a kind of poem that a simple repetition of the precursor's afflatus or godhood could not allow. "Undoing" the precursor's strength *in oneself* serves also to "isolate" the self from the precursor's stance. . . .

Historically, morally, theologically, one cannot be a Jew and stand by this passage.

To recapitulate the idea-germ that exploded into the brilliant hugeness and huge brilliance of the Bloomian system of analysis: a recognition that all of us are disconsolate latecomers; that we are envious and frustrated inheritors; that there have been giants on the earth before us; and what therefore shall we puny latecomers do, how shall we steal the fire that the great ones before us, our fortunate Promethean precursors, have already used up for their own imaginings? The answer comes through modes of discontinuity—*kenosis*, in the term Bloom borrows from Saint Paul, and *shevirat ha-kelim*, the "breaking of the vessels," in the term he borrows from Kabbalah. But the discontinuity does not imply iconoclasm, the Abrahamitic shattering of the idol. On the contrary: it means reinvigorating the ideal of the idol in a new vessel, as Astarte begets Venus, as Rome, through Venus, feels itself possessed by its own goddess.

The notion of " 'undoing' the precursor's strength" has no validity in normative Judaism. Jewish liturgy, for instance, posits just the opposite; it posits *recapturing without revision* the precursor's stance and strength when it iterates "our God, and God of our fathers, God of Abraham, Isaac, and Jacob." Nearly every congeries of Jewish thought is utterly set against the idea of displacing the precursor. "Torah" includes the meanings of *tradition* and *transmittal* together. Although mainstream Judaism rejected the Karaites in favor of an interpretive mode, interpretation never came to stand for disjunction, displacement, ebbing-out, isolation, swerving, deviation, substitution, revisionism. Transmittal signifies the carrying-over of the original strength, the primal monotheistic insight, the force of which drowns out competing power systems. That is what is meant by the recital in the Passover Haggadah, "We ourselves went out from Egypt, and not only our ancestors," and that is what is meant by the *midrash* that declares, "All generations stood together at Sinai," including present and future generations. In Jewish thought there *are* no latecomers.

Consequently the whole nation of "modernism" is, under the illumination of Torah, at best a triviality and for the most part an irrelevance. Modernism has little to do with real chronology, except insofar as it means to dynamite the continuum. Modernism denotes discontinuity: a radical alteration of modes of consciousness. Modernism, perforce, concerns itself with the problem of "belatedness." But modernism and belatedness are notions foreign and irrelevant to the apperceptions of Judaism. Modernism and belatedness induce worry about being condemned to repeat, and therefore anxiously look to break the bond with the old and make over, using the old as the governing standard—or influence—from which to learn deviation and substitution. The mainstream Jewish sense does not regard a hope to recapture the strength, unmediated, of Abraham and Moses as a condemnation. Quite the opposite. In the Jewish view, it is only through such recapture and emulation of the precursor's stance, unrevised, that life can be nourished, that the gift of the Creator can be received, praised, and fulfilled. Jewish thought makes much of its anti-antinomian precursors as given, and lacks both the will and the authority to undo or humble or displace them, least of all to subject them to purposeful misprision. A scribe with the Torah under his hand will live a stringent life in order not to violate a single letter. There is no competition with the text, no power struggle with the original, no envy of the Creator. The aim, instead, is to reproduce a purely transmitted inheritance, free of substitution or incarnation.

But the idol-maker envies the Creator, hopes to compete with the Creator, and schemes to invent a substitute for the Creator; and thereby becomes satanic and ingrown in the search and research that is meant to prise open the shells holding the divine powers. This is the work of "misprision," the chief Bloomian word. Misprision is to Bloom what Satan is to Milton. It is not an accident that the term—before Bloom exercises revisionary misprision upon it—denotes "felony," "wrongdoing," "violation." These definitions proffer a critical judgment of reality; they point, simply, to an Abrahamitic or, better yet, Sinaitic "shalt not." But when Bloom utters "misprision," it is the spirit of Terach that orders it.

Bloom, then, is a struggler between Terach and Abraham. He knows, mutedly, what Abraham knows, but he wants, vociferously, what Terach wants. "To revise is not to fulfill," he is heard to murmur in *Poetry and Repression*, in a voice transfixed by Jewish transmittal. But in all four Prophetic Books one hears, far louder than that, Terach's transfiguring chant: *clinamen, tessera, kenosis, daemonization, askesis, apophrades*. And in the end it is Terach who chiefly claims

155

Bloom. Like Terach, like Freud, like Marx, like the Gnostics, like the classical Christian theologians who are the inheritors of the Gnostics, like the Kabbalists and the Hasidim who are similarly the inheritors of the Gnostics, like all of these, the Bloomian scheme of misprision of the precursor is tainted by a variety of idol-making.

Bloom, giving us Vico's view in quotation, plainly gives his own: "The making that is poetry is god-making, and even the ephebe or starting-poet is as much demon as man or woman." An idol, the product of the demonic *yetzer ha-ra*,* is an internalized system that allows no escape from its terms; and if one tries to escape, the escape itself is subject to interpretation as being predictable within the system. All the avenues of a maze, both the traps and the solutions, belong to the scheme of the maze.

Or think instead of a great crystal globe, perilously delicate yet enduring, with a thousand complex working parts visible within, the parts often exceedingly ingenious and the whole a radiant bauble: an entire man-made world beautiful, above all rational, and complete in itself. But it draws one to intellectual slavery. It signifies bondage to the wheel of self-sufficient idolatry.

The most enduring configurations of Jewish religious idiom are not unfamiliar with Bloom's inventions; they were considered and discarded as long ago as Abraham, and again in Egypt, and again in confrontation with the Hellenizers, and now again in confrontation with so-called modernism, which is only Gnostic syncretism refurbished.

Literature, one should have the courage to reflect, is an idol. We are safe with it when we let the child-part of our minds play with poems and stories as with a pack of dolls; then the role of imaginative literature is only trivial. But what Bloom, anxiously influenced, has done, is to contrive a system of magic set in rational psychological terms, and requiring (as the Jewish religious idiom never will) a mediator. For Freud the mediator or medium is the unconscious. For Bloom the mediator or medium is the precursor-poem. But for each,

* The impulse toward evil, related also to the creative capacity; the desire to compete with the Creator in ordering being and reality.

imagination has devised an inexorable, self-sufficient, self-contained magic system, the most magical aspect of which is the illusion of the superbly rational.

Bloom himself has seen that he began as a desperately serious critic of literature and ended as one inflamed by Cordovero and Luria. Perhaps the trouble—it is every writer's trouble—is that he should not have been serious about literature in the first place; seriousness about an idol leads to the misprision that is violation. As Bloom the system-maker, in book after book, more and more recognizes that what he has invented is magic, i.e., "practical Kabbalah," he turns to the magic system of the actual and historic Kabbalah for confirmation. It is as if Harold Bloom suddenly woke up one morning to discover that he had concocted Kabbalah on his own; only it was already *there*. That is like Venus opening her eyes in a drawing room in Rome to learn that she is Astarte reborn. Astarte will always be reinvented. In the absence of the Second Commandment idolatry will always be reconstituted—if not in wood or stone, then in philosophical or political concept; if not in philosophical or political consent, then in literature.

Through his placing the critic in competition with the creator, Bloom is often regarded as having committed an act of artistic hubris; but those who look askance at Bloom's belief that the poem's interpretation is as much the poem's life as the "original" ought to be more troubled by the hubris of the poet, which the whole body of Bloom's work strives to emphasize and even enlarge. The Bloomian transmutation of critic into poet, after all, is not so innovative as it might seem; it is no news that a critic may feel himself to be in a clandestine contest with the creative artist. It is true that Bloom has significantly altered the meaning of what it is to be "original"; but whether or not his conclusions are found to be attractive or persuasive, what he has made his originals *do* can stop the breath. He has vouchsafed them the temerity to usurp the Throne of Heaven.

Now none of this is to accuse or blame Bloom's position because it is on the side of this grandest usurpation of all. The Second Commandment runs against the grain of our social nature, indeed against human imagination. To observe it is improbable, perhaps impossible; perhaps it has never been, and never will be, wholly observed. But the Second Commandment is nevertheless expressive of one of the essential ideals of Judaism, and like most of the essential ideals of Judaism—consider in this light the institution of the Sabbath—it is uniquely antithetical to the practices and premises of the pre-Judaic and non-Judaic world. In short, it is the Jewish idiom—with regard to art as well as other matters—that is in its deepest strain dissenting, contradictory, frequently irreconcilable, and for Bloom and others to think of his system as "antithetical" is a sizable mistake. What is antithetical goes against the grain of the world at large, while to work at idol-making is not only not to go against the world's grain, but to consort with it in the most ancient, intimate, sibylline, and Delphic way. Bloom stands for the most part as defense counselor for those eternally usurping diviners against whom Zechariah inveighed: "For the idols have spoken vanity, and the diviners have seen a lie, and have told false dreams; they comfort in vain."

But if there *can* be such a chimera as a "Jewish writer," it must be the kind of sphinx or gryphon (part one thing, part another) Bloom himself is, sometimes purifying like Abraham, more often conjuring like Terach, and always knowing that the two are icily, elegically, at war. Bloom as Terach: "The Kabbalists read and interpreted with excessive audacity and extravagance; they knew that the true poem is the critic's mind, or as Emerson says, the true ship is the shipbuilder." Bloom as Abraham: "The Talmund warns against reading Scripture by so inclined a light that the text reveals chiefly the shape of your own countenance."

In an essay called "The Sorrows of American-Jewish Poetry," Bloom writes: "There is no recovery of the covenant, of the Law, without confronting again, in all deep tribulation, the God of the Fathers, Who is beyond image as He is beyond personality, and Who can be met only by somehow again walking His Way."

These words, I think, constitute still another call for misprision; but there is no way they can speak against themselves, or be creatively misread. The recovery of Covenant can be attained only in the living-out of the living Covenant; never among the shamanistic toys of literature.

Alas, like all the others, we drift towards the shamans and their toys.

Sholem Aleichem's Revolution

YIDDISH IS A direct, spirited, and spiritually alert language that is almost a thousand years old—centuries older than Chaucerian English, and, like the robust speech of Chaucer's pilgrims, expressively rooted in the quotidian lives of ordinary folk. It is hard to be pretentious or elevated in Yiddish and easy to poke fun. Yiddish is especially handy for satire, cynicism, familiarity, abuse, sentimentality, resignation, for a sense of high irony, and for putting people in their place and events in bitter perspective: all the defensive verbal baggage an involuntarily migratory nation is likely to need en route to the next temporary refuge. In its tenderer mien, Yiddish is also capable of a touching conversational intimacy with a consoling and accessible God. If Yiddish lacks cathedral grandeur, there is anyhow the compensation of coziness, of smallness, of a lovingly close, empathic, and embracing Creator who can be appealed to in the diminutive. Yiddish is a household tongue, and God, like other members of the family, is sweetly informal in it.

Starting in the early medieval period, the Jews of Europe were rarely allowed a chance to feel at home. Consequently Yiddish developed on the move, evolving out of a mixture of various tenth-century urban German dialects (not exclusively Middle High German, a linguistic misapprehension only recently superseded), and strengthened in its idiosyncrasies by contributions from French, Italian, Slavic, Hebrew, and Aramaic. (The last, the language of the Talmud and of Jesus, was widely in use in the Near East beginning around 300 B.C.E.) Until the end of the eighteenth century, Yiddish was the overwhelming vernacular of European Jewish communi-

160

ties from Amsterdam to Smolensk, from the Baltic to the Balkans, and as far south as Italy. Driven relentlessly eastward by the international brutality of the Crusaders and by the localized brutality of periodic pogroms, the language suffered successive uprootings and took on new morphological influences. In 1492, when Columbus sailed the ocean blue and Ferdinand and Isabella issued their anti-Jewish edict of expulsion, the language of the Spanish Jews—called Judezmo or Ladino—underwent its own upheavals, fleeing the depredations of the Inquisition to Holland, Italy, Turkey, North Africa, and even the New World.

And all the while Yiddish remained a language without a name, or almost so. "Yiddish" means "Jewish," or what Jews speak—but this term became current only toward the close of the nineteenth century. Before then, the everyday speech of Ashkenazi Jews (i.e., Jews without Spanish or Arabic language connections) was designated "Judeo-German," which essentially misrepresented it, since it was steadfastly a language in its own right, with its own regionalisms and dialects. To think of Yiddish (as many German-speakers tend to) merely as a fossilized or corrupted old German dialect would oblige us similarly to think of French as a deformed and slurred vestige of an outlying Latin patois deposited on the Rhône by a defunct Roman colony. But "Judeo-German" at least implied a modicum of dignity; at any rate, it was a scholar's word. The name Jews themselves, intellectuals in particular, habitually clapped on Yiddish was not a name at all; it was, until the miraculous year 1888, an opprobrium: *zhargón*. Gibberish; prattle; a subtongue, something less than a respectably cultivated language. Yiddish was "jargon" to the intellectuals despite its then eleven million speakers (i.e., before the Nazi decimations), despite the profusion of its press, theater, secular educational systems, religious and political movements, and despite its long (though problematical) history of literary productivity.

In 1888—effectively overnight—this contemptuous view of Yiddish was overturned, and by a single powerful pen writing in Yiddish. The pen had a pen name: Sholem Aleichem, a Hebrew salutation that literally means "peace to you" (the familiar Arabic cognate is *salaam aleykum*), and conveys a vigorously affectionate delight in encountering a friend, or someone who can immediately become a friend, if not an instant confidant. Almost no phrase is more common in Yiddish—as common as a handshake. The pseudonym itself declared a revolutionary intention: Yiddish as a literary vehicle was at last to be welcomed, respected, celebrated. The name, like the writer, looked to a program, and Sholem Aleichem was already a prolific author of short stories and feuilletons when, at the age of twenty-nine, he founded a seminal Yiddish literary annual, *Di Yidishe Folksbibliotek* ("The Popular Jewish Library"). The money ran out in a couple of years, and the new periodical vanished. But the revisionist ardor of its first issue alone—an electrifying burst of promulgation and demonstration—permanently changed the fortunes of Yiddish. The despised *zhargón* was all at once removed from scorn and placed in a pantheon of high literary art, complete with a tradition, precursors, genres, a sense of historical development, and uncompromising critical goals— a conscious patrimony that, only the day before, no one had dreamed was there.

It had not been there. The aesthetics of literary self-aware-ness, a preoccupation with generational classifications, issues of precedent and continuity—all these were fictions, the deliberate invention of Sholem Aleichem himself. It was Sholem Aleichem who, invoking Gogol and Turgenev as models, established the genres and identified a radical precur-sor: the novelist and critic Sholem Yankev Abramovitsh, who wrote under the nom de plume of Mendele Moykher-Sforim (Mendele the Book Peddler). In the very hour Sholem Alei-chem was naming him the "grandfather" of Yiddish litera-ture, Mendele was no more than fifty-two years old, in mid-career. According to Professor Dan Miron, a leading scholar of Yiddish letters (who reveals all these marvels in his enchanting study, *A Traveler Disguised*), "What was unim-aginable in 1885 was taken for granted in 1895. In 1880 Yiddish writers did not suspect that they had a history; by the early 1890s they had already produced one 'classic' writer; before the century ended *The History of Yiddish*

Literature in the Nineteenth Century was written in English for American readers by a Harvard instructor." It was, in short, a process of historical mythmaking so rapid and extreme, and so bewitching, that the historians themselves swallowed it whole in no time at all. And Sholem Aleichem was the premier mythmaker and founder of that process.

But why was Yiddish so disreputable that it needed a Sholem Aleichem to fabricate a grand intellectual pedigree for it? Like any other language, it *did* have a genuine history, after all: a living civilization had eaten, slept, wept, laughed, borne babies, earned its bread or failed to, and had, in fact, read and written stories in Yiddish for nearly five centuries. Contempt for Yiddish, moreover, was simultaneously internal and external—Jewish intellectuals as well as Gentiles of every class habitually derided it. The Gentile world despised Yiddish as a marginal tongue because it was spoken by a people deemed marginal by Christendom; that was simple enough. And while it is true that the prejudices of the majority can sometimes manage to leave an unsavory mark on a minority's view of itself, Gentile scorn for Yiddish had almost nothing to do with the contumely Jewish social and intellectual standards reserved for Yiddish. The trouble with Yiddish, from the Jewish standpoint, was that it wasn't Hebrew. Yiddish was the language of exile—temporary, make-do; it belonged to an unfortunate phase of history: an ephemeral if oppressive nightmare only lightened by the unquenchable hope of national restoration. Yiddish was an empty vessel, uncultivated, useless for significant expression and high experience. It was the instrument of women and the ignorant—categories that frequently overlapped.

Hebrew, by contrast, was regarded as synonymous with Jewish reality. Besides being the language of Scripture, of the liturgy, of daily prayer, it was the sole medium of serious life, which could mean one thing only: serious learning. In a society where fundamental literacy was expected of everyone without exception, including women, and where the scholar was situated at the apex of communal distinction, "ignorant" signified insufficient mastery of Hebrew. Everyone, including women—who could recite from the Hebrew prayer book—

had some degree of access to Hebrew. A young boy's basic education began with the Pentateuch; if he never acquired much of anything else, he still had that, along with the daily prayer book, the Passover Haggadah, and a smattering of commentary. And of course Yiddish itself, written in the Hebrew alphabet, is peppered with liturgical and biblical allusions, as well as homelier matter in Hebrew—which is why, while a knowledge of Yiddish may assure an understanding of a sentence in German, the reverse is not so likely. From the time of the destruction of the Second Temple in the year 70, Hebrew remained a living language in everyday reading and writing use. It may have suffered severe popular contraction—practically no one *spoke* it—but it never became moribund. My own father, who wrote a rather formal Victorian-style English, would never consider writing in English or Yiddish when he wanted to address a letter to a person of learning—a rabbi he respected, or perhaps the headmaster of a yeshiva: in the world he was reared in (he was born in White Russia in 1892), Hebrew was the only appropriate vehicle for a civilized pen. It took—and gave— the measure of a mind. You might tie your shoelaces in Yiddish, but Hebrew was the avenue of thought and certainly of civility.

When Enlightenment ideas finally spread to the isolated Yiddish-speaking communities of Eastern Europe, they arrived a century late and turned out to have a somewhat different character. Like the Gentile Enlightenment, Haska-lah—the name for the Enlightenment movement among Jews—fostered the advancement of secularization and an optimistic program for the improvement of the common people. On the face of it, it might seem that Hebrew would have been left behind in the turmoil of the new liberalization, and that the language of the Bible would at least attenuate in an atmosphere where the claims of piety were thinning out—just as Latin, after the decline of the authority of Christ-ian scholasticism, was gradually compelled to give way to a diversity of vernaculars. In Jewish society exactly the opposite happened: the progress of Haskalah only intensified the superior status of Hebrew and accelerated its secular use.

As the temporal more and more replaced the theological (though these phrases don't quite fit the Jewish sense of how spiritual traditions and this-worldliness are intertwined), Hebrew pressed more urgently than ever toward the forefront of intellectual life. Hebrew belles-lettres began to be taken seriously by temperaments that had formerly regarded stories and novels as a species of levity fit only for women and the ignorant—and therefore written exclusively in Yiddish. The first Hebrew novel—*The Love of Zion*, by Abraham Mapu— didn't appear until 1853, but it was very quickly followed by wave after wave of explosively burgeoning literary forms— fiction, essays, poetry. Hebrew composition, which over the last millennium or so had been chiefly employed in scholarly responsa on ethical and juridical issues, was suddenly converted to high imaginative art. Not that original Hebrew literature had never before burst out in European Jewish experience: the majestic poets of medieval Spain had astounded their little historical span with lyrical masterpieces to vie with the Song of Songs; and the experimental poets of Renaissance Italy echoed Petrarch and Dante in Hebrew stanzas.

But the influence—and domination—of Hebrew among nineteenth-century Eastern European Jews was so pronounced that it was presumed the literary stigma attached to Yiddish would never be overcome. And at the same time, a noisy rush of activism expressed in competing currents of idealism, cultural or political, was beginning to awaken a harassed community to the potential of change and renewal. The most ancient of these currents, faithfully reiterated three times a day in the prayer book, refreshed in every season by religious festivals geared to biblical agricultural cycles, seemingly the least political of all in its psychological immanence, was the spirit of national return to Jerusalem. Under the influence of Haskalah, the renascence of literary Hebrew nourished, and was nourished by, this irreducible grain of religio-national aspiration immemorially incorporated in traditional Jewish sensibility. The more secularized Hebrew became, and the more dedicated to belles-lettres, the more it found itself, by virtue of its *being* Hebrew, harking back to the old emotional sources—sometimes even while manifestly repudiating them. The Hebrew belles-lettrists might appear to be focusing on modernist issues of craft and style—particularly at the expense of Yiddish, which the Hebraists declared lacked all possibility of style—but the prestige of Hebrew was also the prestige of national consciousness.

This was the cultural situation into which Sholem Aleichem thrust his manifesto for the equal status of Yiddish.

He was born Sholem Rabinovitsh in a town in the Ukraine in 1859, only three years after the abolition of a Czarist conscription scheme for the assimilation of Jewish children, whereby boys were seized at age twelve and subjected to thirty-one years of military confinement. He died in New York in 1916 (three months after the death of Henry James), having been driven there two years before by the upheavals of war and revolution; but he had already fled Russia a decade before that, after living through the ferocious government-sponsored pogroms of 1905. No version or variety of political or social malevolence failed to touch the Jews of Russia, and Sholem Aleichem—whose fame, after all, was that of sprightly comic artist—omitted few of these brutalities from his tales. The comparison with Mark Twain that emerged in Sholem Aleichem's own lifetime was apt: both men kept people laughing even as they probed the darkness—though Sholem Aleichem, for whom cruelty had an explicit habitation and name, never fell prey to a generalized misanthropy of the *Pudd'nhead Wilson* sort.

As a boy, Sholem Aleichem had Pickwickian propensities, and entertained his family with mimicry and comic skits. His writer's gift—reflecting the normal bilingualism of Jewish life—rapidly turned up in both Yiddish and Hebrew. Not long afterward, though, he acquired a third literary language. After a conventional *cheder* training (Bible and Talmud in a one-room school), he managed to gain admission to a Russian secondary school; the university education that would ordinarily follow was mainly closed to Jews. But his exposure to Russian studies enabled him to get a job as a Russian tutor in a Russified Jewish family of means—he eventually married his young pupil, Olga Loyev—and emphatically opened Russian to him as a literary instrument. Though his earliest serious literary venture of any kind was a novel in imitation of Mapu, called *The Daughter of Zion* and written in Hebrew, his first published articles appeared in Russian, Hebrew, and Yiddish.

When he ultimately settled on Yiddish, he disappointed no one more than his father, a struggling innkeeper who was an enthusiastic disciple of Haskalah, and who had hoped his son would develop into an exclusively Hebrew writer. And much later, after Sholem Aleichem had become virtually an institution, and was celebrated as the soul of Jewish self-understanding wherever Yiddish was spoken, the language that nevertheless prevailed as the mother tongue of his household was not Yiddish but Russian; he raised his children in it. If this suggests itself as a paradox, it also reminds us of Isaac Babel, born thirty-five years after Sholem Aleichem, arrested and silenced by the Soviets in 1939.* Babel too wrote a handful of stories that might be described as revealing the soul of Jewish self-understanding. (One of these, "Shabos Nahamu," with its Hebrew-Yiddish title, could readily pass for a romping fable of Sholem Aleichem's, except for the Chekhovian cadence of its last syllables.) Whether because he chose to write in Russian, or for some other reason, Babel is not usually counted as a Jewish writer. This leads one to imagine what the consequences might have been had Sholem Aleichem, like Babel, committed himself wholly to Russian: it is highly probable that Russian literature might have been augmented by still another dazzling writer. What is certain is that there would have been no Sholem Aleichem. To produce a Sholem Aleichem, Yiddish is a sine qua non.

That may appear to be an unremarkable statement. One might just as well say that to produce a Guy de Maupassant, French is a sine qua non; or that to produce a Selma Lagerlöf, Swedish is indispensable. For these writers, though, there was no difference between the legacy of the literary main-

---

* Patricia Blake, a Babel scholar, notes that at the time of his arrest Babel was engaged in translating Sholem Aleichem into Russian. The manuscript was confiscated by the NKVD.

stream and the daily language that seemed no more a matter of choice than breathing; for them literature was conducted in the vernacular. But Sholem Aleichem was faced with a cultural redundancy—internal bilingualism—known almost nowhere else in Europe (Ireland, with important differences, comes to mind). Yiddish was the common language of breathing—the people's language—and Hebrew was the language of the elitist literary center. In these circumstances, to choose Yiddish, and to insist that it be taken seriously—that it become, if not *the* literary center, then one at least equally respectable—was a mettlesome and revolutionary act.

In a way, a version of this revolution—a revolution in favor of Yiddish—had already occurred a century before, with the advent of the Hasidic movement: romantic, populist, anti-establishment, increasingly cultlike in its attachment to charismatic teachers. The Hasidic leaders, resenting the dominance of the stringently rationalist intellectualism that held pride of place in Jewish communal life, enlisted the Yiddish-speaking masses against the authority of the learned (where learned always meant learned in Hebrew), and offered instead the lively consolations of an emotional pietism. The movement caught on despite—or maybe because of—the fact that scholarliness was unstintingly prized, far above earning power: a scholar-husband was a great catch, and the bride's father would gladly support him if he could; so, often enough, would the bride. (My Russian grandmother, for instance, the mother of eight, ran a dry goods shop while my grandfather typically spent all his waking hours in the study-house.) The corollary of this, not unexpectedly, was that simple people deficient in learning were looked down on. At its inception, Hasidism was a popular rebellion against this sort of intellectual elitism; it threw off rigor and lavished dance, song, legend, story, merriment, and mysticism (the last too frequently fading into superstitious practice) on ordinary mortals whose psalms and prayers were in Hebrew but whose grammar was at best lame.

While there lurked in Hasidism a kind of precedent for an unashamed turn to the Yiddish tale—including at least one fabulist of Kafka-like artistry—Sholem Aleichem's revolution had another source. Like the belletristic passions of the Hebraists, it belonged to the Enlightenment. For the Hasidim, stories told in Yiddish were the appurtenances of a fervent piety; for Sholem Aleichem, they were vessels of a conscious literary art. Hasidism concentrated on devoutness and turned its back on modernism. Haskalah, with its hugely sophisticated modernist aesthetics, had little tolerance for Hasidic revivalism (though it later made literary capital of it). And yet the objectives of the two movements, the popular and the elevated, met in Sholem Aleichem. He had in common with the Hasidic impulse a tenderness toward plain folk and the ambition to address the human heart unassumingly and directly, in its everyday tongue. And he had, through the refinements of Haskalah, all the complexities of high literary seriousness and what we nowadays call the strategies of the text. This combination of irreconcilables—a broad leniency and a channeled pointedness—may be what fashioned him into the master of irony we know as Sholem Aleichem.

Of course we do not really know him—not in English anyhow, and with the passing of the decades since the Nazi extirpation of Yiddish-speaking European civilization, fewer and fewer native readers of literary Yiddish are left. For Americans, Sholem Aleichem has always been no more than a rumor, or two or three rumors, all of them misleading. First there is the rumor of permanent inaccessibility because of the "special flavor" of Yiddish itself—its unfamiliar cultural premises and idiomatic uniqueness. But every language is untranslatable in precisely that sense; Robert Frost's *mot*—poetry is what gets lost in translation—is famous enough, and the Hebrew poet Bialik compared translation to kissing through a handkerchief. Yiddish is as amenable to translation as any other language—which may mean, despite certain glorious exceptions, not very. As for the historical and cultural idiosyncrasies inherent in Yiddish, they are not especially difficult or esoteric, and for the most part require about as much background as, say, managing to figure out what a name day is in Chekhov. If there should be any more trouble than that, the impairment will be in the unaccoutered contemporary reader, not in the passage: Sholem Aleichem is no more disadvantaging than Milton might be to anyone who comes to him innocent of biblical referents. Even so, saturated in allusiveness, Sholem Aleichem is a thousand times closer to Dickens and Mark Twain and Will Rogers than he can possibly be to more encumbered figures; he was a popular presence, and stupendously so. His lectures and readings were mobbed; he was a household friend; he was cherished as a family valuable. His fiftieth birthday was a public event, and at his death hundreds of thousands filled the streets as his cortege wound through the Bronx and Harlem, down to the Lower East Side and into Brooklyn for the burial.

And still he was not what another rumor makes him out to be: simpleminded, sentimental, peasantlike, old-countryish, naive, pre-modern—the occasion of a nostalgia for a sweeter time, pogroms notwithstanding. It would be easy to blame *Fiddler on the Roof* for these distortions, but the Broadway musical—to which all those adjectives *do* apply, plus slickness—didn't arrive until 1964, and Sholem Aleichem had been misrepresented in this way long, long before. In fact, these well-established misconceptions may have been the inspiration for the emptied-out prettified romantic vulgarization (the Yiddish word for it is *shund*) typified by the musical's book and lyrics: exactly the sort of *shund* Sholem Aleichem, in seeking new literary standards for Yiddish, had battled against from the start. Whatever its success as a celebrated musical, the chief non-theatrical accomplishment of *Fiddler on the Roof* has been to reduce the reputation of a literary master to the very thing he repudiated.

That the sophisticated chronicler of a society in transition should be misconstrued as a genial rustic is something worse than a literary embarrassment. Dickens is not interchangeable with Sam Weller, or Mark Twain with Aunt Polly, or Sholem Aleichem with Tevye. (And even the Tevye we think we know isn't the Tevye on the page.) This quandary of misperceived reputation may possibly stem from the garbled attitudes of some of the Yiddish-speaking immigrants' descendants, who inherited a culture—failed to inherit it, rather—only in its most debilitated hour, when it was nearly over and about to

170

give up the ghost. The process of attenuation through competing influences had already commenced in the Jewish villages of Eastern Europe (and was to become Sholem Aleichem's great subject). In the rush to Americanization, the immigrants, zealously setting out to shake off the village ways they had brought with them, ended by encouraging amnesia of the central motifs and texts of their civilization. A certain text-orientation remained, to be sure, which their American-born successors would learn to bring to bear on Whitman and James and Emerson and Faulkner, not to mention Bloomsbury; but the more intrinsic themes of Jewish conceptual life came to be understood only feebly, vestigially, when, substantially diluted by the new culture, they were almost beyond recognition, or were disappearing altogether. Among the immigrants' children and grandchildren, the misshapen shard was mainly taken for the original cup. And generations that in the old country had been vividly and characteristically distinct from the surrounding peasant society were themselves dismissed as peasants by their "modern" offspring—university-educated, perhaps, but tone-deaf to history.

Now, toward the end of the twentieth-century—with a startling abundance that seems close to mysterious—we are witnessing a conscientious push toward a kind of restitution. Something there is that wants us finally to see—to see fairly, accurately, richly—into the substance of Yiddish prose and poetry, even if necessarily through the seven veils of translation. The buzz of anthologists hopeful of gaining attention for Yiddish has always been with us, but a worshipful air of do-goodism, whether hearty or wistful or polemical, frequently trails these votary efforts. A serious critical focus was inaugurated more than thirty years ago by Irving Howe and his then-collaborator, the late Yiddish poet Eliezer Greenberg, with their thick pair of "Treasuries"—collections of Yiddish stories and poems enhanced by first-rate introductions. These were succeeded in 1972 by the Howe-Greenberg *Voices from the Yiddish*, a compilation of literary and historical essays, memoirs, and diaries, and again in 1974 by selections from the tales of I. L. Peretz, one of the three classic

writers of the Yiddish narrative. (Mendele and Sholem Aleichem are the others.) The last two or three years, however,
have brought about an eruption—if this word is too strong,
"efflorescence" is not nearly strong enough—of dedicated
translation: *My Mother's Sabbath Days*, a memoir by Chaim
Grade, translated by Chana Kleinerman Goldstein and Inna
Hecht Grade; the extant parts of *The Family Mashber*, an
extraordinary work long quiescent in the Soviet Union, by
Der Nister ("The Hidden One," the pen name of Pinkhas
Kahanovitsh, who died in a Soviet prison in 1950), translated
by Leonard Wolf; *American Yiddish Poetry*, the first of a
series of scholarly anthologies projected by Benjamin and
Barbara Harshav and designed to support the thesis that
poetry written in Yiddish, composed on American soil and
expressive of American experience, counts significantly as
American poetry; the splendid new *Penguin Book of Modern
Yiddish Verse*, a landmark volume brilliantly edited and
introduced by Irving Howe, Ruth R. Wisse, and Khone
Shmeruk; *In the Storm* and *The Nightingale*, novels by
Sholem Aleichem, lucidly translated by Aliza Shevrin;
Richard J. Fein's devoted rendering of the poetry of Jacob
Glatstein, and Ruth Whitman's of Abraham Sutzkever; and
doubtless others that have escaped me. One result of all
this publishing activity is that Isaac Bashevis Singer, the sole
Yiddish-language Nobel winner and the only Yiddish writer
familiar in any substantial degree to American readers, can
finally be seen as one figure among a multitude of others in
a diverse, complex, and turbulent community of letters. Too
often—lacking an appropriate cultural horizon and seemingly
without an ancestry—Singer has had the look in English of
an isolated hermit of language fallen out of a silent congregation and standing strangely apart. The current stir of industry among translators begins at last to hint at the range and
amplitude of modern Yiddish literature.

All these freshly revealed novelists and poets are, in one
respect or another, the heirs of Sholem Aleichem, and if there
is a single work among those now emerging in English that is
the herald and signature of the rest, it is, unsurprisingly,
Sholem Aleichem's *Tevye the Dairyman and the Railroad*

Stories, issued under the auspices of the newly organized Library of Yiddish Classics, of which Professor Ruth R. Wisse is the series editor. The translator, Hillel Halkin, an Israeli born and reared in the United States, an accomplished translator from Hebrew here tackling Yiddish for the first time, has supplied a superb historical introduction and a clarifying biblical glossary. If it is true that one need not be familiar with Wordsworth, say, before starting on Marianne Moore or the nature prose of Edward Hoagland, then it is just as true that one need not have assimilated Sholem Aleichem before entering the fiction of Chaim Grade or the poetry of Jacob Glatstein, but in both cases it's not a bad idea. Sholem Aleichem provides, in ways weblike and plain, the exegetical groundwork for his literary successors: to race along behind his footsteps brings one quickly and intensely into a society, an atmosphere, a predicament, and, more than anything else, a *voice*. The voice is monologic, partly out of deepest intimacy, a sense of tête-á-tête (with God or the reader), and partly out of verbal ingenuity, comedy, theatricality—even the sweep of aria. "While the crowd laughed, clapped, and frolicked, he wept unseen" is a line from an early version of an epitaph Sholem Aleichem wrote for himself; *Pagliacci* was brand-new in 1892, and its imagery of the clown in pain, trite for us, struck hard at the inventor of Tevye. (An oddity of resemblance: the late Gershom Scholem, the monumental scholar of Jewish mysticism, also identified himself with the idea of a clown.)

The eight Tevye stories are without doubt the nucleus of any understanding of how Yiddish leaped into world literature a hundred years ago (even though world literature may not have taken note of it, then or since). Professor Miron speaks of "the homiletic-sentimental streak" in Yiddish fiction before Mendele and Sholem Aleichem: "definitely antiartistic, inimical to irony, to conscious structural artistry, to the idea of literary technique, to stylistic perfection, and favorable to moralistic sermonizing, to unbridled emotionalism, and to stylistic sloppiness." Tevye stands for everything antithetical to such a catalogue. What one notices first is not the comedy—because the comedy is what Sholem Aleichem is famous for, the comedy is what is expected—but the shock of darkness. Poverty and persecution: while not even Sholem Aleichem can make these funny, he can satirize their reasons for being, or else he can set against them the standard and example of Tevye (as Mark Twain does with Huck Finn). Tevye is not any sort of scholar, this goes without saying: he is a *milckhiger*, meaning that he owns a cow; "dairyman" is too exalted a word for the owner of a cow, a horse, and a wagon. But he is not a fool, he is certainly not a peasant, and he is by no means the malaprop he is reputed to be. Tevye is intelligent; more, he is loving, witty, virtuous, generous, open, unwilling to sacrifice human feeling to grandiose aims—and all without a grain of heroism or sentimentality. He is never optimistic—he is too much at home with the worst that can happen. And he is never wiped out by despair—he is too much at home with Scripture and with the knowledge of frailty, mutability, mortality. When his wife, Golde, dies, he quotes from the morning prayer—"What are we and what is our life?"; and also from Ecclesiastes—"Let us hear the conclusion of the whole matter: fear God and keep His commandments, for that is the whole of man."

Tevye's play with sources, biblical and liturgical, is the enchantment—and brevity—of his wit. (Halkin's glossary insures that nearly all of it is gratifyingly at our fingertips.) Though his citations are mostly designed for comical juxtaposition—"And it came to pass," he will chant, with biblical sonorousness, about an ordinary wagon ride from Yehupetz to Boiberik—now and then a passage is straightforwardly plumbed, and then the glancingness of Tevye's brush stroke only abets the resonance of the verse. That sentence from Ecclesiastes, for instance: Tevye doesn't recite it in its entirety. What he actually says is *"ki zeh koyl ha'odom,"* "for that is the whole of man"—and the six scant Hebrew syllables instantly call up, for Tevye and his readers, the full quotation, the tremor of memory aroused by its ancestral uses, the tone and heft of the surrounding passages. Again it is worth keeping in mind that Tevye is not to be regarded as an educated man: he is a peddler of milk and cheese. And still he has a mastery of a plenitude of texts that enables him to

174

send them aloft like experimental kites, twisting their lines as they sail. By contrast, it would be unimaginable for a rustic in a novel by Thomas Hardy (Sholem Aleichem's contemporary, who outlived him by more than a decade) to have memorized a representative handful of Shakespeare's plays from earliest childhood, and to have the habit of liberally quoting from one or the other of these dozens and dozens of times, not only accurately and aptly but stingingly, pointedly, absurdly, and always to an immediate purpose; we would reject such a character as madly idiosyncratic if not wholly implausible. Country people don't get *Macbeth* or *Timon of Athens* by heart, if they are literate at all. And yet Tevye is a vivacious, persuasive creature, warm with the blood of reality. In his world it is not only plausible, it is not unusual, for a milkman or a carpenter to know the Pentateuch and the Psalms inside out, as well as considerable other scriptural and rabbinic territory, and to have the daily and holiday prayer books—no slender volumes, these—backwards and forwards. Tevye's cosmos is verbal. Biblical phrases are as palpable to him as his old horse. When he wants to remark that he has no secrets, he tosses in a fragment from Genesis: "And the Lord said, Shall I hide from Abraham that thing which I do?" When his only cow dies on him, he invokes a Psalm: "The sorrows of death compassed me, and the pains of hell got hold upon me; I found trouble and sorrow." When his daughter Shprintze is being courted by an unsuitable young man, he draws from the Songs of Songs: "a lily among thorns." Chaffing a utopian socialist, he turns to a rabbinic tractate, the Ethics of the Fathers, for its illumination of a type of artlessness: "What's mine is yours and what's yours is mine." It is all done with feather-light economy; he drops in only two or three words of the verse in question—an elegant minimalism—confident that his audience will recognize the source and fill in the rest. Or perhaps sometimes not so confident. Tevye's quotations, Halkin comments, "depending on the situation and the person he is talking to, can serve any conceivable purpose: to impress, to inform, to amuse, to intimidate, to comfort, to scold, to ridicule, to show off, to avoid, to put down, to stake a claim of equality or create a mood of intimacy." And he is not above "deliberately inventing, confusing, or misattributing a quote," Halkin continues, "in order to mock an ignoramus who will never know the difference, thus scoring a little private triumph of which he himself is the sole witness."

These virtuoso dartings of language—the prestidigitator's flash from biblical eloquence to its mundane applicability—have a cavorting brilliance reminiscent of the tricks and coruscations of *Finnegans Wake*, where sentences are also put under the pressure of multiple reverberations. Or think of Harold Bloom's thesis of "misprison," whereby an influential resource is usurped for purposeful "misinterpretation," engendering new life in a new text. While these macaronic comparisons—Tevye in the company of James Joyce and Harold Bloom!—may have the selfsame farcical impact as Tevye's own juxtapositions, they serve the point: which is that Sholem Aleichem's Tevye is about as far from the mind, tone, temperament, and language of either folk art or *Fiddler*-type showbiz as Boiberik is from Patagonia. Tevye is the stylistic invention of a self-conscious verbal artist, and if he stands for, and speaks for, the folk, that is the consequence of the artist's power. Tevye's manner emerges from the wit and genius of Sholem Aleichem.

Tevye's matter, however—his good and bad luck, his daily travail and occasional victory, the events in his family and in his village and in the next village—belongs unalloyedly to the folk. What happens to Tevye is what is happening to all Jews in the Russian Pale of Settlement; his tales are as political as they are individual, and it is entirely pertinent that Halkin provides a list of government-instigated depredations against Russian Jews from 1881 to 1904, including numbers of pogroms, blood libel charges, restrictions, expulsions, closed towns and cities, special taxes, identity passes, quotas, and other oppressive and humiliating measures. Tevye's life (and the lives of the characters in "The Railroad Stories") is assaulted by them all.

Tevye starts off, in the first of the eight tales, gently enough, with a generous ladling of burlesque. Ten years ago, he recounts in "Tevye Strikes It Rich," "I was such a miserable beggar that rags were too good for me." Unexpectedly he and his nag stumble into an act of slapstick kindness, he is rewarded with a cow, and his career as a *milkhiger* is launched. In the second story, "Tevye Blows a Small Fortune," he is taken in by a con man, a Jew even poorer than himself; when he catches up with the swindler, who by then has lost everything and looks it, Tevye ends by forgiving him and blaming himself. "The Lord giveth and the Lord taketh away," he quotes from Job. But with the third story, "Today's Children," and the remaining five, social and cultural disintegrations begin to rule the narrative. Against the stiff precedents of arranged marriage, Tevye's daughter Tsaytl and a poor young tailor decide to marry for love. Tevye accedes, but he is discontent on three strong counts: custom has been violated and the world turned upside down; Tsaytl has rejected an older widower of some means, a butcher in whose household there will always be enough to eat; and, foremost, Tevye himself is a textual snob with aristocratic aspirations who would like to claim a learned son-in-law. Neither the butcher nor the tailor is capable of the nuanced study of *di kleyne pintelakh*, "the fine points." Still, Tevye defends his daughter's autonomy for the sake of her happiness, despite his certainty that she will go hungry. "What do you have against her that you want to marry her?" he teases the young tailor. In "Hodl," a story that extends the theme of social decomposition, Tevye's daughter by that name also makes her own marital choice—a student revolutionary, a socialist intellectual who is arrested and sent to Siberia. Hodl insists on following him into exile, and when Tevye has driven her in his wagon to the railroad station, he closes the tale in sardonic melancholy: "Let's talk about something more cheerful. Have you heard any news of the cholera in Odessa?"

But the truly unthinkable is yet to come: in "Chava," Tevye's most rebellious daughter elopes with Chvedka, an educated Gentile village boy (a social rarity in himself), and Tevye is torn by anguish and terror. Chava has not only cut the thread of religious and historic continuity, she has joined up with the persecutors. The village priest takes charge of her because, he says, "we Christians have your good in mind," and Tevye cries: "... it would have been kinder to poison me or put a bullet in my head. If you're really such a good friend of mine, do me a favor: leave my daughter alone!" In Tevye's universe the loss of a daughter to Christianity—which for him has never shown anything but a murderous face—is the nadir of tragedy; he sobs for her as for a kidnapped child. (*Fiddler on the Roof* conspicuously Americanizes these perceptions. When a pogrom is threatened, Chava reappears with her suitably liberal and pluralist-minded husband, who announces in solidarity, "We cannot stay among people who can do such things to others," and even throws in a post-Holocaust declaration against Gentile "silence." But Sholem Aleichem's Chava returns "to her father and her God," chastened, remorseful, and without Chvedka.) In "Shprintze," the daughter of the sixth tale—her name, by the way, is more decorous than it sounds, deriving from the Italian *speranza*—is jilted by a well-off young rattlebrain who is fond of horses, and drowns herself. Beilke, the daughter of "Tevye Leaves for the Land of Israel," marries a coarse parvenu who, ashamed of a "cheesemonger" father-in-law, wants to pay Tevye off to get him out of the way, even offering him the fulfillment of a dream—a ticket to Palestine. Shprintze and Beilke are the center of "class" stories: as traditional influences lose hold, position based on material possessions begins to count over the authority of intellectual accomplishment, marking a growing leniency toward Gentile ways (typified by Shprintze's feckless suitor's preoccupation with "horses, fishing, and bicycles"). The aristocracy of learning—the essential principle and pillar of *shtetl* life—is breaking down; the mores of the outer society are creeping, even streaming, in.

In the final narrative, "Lekh-Lekho" (the opening words of God's command to Abraham: "Get thee out of thy country"), everything has come apart. Golde, Tevye's wife, the pragmatic foil for his idealism, is dead. Beilke and her husband have lost their money and are now laboring in the sweatshops of America. Tsaytl's husband, the young tailor, is struck down by consumption; and the hope of Palestine vanishes for Tevye as he takes in his impoverished daughter and her orphans.

On top of all this, it is the time of the Beilis blood libel trial—a Jew accused, as late as 1911, of killing a Christian child for its blood. (This grisly anti-Semitic fantasy turns up as far back as Chaucer's "Prioress's Tale.") Tevye's neighbors, after a meeting of the village council, are preparing for a pogrom. "Since you Jews have been beaten up everywhere, why let you get away with it here?" argues Ivan Paparilo, the village elder. "We just aren't certain what kind of pogrom to have. Should we just smash your windows, should we tear up your pillows and blankets and scatter all the feathers, or should we also burn down your house and barn with everything in them?" To which Tevye replies: "If that's what you've decided, who am I to object? You must have good reasons for thinking that Tevye deserves to see his life go up in smoke . . . You do know that there's a God above, don't you? Mind you, I'm not talking about my God or your God—I'm talking about the God of us all . . . It may very well be that He wants you to punish me for nothing at all. But the opposite may also be true . . ." Ultimately the villagers are talked out of the pogrom—they want it, they explain, only to save face with the towns that have already had one. Instead, all the Jews in the village—among them Tevye's family, including the returned Chava—are expelled by order of the provincial governor; and there the Tevye tales end. "Anyone can be a goy," Tevye concludes, "but a Jew must be born one . . . it's a lucky thing I was, then, because otherwise how would I ever know what it's like to be homeless and wander all over the world without resting my head on the same pillow two nights running?"

Thus the somber matter of Sholem Aleichem's comedy. Tevye's dicta run all through it: what he thinks about God ("Why doesn't He do something? Why doesn't He say something?"), about wickedness ("My problem was men. Why did they have to be so bad when they could just as well have been good?"), about the goals of life ("to do a little good in His world before you die—to give a bit of money to charity, to take someone needy under your wing, even to sit down with educated Jews and study some Torah"), about the situation in Russia ("pogroms in Kishinev, riots, troubles, the new Constantution* [Constitution] ... God wanted to do us Jews a favor and so He sent us a new catastrophe, a Constantution"), about education ("I'd sooner eat a buttered pig than sit down to a meal with an illiterate. A Jew who can't read a Jewish book is a hundred times worse than a sinner"), about reserve ("secretive people annoy me"), about opportunity ("A cow can sooner jump over a roof than a Jew get into a Russian university! ... they guard their schools from us like a bowl of cream from a cat"), about faith and resignation ("A Jew has to hope. So what if things couldn't be worse? That's why there are Jews in the world!"), about what to do with money if one ever got any ("make a contribution to charity that would be the envy of any rich Jew"), about ignorance, love, decency, poverty, misery, anti-Semitism, and the tardiness of the Messiah.

"The Railroad Stories," the second half of the Halkin volume, are similar in their use of a monologic narrator, and certainly in their cheerless subject matter. The storyteller of "Baranovich Station" sums up what Jews traveling by train—men scrambling for a living—talk about: "From the Revolution we passed to the Constitution, and from the Constitution it was but a short step to the pogroms, the massacres of Jews, the new anti-Semitic legislation, the expulsion from the villages, the mass flight to America, and all the other trials and tribulations that you hear about these fine days: bankruptcies, expropriations, military emergencies, executions, starvation, cholera, Perushkevich [the founder of the anti-Semitic Black Hundreds] ..." If we did not absolutely grasp it before, we can profoundly recognize it now: Sholem Aleichem's is a literature of crisis.

And yet "The Railroad Stories," in their slightness and vitality and scattershot abundance—there are twenty of them—strike with a comic sharpness that to my mind exceeds even the effervescent artistry of the Tevye tales. Tevye's voice is elastic, simultaneously innocent and knowing, never short on acuteness of energy or observation or ironic fervor; but "The Railroad Stories," perhaps because they are largely

* Possibly a pun on Konstantin Petrovich Pobedonostsev, an influential anti-Semite of the time. (I am indebted to Abraham J. Karp for this insight.)

unfamiliar to us and have never been contaminated by reductiveness, yield the plain shock of their form. Their form is all plotless trajectory: one doesn't apprehend the mark until after the mark has been hit. To come on these stories with no inkling of their existence beforehand (I imagine this will be the experience of numbers of readers) is to understand what it is to marvel at form—or formlessness—in the hands of literary genius. There are pronounced resemblances to early Chekhov and to Babel and Gorky, as well as a recognizable source—the casual sketch that is the outgrowth of the feuilleton, here strengthened and darkened by denser resonances. Nevertheless the landscape is for the most part uniquely Sholem Aleichem's, a Russia not easily duplicated even by the sympathetic Chekhov, who in his letters could now and then toss off an anti-Semitic crack as lightly as a shrug. The most Chekhovian of these stories, "Eighteen from Pereshchepena"—a vignette of comic misunderstanding that, when untangled, is seen to be tragic—appears at first to be about the quota system in schools, but actually turns on the dread of forced military service: the eighteen Jewish youths "taken" from the town of Pereshchepena are revealed to be unlucky conscripts, not lucky students. "The Wedding That Came Without Its Band" lustily caricatures a pogrom that doesn't come off: a trainload of hooligans, "in full battle gear, too, with clubs, and tar," get so drunk—"the conductor and the stoker and even the policeman"—that they are left behind by the locomotive intended to carry them to their prey. In "The Miracle of Hoshana Rabbah," a venturesome Jew named Berl and an anti-Semitic priest find themselves improbably but perilously alone together aboard a runaway engine; the priest, exasperated with Berl, threatens to push him off. "Just look at the difference, Father, between you and me," says Berl, as the engine hurtles wildly on. "I'm doing my best to stop this locomotive, because I'm trying to save us both, and all you can think of is throwing me out of it—in other words, of murdering your fellow man!" An antic moral fable, wherein the priest is shamed and tamed. But there are plenty of Jewish rascals too—con men and card-sharps and thieves, and a pimp and a cowardly apostate and even an insurance arsonist; and desolate Jews—a teenage suicide, a desperate father who pursues a Gentile "professor of medicine" to beg him to tend his dying boy, Jews without residence permits who risk arrest by sneaking into town to see a doctor.

All these characters, whether avoiding or perpetrating pogroms, whether hostile or farcical or pathetic or paradoxical, are flushed with the rosiness of comedy. Comedy, the product of ridicule, is too brittle a mode in the absence of compassion, and too soppy a mode in the absence of briskness. Sholem Aleichem is always brisk and always ready to display just enough (sparing) kindliness to keep the tone on the far side of soppiness. Here he is, in "Third Class," matter-of-fact without coldness, satiric without meanness, loving without mawkishness:

> When you go third class and wake up in the morning to discover that you've left your tefillin and your prayer shawl at home, there isn't any cause for alarm—you only need to ask and you'll be given someone else's, along with whatever else you require. All that's expected of you in return, once you're done praying, is to open your suitcase and display your own wares. Vodka, cake, a hard-boiled egg, a drumstick, a piece of fish—it's all grist for the mill. Perhaps you have an apple, an orange, a piece of strudel? Out with it, no one stands on ceremony here . . . Before long each of us not only knows all about the other's troubles, he knows about every trial and tribulation that ever befell a Jew anywhere. It's enough to warm the cockles of your heart!

The close-knittedness—or huddling, or nestling—of frequently threatened poor Jews, collectively and individually powerless, who bloom in the fond and comradely safety of fellow Jews on a train; the caustic notion of adversity as one's oldest intimate; trials and tribulations that nevertheless warm the cockles—this is Sholem Aleichem defining, so to speak, the connotations of his nom de plume. That these ironies can rise so pungently from the translated page testifies to how clear and broad an opening Hillel Halkin has bored into the original, where psychological sighs and skeptical gestures are more slender than a hair, or else hidden—a grain here, a grain there, in the crannies of language. A translator's triumph occurs when the reader comes away from the text in the security of having been given a reasonable measure of access. Halkin now and then achieves much more than the merely reasonable—a true bridge across languages, happy moments like this: "Menachem Mendel was his name: a wheeler, a dealer, a schemer, a dreamer, a bag of hot air." Or this: "He called him a scoundrel, a degenerate, a know-nothing, a leech, a bloodsucker, a fiend, a traitor, a disgrace to the Jewish people." Such jubilant and exuberant flights let us know without question that we have been catapulted right inside what Maurice Samuel once called "the world of Sholem Aleichem."

But even where there is generous overall access, there can be problems and irritations. Especially with Sholem Aleichem, tone is everything. Halkin's work, stemming perhaps from his frank belief in "untranslatabilities," is too often jarred by sudden clangs that do violence to both tongues, bringing on startling distractions in the English while derailing our expectations of the Yiddish. Either we are in Sholem Aleichem's milieu or we are not—that is the crux. To transmute Sholem Aleichem's easy idiomatic language into familiar slang is not necessarily a bad or inept solution; it requires of the translator a facile and supple ear, alert to the equation of idioms in two cultures. And it isn't that Hillel Halkin lacks such an ear; just the opposite. What he lacks, I am afraid, is an instinct for what is apropos. American street talk is preposterous in the mouths of people in a forest outside Yehupetz on the way to Boiberik—and the more skillfully and lavishly these relaxed Americanisms are deployed, the more preposterous they seem. "He looks at me like the dumb bunny he is," "I blew in this morning," "It drives me up the wall," "holy suffering catfish!"—absurd locutions for poor Jews in a Russian railway carriage at the turn of the century, especially in the company of the occasional British "quite" and a stilted "A black plague take them all" (a stock imprecation that in Yiddish stings without sounding rococo). And what are we to do with a Tevye who is "bushed," who downs his brandy with "Cheers!" (even *Fiddler* stuck by *l'khayim*), who tells someone, "You're off your trolley"? With ripe improbability the Jews on the train say "the gospel truth," "doesn't that beat all for low-down-ness," "tried to pin such a bum rap on me," "you're all bollixed up," "some meatball he was," "a federal case," and painfully, for dancing, "everyone cut the rug up." Somewhere there is an agonizing 1940s "swell." Under such an assault, tone collapses and imagination dies.

But these are phrases snatched out of context. Here, by contrast, is a bit of dialogue between Tevye and his daughter Chava concerning Chvedka, the young Gentile she will eventually run off with:

> "Well, then," I say, "what sort of person is he? Perhaps you could enlighten me."
>
> "Even if I told you," she said, "You wouldn't understand. Chvedka is a second Gorky."
>
> "A second Gorky?" I said. "And who, pray tell, was the first?"
>
> "Gorky," she says, "is only just about the most important man alive."
>
> "Is he?" I say. "And just where does he live, this Mr. Important of yours? What's his act and what makes him such a big deal?"

In the Yiddish, Tevye's bitterness is less elaborately spoken, and effectively more cutting. Instead of "Perhaps you could enlighten me," Tevye comes back with a curt "Let's hear," all the more biting for its brevity. "Pray tell," absent in the original, is too fancy; Tevye grunts out his sardonic helplessness in a single fricative, a *zhe* attached to the sentence's opening word. This *zhe*, in no way portable into English, is none the less rawly expressive, and deserves better than the tinkle of Halkin's "Pray tell." But the real blow to Tevye's language (and his moral cosmos) is struck in the last line quoted above, which, in the light of the Yiddish original, is insupportably charmless and hollow—lingo far too carelessly parochial to reflect Tevye's sufferings in a pharaonic Russia.

Agreed, the original is intimidating. "*Vu zitst er, der tane dayner, vos iz zayn gesheft un vos far a droshe hot er gedarshnt?*" Literally, "Where does he sit, that *tane* of yours, how does he get his living, and what kind of a *droshe* has he preached?" A *tane* is one of the classical scholastics known as *tannaim*, whose hermeneutics appear in the Mishnah, a collection of sixty-three tractates of law and ethics that constitute the foundation of the Talmud; a *droshe* is a commentary, often formidably allusive, prepared by a serious student of homiletics. For Tevye to compare a Russian peasant boy, whose father he judges to be a swineherd and a drunk, with the most influential sages of antiquity is bruising sarcasm—and not only because Chvedka's family outlook is so remote from the impassioned patrimony of Jewish learning.

More appositely, Tevye is making the point that the Gorky he has never heard of stands as a mote in relation to that patrimony. From Tevye's perspective—and his perspective always includes historical memory, with its emphasis on survival and continuity—Chava, in pursuing Chvedka, is venturing into the transgressions of spiritual self-erasure: Tevye is altogether untouched by that cosmopolitan Western liberalism that will overwhelmingly claim his deracinated descendants. In half a moment, the dialogue has moved from the joke of "a second Gorky" to the outcry of a crumbling tradition wherein a secular Russian author is starting to assume major cultural authority for Jews. However difficult it may be for a translator to convey all this—so complex and hurtful a knot of social and emotional attitudes ingeniously trapped in a two-syllable word—it is certain that Halkin's "this Mr. Important of yours," with its unerring echoes of old radio programs (Molly Goldberg, Fred Allen's Mrs. Nussbaum), has not begun to achieve a solution.

Even so, given its strengths, this volume is likely to serve as the indispensable Sholem Aleichem for some time to come.

RUTH

For
Muriel Dance, In New York;
Lee Gleichmann, in Stockholm;
Sarah Halevi, in Jerusalem; and
Inger Mirsky, in New York

I. FLOWERS

THERE WERE ONLY two pictures on the walls of the house
I grew up in. One was large, and hung from the molding on
a golden cord with a full golden tassel. It was a painting
taken from a photograph—all dark, a kind of grayish-brown;
it was of my grandfather Hirshl, my father's father. My
grandfather's coat had big foreign-looking buttons, and he
wore a tall stiff square yarmulke that descended almost to
the middle of his forehead. His eyes were severe, pale, concentrated. There was no way to escape those eyes; they came
after you wherever you were. I had never known this grandfather: he died in Russia long ago. My father, a taciturn man,
spoke of him only once, when I was already grown: as a boy,
my father said, he had gone with his father on a teaching
expedition to Kiev; he remembered how the mud was deep
in the roads. From my mother I learned a little more. Zeyde
Hirshl was frail. His wife, Bobe Sore-Libe, was the opposite:
quick, energetic, hearty, a skilled *zogerke*—a women's prayer
leader in the synagogue—a whirlwind who kept a dry goods
store and had baby after baby, all on her own, while Zeyde
Hirshl spent his days in the study-house. Sometimes he

186

fainted on his way there. He was pale, he was mild, he was delicate, unworldly; a student, a *melamed*, a fainter. Why, then, those unforgiving stern eyes that would not let you go?

My grandfather's portrait had its permanent place over the secondhand piano. To the right, farther down the wall, hung the other picture. It was framed modestly in a thin black wooden rectangle, and was, in those spare days, all I knew of "art." Was it torn from a magazine, cut from a calendar? A barefoot young woman, her hair bound in a kerchief, grasping a sickle, stands alone and erect in a field. Behind her a red sun is half-swallowed by the horizon. She wears a loose white peasant's blouse and a long dark skirt, deeply blue; her head and shoulders are isolated against a limitless sky. Her head is held poised: she gazes past my gaze into some infinity of loneliness stiller than the sky.

Below the picture was its title: *The Song of the Lark*. There was no lark. It did not come to me that the young woman, with her lifted face, was straining after the note of a bird who might be in a place invisible to the painter. What I saw and heard was something else: a scene older than this French countryside, a woman lonelier even than the woman alone in the calendar meadow. It was, my mother said, Ruth: Ruth gleaning in the fields of Boaz.

For many years afterward—long after *The Song of the Lark* had disappeared from the living room wall—I had the idea that this landscape (a 1930s fixture, it emerged, in scores of American households and Sunday-school classrooms) was the work of Jean-François Millet, the French painter of farm life. "I try not to have things look as if chance had brought them together," Millet wrote, "but as if they had a necessary bond between them. I want the people I represent to look as if they really belonged to their station, so that imagination cannot conceive of their ever being anything else."

Here is my grandfather. Imagination cannot conceive of his ever being anything else: a *melamed* who once ventured with his young son (my blue-eyed father) as far as Kiev, but mainly stayed at home in his own town, sometimes fainting on the way to the study-house. The study-house was his "station." In his portrait he looks as if he really belonged there; and he did. It was how he lived.

And here is Ruth, on the far side of the piano, in Boaz's field, gleaning. Her mouth is remote: it seems somehow damaged; there is a blur behind her eyes. All the sadness of the earth is in her tender neck, all the blur of loss, all the damage of rupture: remote, remote, rent. The child who stands before the woman standing barefoot, sickle forgotten, has fallen through the barrier of an old wooden frame into the picture itself, into the field; into the smell of the field. There is no lark, no birdcall: only the terrible silence of the living room when no one else is there. The grandfather is always there; his eyes keep their vigil. The silence of the field swims up from a time so profoundly lost that it annihilates time. There is the faint weedy smell of thistle: and masses of meadow flowers. In my childhood I recognized violets, lilacs, roses, daisies, dandelions, black-eyed Susans, tiger lilies, pansies (I planted, one summer, a tiny square of pansies, one in each corner, one in the middle), and no more. The lilacs I knew because of the children who brought them to school in springtime: children with German names, Koechling, Behrens, Kuntz.

To annihilate time, to conjure up unfailingly the fragrance in Boaz's field (his field in *The Song of the Lark*), I have the power now to summon what the child peering into the picture could not. "Tolstoy, come to my aid," I could not call then: I had never heard of Tolstoy: my child's Russia was the grandfather's portrait, and stories of fleeing across borders at night, and wolves, and the baba yaga in the fairy tales. But now: "Tolstoy, come to my aid," I can chant at this hour, with my hair turned silver, and lo, the opening of *Hadji Murad* spills out all the flowers in Boaz's field:

It was midsummer, the hay harvest was over and they were just beginning to reap the rye. At that season of the year there is a delightful variety of flowers—red, white, and pink scented tufty clover; milk-white ox-eye daisies with their bright yellow centers and pleasant spicy smell; yellow honey-scented rape blossoms; tall campanulas with white and lilac bells, tulip-shaped; creeping vetch; yellow, red, and pink scabious; faintly scented, neatly arranged purple plantains with blossoms slightly tinged with pink; cornflowers, the newly opened blossoms bright blue in the sunshine but growing paler and redder towards evening or when growing old; and delicate almond-scented dodder flowers that withered quickly.

Dodder? Vetch? (Flash of Henry James's Fleda Vetch.) Scabious? Rape and campanula? The names are unaccustomed; my grandfather in the study-house never sees the flowers. In the text itself—in the book of Ruth—not a single flower is mentioned. And the harvest is neither hay nor rye; in Boaz's field outside Bethlehem they are cutting down barley and wheat. The flowers are there all the same, even if the text doesn't show them, and we are obliged to take in their scents, the weaker with the keener, the grassier with the meatier: without the smell of flowers, we cannot pass through the frame of history into that long ago, ancientness behind ancientness, when Ruth the Moabite gleaned. It is as if the little spurts and shoots of fragrance form a rod, a rail of light, along which we are carried, drifting, into that time before time "when the judges ruled."

Two pictures, divided by an old piano—Ruth in *The Song of the Lark*, my grandfather in his yarmulke. He looks straight out; so does she. They sight each other across the breadth of the wall. I stare at both of them. Eventually I will learn that *The Song of the Lark* was not painted by Millet, not at all; the painter is Jules Breton—French like Millet, like Millet devoted to rural scenes. *The Song of the Lark* hangs in the Art Institute of Chicago; it is possible I will die without ever having visited there. Good: I never want to see the original, out of shock at what a reproduction now discloses: a mistake, everything is turned the other way! On our living room wall Ruth faced right. In the Art Institute of Chicago she faces left. A calendar reversal!—but of course it feels to me that the original is in sullen error. Breton, unlike Millet, lived into our century—he died in 1906, the year my nine-year-old mother came through Castle Garden on her way to framing *The Song of the Lark* two decades later. About my grandfather Hirshl there is no "eventually"; I will not learn anything new about him. He will not acquire a different maker. Nothing in his view will be reversed. He will remain a dusty indoor *melamed* with eyes that drill through bone.

Leaving aside the wall, leaving aside the child who haunts and is haunted by the grandfather and the woman with the sickle, what is the connection between this dusty indoor *melamed* and the nymph in the meadow, standing barefoot amid the tall campanula?

Everything, everything. If the woman had not been in the field, my grandfather, three thousand years afterward, would not have been in the study-house. She, the Moabite, is why he, when hope is embittered, murmurs the Psalms of David. The track her naked toes make through spice and sweetness, through dodder, vetch, rape, and scabious, is the very track his forefinger follows across the letter-speckled sacred page.

II. MERCY

When my grandfather reads the Book of Ruth, it is on Shavuot, the Feast of Weeks, with its twin furrows: the text's straight furrow planted with the alphabet; the harvest's furrow, fuzzy with seedlings. The Feast of Weeks, which comes in May, is a reminder of the late spring crops, but only as an aside. The soul of it is the acceptance of the Torah by the Children of Israel. If there is a garland crowning this festival of May, it is the arms of Israel embracing the Covenant. My grandfather will not dart among field flowers after Ruth and her sickle; the field is fenced round by the rabbis, and the rabbis—those insistent interpretive spirits of Commentary whose arguments and counter-arguments, from generation to generation, comprise the Tradition—seem at first to be vexed with the Book of Ruth. If they are not actually or openly vexed, they are suspicious; and if they are not willing to be judged flatly suspicious, then surely they are cautious.

The Book of Ruth is, after all, about exogamy, and not simple exogamy—marriage with a stranger, a member of a foreign culture: Ruth's ancestry is hardly neutral in that sense. She is a Moabite. She belongs to an enemy people, callous, pitiless; a people who deal in lethal curses. The children of the wild hunter Esau—the Edomites, who will ultimately stand for the imperial oppressors of Rome—cannot be shut out of the family of Israel. Even the descendants of the enslaving Egyptians are welcome to marry and grow into intimacy. "You shall not abhor an Edomite, for he is your kinsman. You shall not abhor an Egyptian, for you were a stranger in his land. Children born to them may be admitted into the congregation of the Lord in the third generation" (Deut. 23:8–9). But a Moabite, never: "none of their descendants, even in the tenth generation, shall ever be admitted into the congregation of the Lord, because they did not meet you with food and water on your journey after you left Egypt, and because they hired Balaam . . . to curse you" (Deut. 23:4–5). An abyss of memory and hurt in that: to have passed through the furnace of the desert famished, parched, and to be chased after by a wonder-worker on an ass hurling the king's maledictions, officially designed to wipe out the straggling mob of exhausted refugees! One might in time reconcile with Esau, one might in time reconcile with hard-hearted Egypt. All this was not merely conceivable— through acculturation, conversion, family ties, and new babies, it could be implemented, it *would* be implemented. But Moabite spite had a lasting sting.

What, then, are the sages to do with Ruth the Moabite as in-law? How account for her presence and resonance in Israel's story? How is it possible for a member of the congregation of the Lord to have violated the edict against marriage with a Moabite? The rabbis, reflecting on the pertinent verses, deduce a rule: *Moabite, not Moabitess.* It was customary for men, they conclude, not for women, to succor travelers in the desert, so only the Moabite males were guilty of a failure of humanity. The women were blameless, hence are exempt from the ban on conversion and marriage.

Even with the discovery of this mitigating loophole (with

its odd premise that women are descended only from women, and men from men; or else that all the women, or all the men, in a family line are interchangeable with one another, up and down the ladder of the generations, and that guilt and innocence are collective, sex-linked, and heritable), it is hard for the rabbis to swallow a Moabite bride. They are discomfited by every particle of cause-and-effect that brought about such an eventuality. Why should a family with a pair of marriageable sons find itself in pagan Moab in the first place? The rabbis begin by scolding the text—or, rather, the characters and events of the story as they are straightforwardly set out.

Here is how the Book of Ruth begins:

> In the days when the judges ruled, there was a famine in the land; and a man of Bethlehem in Judah, with his wife and two sons, went to reside in the country of Moab. The man's name was Elimelech, his wife's name was Naomi, and his two sons were named Mahlon and Chilion—Ephrathites of Bethlehem in Judah. They came to the country of Moab and remained there.
>
> Elimelech, Naomi's husband, died; and she was left with her two sons. They married Moabite women, one named Orpah and the other Ruth, and they lived there about ten years. Then those two—Mahlon and Chilion—also died; so the woman was left without her two sons and without her husband.

Famine; migration; three deaths in a single household; three widows. Catastrophe after catastrophe, yet the text, plain and sparse, is only matter-of-fact. There is no anger in it, no one is condemned. What happened, happened—though not unaccoutred by echo and reverberation. Earlier biblical families and journeys-toward-sustenance cluster and chatter around Elimelech's decision: "There was a famine in the land, and Abram went down to Egypt to sojourn there, for the famine was severe in the land" (Gen. 12:10). "So ten of Joseph's brothers went down to get rations in Egypt . . . Thus the sons of Israel were among those who came to procure rations, for the famine extended to the land of Canaan"

(Gen. 42: 3.5). What Abraham did, what the sons of Jacob did, Elimelech also feels constrained to do: there is famine, he will go where the food is.

And the rabbis subject him to bitter censure for it. The famine, they say, is retribution for the times—"the days when the judges ruled"—and the times are coarse, cynical, lawless. "In those days there was no king in Israel; everyone did what he pleased" (Judges 17:6). Ironic that the leaders should be deemed "judges," and that under their aegis the rule of law is loosened, each one pursuing "what is right in his own eyes," without standard or conscience. Elimelech, according to the rabbis, is one of these unraveled and atomized souls: a leader who will not lead. They identify him as a man of substance, distinguished, well-off, an eminence; but arrogant and selfish. Even his name suggests self-aggrandizement: *to me shall kingship come.** Elimelech turns his back on the destitute conditions of hungry Bethlehem, picks up his family, and, because he is rich enough to afford the journey, sets out for where the food is. He looks to his own skin and means to get his own grub. The rabbis charge Elimelech with desertion; they accuse him of running away from the importunings of the impoverished, of provoking discouragement and despair; he is miserly, there is no charitableness in him, he is ungenerous. They call him a "dead stump"—he attends only to his immediate kin and shrugs off the community at large. Worse yet, he is heading for Moab, vile Moab! The very man who might have heartened his generation in a period of upheaval and inspired its moral repair leaves his own country, a land sanctified by Divine Covenant, for a historically repugnant region inhabited by idolators—and only to fill his own belly, and his own wife's, and his own sons'.

Elimelech in Moab will die in his prime. His widow will suffer radical denigration—a drop in status commonly enough observed even among independent women of our

---

* Latter-day scholarship avers that Elimelech is a run-of-the-mill name in pre-Israelite Canaan, "and is the one name in the Ruth story that seems incapable of being explained as having a symbolic meaning pertinent to the narrative" (Edward F. Campbell, Jr., *Ruth*, The Anchor Bible, p. 52). The rabbis, however, are above all metaphor-seekers and symbolists.

era—and, more seriously, a loss of protection. The rabbis will compare Naomi in her widowhood with "the remnants of the meal offerings"—i.e., with detritus and ash. Elimelech's sons—children of a father whose example is abandonment of community and of conscience—will die too soon. Already grown men after the death of Elimelech, they have themselves earned retribution. Instead of returning with their unhappy mother to their own people in the land dedicated to monotheism, they settle down to stay, and marry Moabite women. "One transgression leads to another," chide the rabbis, and argue over whether the brides of Mahlon and Chilion were or were not ritually converted before their weddings. In any case, a decade after those weddings, nothing has flowered for these husbands and wives, fertility eludes them, there will be no blossoming branches: the two young husbands are dead—dead stumps—and the two young widows are childless.

This is the rabbis' view. They are symbolists and metaphor-seekers; it goes without saying they are moralists. Punishment is truthful; punishment is the consequence of reality, it instructs in what happens. It is not that the rabbis are severe; they are just the opposite of severe. What they are after is simple mercy: where is the standard of mercy and humanity in a time when careless men and women follow the whim of their own greedy and expedient eyes? It is not merciful to abandon chaos and neediness; chaos and neediness call out for reclamation. It is not merciful to forsake one's devastated countrymen; opportunism is despicable; desertion is despicable; derogation of responsibility is despicable; it is not merciful to think solely of one's own family: if I am only for myself, what am I? And what of the hallowed land, that sacral ground consecrated to the unity of the Creator and the teaching of mercy, while the babble and garble of polymyth pullulate all around? The man who throws away the country of aspiration, especially in a lamentable hour when failure overruns it—the man who promotes egotism, elevates the material, and deprives his children of idealism—this fellow, this Elimelech, vexes the rabbis and afflicts them with shame.

Of course there is not a grain of any of this in the text

itself—not a word about Elimelech's character or motives or even his position in Bethlehem. The rabbis' commentary is all extrapolation, embroidery, plausible invention. What is plausible in it is firmly plausible: it stands to reason that only a wealthy family, traveling together as a family, would be able to contemplate emigration to another country with which they have no economic or kinship ties. And it follows also that a wealthy householder is likely to be an established figure in his home town. The rabbis' storytelling faculty is not capricious or fantastic: it is rooted in the way the world actually works, then and now.

But the rabbis are even more interested in the way the world *ought* to work. Their parallel text hardly emerges *ex nihilo*. They are not oblivious to what-is: they can, in fact, construct a remarkably particularized social density from a handful of skeletal data. Yet, shrewd sociologists though they are, it is not sociology that stirs them. What stirs them is the aura of judgment—or call it ethical interpretation—that rises out of even the most comprehensively imagined social particularity. The rabbis are driven by a struggle to uncover a moral immanence in every human being. It signifies, such a struggle, hopefulness to the point of pathos, and the texture and pliability of this deeply embedded matrix of optimism is more pressing for the rabbis than any other kind of speculation or cultural improvisation. Callousness and egotism are an affront to their expectations. What are their expectations in the Book of Ruth? That an established community figure has an obligation not to demoralize his constituency by walking out on it. And that the Holy Land is to be passionately embraced, clung to, blessed, and defended as the ripening center and historic promise of the covenanted life. Like the Covenant that engendered its sanctifying purpose, Israel cannot be "marginalized." One place is not the same as another place. The rabbis are not cultural relativists.

From the rabbis' vantage, it is not that their commentary is "implicit" in the plain text under their noses; what they see is not implicit so much as it is fully intrinsic. It is there already, like invisible ink gradually made to appear. A system of values produces a story. A system of values? Never mind such Aristotelian language. The rabbis said, and meant, the quality of mercy: human feeling.

III. NORMALITY

I have been diligent in opening the first five verses of the Book of Ruth to the rabbis' voices, and though I am unwilling to leave their voices behind—they painstakingly accompany the story inch by inch, breath for breath—I mean for the rest of my sojourn in the text (perforce spotty and selective, a point here, a point there) to go on more or less without them. I say "more or less" because it is impossible, really, to go on without them. They are (to use an unsuitable image) the Muses of exegesis: not the current sort of exegesis that ushers insights out of a tale by scattering a thousand brilliant fragments, but rather the kind that ushers things *toward*: a guide toward principle. The Book of Ruth presents two principles. The first is what is normal. The second is what is singular.

Until Elimelech's death, Naomi has been an exemplum of the normal. She has followed her husband and made no decisions or choices of her own. What we nowadays call feminism is of course as old as the oldest society imaginable; there have always been feminists: women (including the unsung) who will allow no element of themselves—gift, capacity, natural authority—to go unexpressed, whatever the weight of the mores. Naomi has not been one of these. Until the death of her husband we know nothing of her but her compliance, and it would be foolish to suppose that in Naomi's world a wife's obedience is not a fundamental social virtue. But once Naomi's husband and sons have been tragically cleared from the stage, Naomi moves from the merely passive virtue of an honorable dependent to risks and contingencies well beyond the reach of comfortable common virtue. Stripped of every social support,* isolated in a foreign land, pitifully unprotected, her anomalous position apparently wholly ignored by Maobite practices, responsible for the lives

* The rabbis' notion of Elimelech as a man of substance is no help to his widow. She has not been provided for; we see her as helpless and impoverished.

of a pair of foreign daughters-in-law (themselves isolated and unprotected under her roof), Naomi is transformed over-night. Under the crush of mourning and defenselessness, she becomes, without warning or preparation, a woman of valor.

She is only a village woman, after all. The Book of Ruth, from beginning to end, is played out in village scenes. The history of valor will not find in Naomi what it found in another village woman: she will not arm herself like a man or ride a horse or lead a military expedition. She will never cross over to another style of being. The new ways of her valor will not annul the old ways of her virtue.

And yet—overnight!—she will set out on a program of autonomy. Her first act is a decision: she will return to Bethlehem, "for in the country of Moab she had heard that the Lord had taken note of His people and given them food." After so many years, the famine in Bethlehem is spent—but since Naomi is cognizant of this as the work of the Lord, there is a hint that she would have gone back to Bethlehem in Judah in any event, even if that place were still troubled by hunger. It is no ordinary place for her: the Lord hovers over Judah and its people, and Naomi in returning makes restitution for Elimelech's abandonment. Simply in her deter-mination to go back, she rights an old wrong.

But she does not go back alone. Now, willy-nilly, she is herself the head of a household bound to her by obedience. "Accompanied by her two daughters-in-law, she left the place where she had been living; and they set out on the road back to the land of Judah." On the road, Naomi reflects. What she reflects on—only connect! she is herself an exile—is the ache of exile and the consolations of normality.

Naomi said to her two daughters-in-law, "Turn back, each of you to her mother's house. May the Lord deal kindly with you, as you have dealt with the dead and with me! May the Lord grant that each of you find security in the house of a husband!" And she kissed them farewell. They broke into weeping and said to her, "No, we will return with you to your people."

But Naomi replied, "Turn back, my daughters! Why

should you go with me? Have I any more sons in my body who might be husbands for you? Turn back, my daughters, for I am too old to be married. Even if I thought there was hope for me, even if I were married tonight and I also bore sons, should you wait for them to grow up? Should you on their account debar your-selves from marriage? Oh no, my daughters!"

In a moment or so we will hear Ruth's incandescent reply spiraling down to us through the ardors of three thousand years; but here let us check the tale, fashion a hiatus, and allow normality to flow in: let young stricken Orpah not be overlooked. She is always overlooked; she is the daughter-in-law who, given the chance, chose not to follow Naomi. She is no one's heroine. Her mark is erased from history; there is no Book of Orpah. And yet Orpah *is* history. Or rather, she is history's great backdrop. She is the majority of humankind living out its usualness on home ground. These young women—both of them—are cherished by Naomi; she cannot speak to them without flooding them in her fellow feeling. She *knows* what it is to be Orpah and Ruth. They have all suffered and sorrowed together, and in ten years of living in one household much of the superficial cultural strangeness has worn off. She pities them because they are childless, and she honors them because they have "dealt kindly" with their husbands and with their mother-in-law. She calls them—the word as she releases it is accustomed, familiar, close, ripe with dearness—*b'notai*, "my daughters," whereas the voice of the narrative is careful to identify them precisely, though neutrally, as *khalotekha*, "her daughters-in-law."

Orpah is a loving young woman of clear goodness; she has kisses and tears for the loss of Naomi. "They broke into weeping again, and Orpah kissed her mother-in-law fare-well." Her sensibility is ungrudging, and she is not in the least narrow-minded. Her upbringing may well have been liberal. Would a narrow-minded Moabite father have given over one of his daughters to the only foreign family in town? Such a surrender goes against the grain of the ordinary. Exogamy is never ordinary. So Orpah has already been stamped with the "abnormal"; she is already a little more daring than most, already somewhat offbeat—she is one of only two young Moabite women to marry Hebrews, and Hebrews have never been congenial to Moabites. If the Hebrews can remember how the Moabites treated them long ago, so can the Moabites: traditions of emnity work in both directions. The mean-spirited have a habit of resenting their victims quite as much as the other way around. Orpah has cut through all this bad blood to plain humanity; it would be unfair to consider her inferior to any other kindhearted young woman who ever lived in the world before or since. She is in fact superior; she has thrown off prejudice, and she has had to endure more than most young women of her class, including the less spunky and the less amiable: an early widowhood and no babies. And what else is there for a good girl like Orpah, in her epoch, and often enough in ours, but family happiness?

Her prototype abounds. She has fine impulses, but she is not an iconoclast. She can push against convention to a generous degree, but it is out of the generosity of her temperament, not out of some large metaphysical idea. Who will demand of Orpah—think of the hugeness of the demand!— that she admit monotheism to the concentration and trials of her mind? Offer monotheism to almost anyone—offer it as something to take seriously—and ninety-nine times out of a hundred it will be declined, even by professing "monotheists." A Lord of History whose intent is felt, whose Commandments stand with immediacy, whose Convenant summons perpetual self-scrutiny and a continual Turning toward moral renewal, and yet *cannot, may not, be physically imagined*? A Creator neither remote and abstract like the God of the philosophers, nor palpable like the "normal" divinities, both ancient and contemporary, both East and West? Give us (cries the nature of our race) our gods and goddesses, give us the little fertility icons with their welcoming breasts and elongated beckoning laps, give us the resplendent Virgin with her suffering brow and her arms outstretched in blessing, give us the Man on the Cross through whom to learn pity and love, and sometimes brutal exclusivity! Only give us what our eyes can see and our understanding understand: who can imagine the unimaginable? That may be for the philosophers; *they* can do it; but then they lack the imagination of the Covenant. The philosophers leave the world naked and blind and deaf and mute and relentlessly indifferent, and the village folk—who refuse a lonely cosmos without consolation—fill it and fill it and fill it with stone and wood and birds and mammals and miraculous potions and holy babes and animate carcasses and magically divine women and magically divine men: images, sights, and swallowings comprehensible to the hand, to the eye, to plain experience. For the nature of our race, God is one of the visual arts.

Is Orpah typical of these plain village folk? She is certainly not a philosopher, but neither is she, after ten years with Naomi, an ordinary Moabite. Not that she has altogether absorbed the Hebrew vision—if she had absorbed it, would she have been tempted to relinquish it so readily? She is somewhere in between, perhaps. In this we may suppose her to be one of us: a modern, no longer a full-fledged member of the pagan world, but always with one foot warming in the seductive bath of those colorful, comfortable, often beautiful old lies (they can console, but because they are lies they can also hurt and kill); not yet given over to the Covenant and its determination to train us away from lies, however warm, colorful, beautiful, and consoling.

Naomi, who is no metaphysician herself, who is, rather, heir to a tradition, imposes no monotheistic claim on either one of her daughters-in-law. She is right not to do this. In the first place, she is not a proselytizer or polemicist or preacher or even a teacher. She is none of those things: she is a bereaved woman far from home, and when she looks at her bereaved daughters-in-law, it is home she is thinking of, for herself and for them. Like the rabbis who will arrive two millennia after her, she is not a cultural relativist: God is God, and God is One. But in her own way, the way of empathy—three millennia before the concept of a democratic pluralist polity—she is a kind of pluralist. She does not require that Orpah accept what it is not natural for her, in

the light of how she was reared, to accept. She speaks of
Orpah's return not merely to her people but to her gods.
Naomi is the opposite of coercive or punitive. One cannot
dream of Inquisition or jihad emerging from her loins. She
may not admire the usages of Orpah's people—they do not
concern themselves with the widow and the destitute; no one
in Moab comes forward to care for Naomi—but she knows
that Orpah has a mother, and may yet have a new husband,
and will be secure where she is. It will not occur to Naomi
to initiate a metaphysical discussion with Orpah! She sends
her as a lost child back to her mother's hearth. (Will there
be idols on her mother's hearth? Well, yes. But this sour
comment is mine, not Naomi's.)

So Orpah goes home; or, more to the point, she goes
nowhere. She stays home. She is never, never, never to be
blamed for it. If she is not extraordinary, she is also normal.
The extraordinary is what is not normal, and it is no fault
of the normal that it does not, or cannot, aspire to the
extraordinary. What Orpah gains by staying home with her
own people is what she always deserved: family happiness.
She is young and fertile; soon she will marry a Moabite
husband and have a Moabite child.

What Orpah loses is the last three thousand years of being
present in history. Israel continues; Moab is not. Still, for
Orpah, historic longevity—the longevity of an Idea to which
a people attaches itself—may not be a loss at all. It is only
an absence, and absence is not felt as loss. Orpah has her
husband, her cradle, her little time. That her gods are false
is of no moment to her; she believes they are true. That her
social system does not provide for the widow and the destitute is of no moment to her; she is no longer a widow, and
as a wife she will not be destitute; as for looking over her
shoulder to see how others fare, there is nothing in Moab to
require it of her. She once loved her oddly foreign mother-
in-law. And why shouldn't openhearted Orpah, in her little
time, also love her Moabite mother-in-law, who is as like her
as her own mother, and will also call her "my daughter"?
Does it matter to Orpah that her great-great-great-grand-
children have tumbled out of history, and that there is no

Book of Orpah, and that she slips from the Book of Ruth in only its fourteenth verse?

Normality is not visionary. Normality's appetite stops at satisfaction.

IV. SINGULARITY

No, Naomi makes no metaphysical declaration to Orpah. It falls to Ruth, who has heard the same compassionate discourse as her sister-in-law, who has heard her mother-in-law three times call out "Daughter, turn back"—it falls to Ruth to throw out exactly such a declaration to Naomi.

Her words have set thirty centuries to trembling: "Your God shall be my God," uttered in what might be named visionary language. Does it merely "fall" to Ruth that she speaks possessed by the visionary? What is at work in her? Is it capacity, seizure, or the force of intent and the clarity of will? Set this inquiry aside for now, and—apart from what the story tells us she really did say—ask instead what Ruth might have replied in the more available language of pragmatism, answering Naomi's sensible "Turn back" exigency for exigency. What "natural" reasons might such a young woman have for leaving her birthplace? Surely there is nothing advantageous in Ruth's clinging to Naomi. Everything socially rational is on the side of Ruth's remaining in her own country: what is true for Orpah is equally true for Ruth. But even if Ruth happened to think beyond exigency—even if she were exceptional in reaching past common sense toward ideal conduct—she need not have thought in the framework of the largest cosmic questions. Are we to expect of Ruth that she be a prophet? Why should she, any more than any other village woman, think beyond personal relations?

In the language of personal relations, in the language of pragmatism and exigency, here is what Ruth might have replied:

Mother-in-law, I am used to living in your household, and have become accustomed to the ways of your family.

I would no longer feel at home if I resumed the ways of my own people. After all, during the ten years or so I was married to your son, haven't I flourished under your influence? I was so young when I came into your family that it was you who completed my upbringing. It isn't for nothing that you call me daughter. So let me go with you.

Or, higher on the spectrum of ideal conduct (rather, the conduct of idealism), but still within the range of reasonable altruism, she might have said:

Mother-in-law, you are heavier in years that I and alone in a strange place, whereas I am stalwart and not likely to be alone for long. Surely I will have a second chance, just as you predict, but you—how helpless you are, how unprotected! If I stayed home in Moab, I would be looking after my own interests, as you recommend, but do you think I can all of a sudden stop feeling for you, just like that? No, don't expect me to abandon you— who knows what can happen to a woman of your years all by herself on the road? And what prospects can there be for you, after all this long time away, in Bethlehem? It's true I'll seem a little odd in your country, but I'd much rather endure a little oddness in Bethlehem than lose you forever, not knowing what's to become of you. Let me go and watch over you.

There is no God in any of that. If these are thoughts Ruth did not speak out, they are all implicit in what has been recorded. Limited though they are by pragmatism, exigency, and personal relations, they are already anomalous. They address extraordinary alterations—of self, of worldly expectation. For Ruth to cling to Naomi as a daughter to her own mother is uncommon enough; a universe of folklore confirms that a daughter-in-law is not a daughter. But for Ruth to become the instrument of Naomi's restoration to safekeeping within her own community—and to prosperity and honor as well—is a thing of magnitude. And, in fact, all these praiseworthy circumstances do come to pass: though circumscribed by pragmatism, exigency, and personal relations. And without the visionary. Ideal conduct—or the conduct of idealism—is possible even in the absence of the language of the visionary. Observe:

> They broke into weeping again, and Orpah kissed her mother-in-law farewell. But Ruth clung to her. So she said, "See, your sister-in-law has returned to her people. Go follow your sister-in-law." But Ruth replied: "Do not urge me to leave you, to turn back and not follow you. For wherever you go, I will go; wherever you lodge, I will lodge; your people shall be my people. Where you die, I will die, and there I will be buried. Only death will part me from you." When Naomi saw how determined she was to go with her, she ceased to argue with her, and the two went on until they reached Bethlehem.

Of course this lovely passage is not the story of the Book of Ruth (any more than my unpoetic made-up monologues are), though it might easily have been Ruth's story. In transcribing from the text, I have left out what Ruth passionately put in: God. And still Ruth's speech, even with God left out, and however particularized by the personal, is a stupendous expression of loyalty and love.

But now, in a sort of conflagration of seeing, the cosmic sweep of a single phrase transforms these spare syllables from the touching language of family feeling to the unearthly tongue of the visionary:

> "See, your sister-in-law has returned to her people and her gods. Go and follow your sister-in-law." But Ruth replied, "Do not urge me to leave you, to turn back and not follow you. For wherever you go, I will go; wherever you lodge, I will lodge; your people shall be my people, and your God my God. Where you die, I will die, and there I will be buried. Thus and more may the Lord do to me if anything but death parts me from you."

Your God shall be my God: Ruth's story is kindled into the Book of Ruth by the presence of God on Ruth's lips, and her act is far, far more than a ringing embrace of Naomi, and far, far more than the simple acculturation it resembles. Ruth leaves Moab because she intends to leave childish ideas behind. She is drawn to Israel because Israel is the inheritor of the One Universal Creator.

Has Ruth "learned" this insight from Naomi and from Naomi's son? It may be; the likelihood is almost as pressing as evidence: how, without assimilation into the life of an Israelite family, would Ruth ever have penetrated into the great monotheistic cognition? On the other hand: Orpah too encounters that cognition, and slips back into Moab to lose it again. Inculcation is not insight, and what Orpah owns is only that: inculcation without insight. Abraham—the first Hebrew to catch insight—caught it as genius does, autonomously, out of the blue, without any inculcating tradition. Ruth is in possession of both inculcation *and* insight.

And yet, so intense is her insight, one can almost imagine her as a kind of Abraham. Suppose Elimelech had never emigrated to Moab; suppose Ruth had never married a Hebrew. The fire of cognition might still have come upon her as it came upon Abraham—autonomously, out of the blue, without any inculcating tradition. Abraham's cognition turned into a civilization. Might Ruth have transmuted Moab? Ruth as a second Abraham! We see in her that clear power; that power of consummate clarity. But whether Moab might, through Ruth, have entered the history of mono-theism, like Israel, is a question stalled by the more modest history of kinship entanglement. In Ruth's story, insight is inexorably accompanied by, fused with, inculcation; how can we sort out one from the other? If Ruth had not been married to one of Naomi's sons, perhaps we would have heard no more of her than we will hear henceforth of Orpah. Or: Moab might have ascended, like Abraham's seed, from the gods to God. Moab cleansed and reborn through Ruth! The story as it is given is perforce inflexible, not amenable to experiment. We cannot have Ruth without Naomi; nor would we welcome the loss of such loving-kindness. All the same, Ruth may not count as a second Abraham because her tale is enfolded in a way Abraham's is not: she has had her saturation in Abraham's seed. The ingredient of inculcation cannot be expunged: there it is.

Nevertheless it seems insufficient—it seems askew—to leave it at that. Ruth marries into Israel, yes; but her mind is vaster than the private or social facts of marriage and inculcation; vaster than the merely familial. Insight, cognition, intuition, religious genius—how to name it? It is not simply because of Ruth's love for Naomi—a love unarguably resplendent—that Naomi's God becomes Ruth's God. To stop at love and loyalty is to have arrived at much, but not all; to stop at love and loyalty is to stop too soon. Ruth claims the God of Israel out of her own ontological understanding. She knows—she knows directly, prophetically—that the Creator of the Universe is One.

V. UNFOLDING

The greater part of Ruth's tale is yet to occur—the greater, that is, in length and episode. The central setting of the Book of Ruth is hardly Moab; it is Bethlehem in Judah. But by the time the two destitute widows, the older and the younger, reach Bethlehem, the volcanic heart of the Book of Ruth— the majesty of Ruth's declaration—has already happened. All the rest is an unfolding.

Let it unfold, then, without us. We have witnessed normality and we have witnessed singularity. We will, if we linger, witness these again in Bethlehem; but let the next events flash by without our lingering. Let Naomi come with Ruth to Bethlehem; let Naomi in her distress name herself Mara, meaning bitter, "for the Lord has made my lot very bitter"; let Ruth set out to feed them both by gleaning in the field of Elimelech's kinsman, Boaz—fortuitous, God-given, that she should blunder onto Boaz's property! He is an elderly landowner, an affluent farmer who, like Levin in *Anna Karenina*, works side by side with his laborers. He is at once aware that there is a stranger in his field, and is at once solicitous. He is the sort of man who, in the heat of the harvest, greets the reapers with courteous devoutness: "The Lord be with you!" A benign convention, perhaps, but when he addresses Ruth it is no ordinary invocation: "I have been told of all that you did for your mother-in-law after the death of her husband, how you left your father and mother and the land of your birth and came to a people you had not known before. May the Lord reward your deeds. May you have a full recompense from the Lord, the God of Israel, under whose wings you have sought refuge!" Like Naomi, he calls Ruth "daughter," and he speaks an old-fashioned Hebrew; he and Naomi are of the same generation.*

But remember that we are hurrying along now; so let Naomi, taking charge behind the scenes, send Ruth to sleep at Boaz's feet on the threshing floor in order to invite his special notice—a contrivance to make known to Boaz that he is eligible for Ruth's salvation within the frame of the levirate code. And let the humane and flexible system of the levirate code work itself out, so that Boaz can marry Ruth, who will become the mother of Obed, who is the father of Jesse, who is the father of King David, author of the Psalms.

The levirate law in Israel—like the rule for gleaners—is designed to redeem the destitute. The reapers may not sweep up every stalk in the meadow; some of the harvest must be left behind for bread for the needy. And if a woman is widowed, the circle of her husband's kin must open their homes to her; in a time when the sole protective provision for a woman is marriage, she must have a new husband from her dead husband's family—the relative closest to the husband, a brother if possible. Otherwise what will become of her? Dust and cinders. She will be like the remnants of the meal offerings.

Boaz in his tenderness (we have hurried past even this, which more than almost anything else merits our hanging back; but there it is on the page, enchanting the centuries—a tenderness sweetly discriminating, morally meticulous, wide-

---

* "Boaz and Naomi talk like older people. Their speeches contain archaic morphology and syntax. Perhaps the most delightful indication of this is the one instance when an archaic form is put into Ruth's mouth, at 2:21—where she is quoting Boaz!" (Edward F. Campbell, Jr., *Ruth*, The Anchor Bible, p. 17)

hearted and ripe)—Boaz is touched by Ruth's appeal to become her husband-protector. It is a fatherly tenderness, not an erotic one—though such a scene might, in some other tale, burst with the erotic: a young woman, perfumed, lying at the feet of an old man at night in a barn. The old man is not indifferent to the pulsing of Eros in the young: "Be blessed of the Lord, daughter! Your latest deed of loyalty is greater than the first, in that you have not turned to younger men." The remark may carry a pang of wistfulness, but Boaz in undertaking to marry Ruth is not animated by the lubricious. He is no December panting after May. A forlorn young widow, homeless in every sense, has asked for his guardianship, and he responds under the merciful levirate proviso with all the dignity and responsibility of his character, including an ethical scruple: "While it is true that I am a redeeming kinsman, there is another redeemer closer than I"—someone more closely related to Elimelech than Boaz, and therefore first in line to assume the right, and burden, of kinship protection.

In this closer relative we have a sudden pale reminder of Orpah. Though she has long vanished from the story, normality has not. Who conforms more vividly to the type of Average Man than that practical head of a household we call John Doe? And now John Doe (the exact Hebrew equivalent is Ploni Almoni) briefly enters the narrative and quickly jumps out of it; averageness leaves no reputation, except for averageness. John Doe, a.k.a. Ploni Almoni, is the closer relative Boaz has in mind, and he appears at a meeting of town elders convened to sort out the levirate succession in Naomi's case. The hearing happens also to include some business about a piece of land that Elimelech owned; if sold, it will bring a little money for Naomi. Naomi may not have known of the existence of this property—or else why would she be reduced to living on Ruth's gleaning? But Boaz is informed of it, and immediately arranges for a transaction aimed at relieving both Naomi and Ruth. The sale of Elimelech's property, though secondary to the issue of marital guardianship for Naomi's young daughter-in-law, is legally attached to it: whoever acquires the land acquires Ruth. The

closer relative, Ploni Almoni (curious how the text refuses
him a real name of his own, as if it couldn't be bothered, as
if it were all at once impatient with averageness), is willing
enough to buy the land: John Doe always understands money
and property. But he is not at all willing to accept Ruth. The
moment he learns he is also being asked to take on the care
of a widow—one young enough to bear children, when very
likely he already has a family to support—he changes his
mind. He worries, he explains, that he will impair his estate.
An entirely reasonable, even a dutiful, worry, and who can
blame him? If he has missed his chance to become the great-
grandfather of the Psalmist, he is probably, like Ploni Almoni
everywhere, a philistine scorner of poetry anyhow.

And we are glad to see him go. In this he is no reminder
of Orpah; Orpah, a loving young woman, is regretted. But
like Orpah he has only the usual order of courage. He avoids
risk, the unexpected, the lightning move into imagination.
He thinks of what he has, not of what he might do: he recoils
from the conduct of idealism. He is perfectly conventional,
and wants to stick with what is familiar. Then let him go in
peace—he is too ordinary to be the husband of Ruth. We
have not heard him make a single inquiry about her. He has
not troubled over any gesture of interest or sympathy. Ruth
is no more to him than an object of acquisition offered for
sale. He declines to buy; he has his own life to get on with,
and no intention of altering it, levirate code or no levirate
code. "You do it," he tells Boaz.

Boaz does it. At every step he has given more than full
measure, whether of barley or benevolence. We have watched
him load Ruth's sack with extra grain to take back to Naomi.
He has instructed the reapers to scatter extra stalks for her
to scoop up. He has summoned her to his own table for
lunch in the field. He is generous, he is kindly, he is old, and
in spite of his years he opens his remaining strength to the
imagination of the future: he enters on a new life inconceivable to him on the day a penniless young foreigner wandered
over his field behind the harvest workers. *Mercy, pity, peace,
and love*: these Blakean words lead, in our pastoral, to a
beginning.

The beginning is of course a baby, and when Naomi cradles her grandchild in her bosom, the village women cry: "A son is born to Naomi!" And they cry: "Blessed be the Lord, who hath not withheld a redeemer from you today! May his name be perpetuated in Israel! He will renew your life and sustain your old age; for he is born of your daughter-in-law, who loves you and is better to you than seven sons."

Only eighty-five verses tell Ruth's and Naomi's story. To talk of it takes much longer. Not that the greatest stories are the shortest—not at all. But a short story has a stalk—or shoot—through which its life rushes, and out of which the flowery head erupts. The Book of Ruth—wherein goodness grows out of goodness, and the extraordinary is found here, and here, and here—is sown in desertion, bereavement, barrenness, death, loss, displacement, destitution. What can sprout from such ash? Then Ruth sees into the nature of Covenant, and the life of the story streams in. Out of this stalk mercy and redemption unfold; flowers flood Ruth's feet; and my grandfather goes on following her track until the coming of Messiah from the shoot of David, in the line of Ruth and Naomi.

The Way We Live Now

THREE-QUARTERS OF A century have slipped away since
Bloomsbury last sneered at the British Victorians; fiction's
new career, in the form of *Ulysses*, began over seventy years
ago. We postmoderns are by now so far from the modernist
repudiation of Victorian influence that we can look with an
unembarrassed eye—an eye of one's own, we might say—at
the three-decker Victorian novel's subplots and coincidences,
its bloated serializations, its unnaturally heightened and
speechifying dialogue. We can see past their potboiler mech-
anisms into what these baggy old novelists humanly, and
sometimes, half-divinely, *knew*.

Anthony Trollope has long been excluded from this percip-
ent, and undeceived, reassessment. He is nearly the only
Victorian novelist who has been critically doomed to remain
a Victorian. He alone appears to be unforgiven. Dickens and
Henry James and George Eliot and Thackeray—even the
colonialist-imperialist Kipling!—are permitted, and sometimes prodded, to transcend the accident of their chronology
and the confines of their mores. Only Trollope is regarded as
still mired in his devices—devices that are, in their pre-video
yet cinematic way, archetypes of our present-day story-
machines, glowing like colored apothecary globes in rooms
where pianos used to stand. Trollope, in brief, is dismissed
as a kind of antiquated television set; he is said to be "unde-
manding." Dickens, by contrast, survives in all his greatness
as caricaturist; George Eliot as moralist; Thackeray as ironist;
Hardy as determinist. (Shorthand, it goes without saying, for
the orchestrally manifold.)

But there is no organizing epithet or central insight for

211

Trollope. He is all those sharp-edged things: caricaturist, moralist, ironist (very strong here), determinist (to a degree). And still he is flicked off as shallow. So he is left behind among the unemerged Victorians, deprived of the stature of transcendence. Much of the fault is extrinsic: a case can be made that the blame falls on those preening bands of Trollope cultists, far-flung votaries in Papua, Tel Aviv, and Hay-on-Wye (not to mention certain pockets of the Upper West Side)—coterie enthusiasts and credit-seekers who suppose that to esteem a writer is to take on some of that writer's cachet. Trollope's reputation has rested (or foundered) too long and too stickily on the self-congratulation and misdirection of Trollopean zealots. These, like the even more notorious Janeites, or like the pious devotees of an apotheosized George Eliot, are misled in assuming that their hero is all tea-cozies and country comforts, in the style of Masterpiece Theater's bright palette. Worse, single-author addicts have the naïve habit of equating literature with the easy pleasures of self-approval.

But there is, I think, a much more significant reason for the omission of Trollope from most contemporary reappraisals. It isn't only that serious readers will run from what the zealots praise. The truth is that Trollope is more *ours* than any of those honored others (Dickens, for instance)—which may be why the current generation has the instinct to undervalue him. Writers who describe for us precisely the way we live now tend to be scorned—a single glance at how the so-called multiculturalists and other politico-literary trendists have slighted Saul Bellow is a sufficient sampling. Trollope is ten times slyer than his adorers (adorers of village parsonages) can dream—slyer and colder, with a brainy analytic laughter so remote it can register nearly as indifference. Trollope, like Bellow, is a meticulous and often ferocious anatomizer of character and society. His hand can be both light and weighty; he gets to the bottom of vileness, and also of decency; he is magisterially shrewd—shrewd in the manner of Cervantes; he likes to write about churchmen but is easy on belief; nothing in the pragmatic workings of worldliness escapes him.

Henry James complained early and nastily about Trollope's "devotion to little things," and charged him with "the virtues of the photograph." "Mr. Trollope is a good observer," James said, "but he is literally nothing else." A surprisingly grudging comment from the novelist whose most celebrated dictum is "Try to be one of the people on whom nothing is lost," and who was himself possessed by the voyeurism of the ardent observer. Well, yes, there *is* in Trollope something of a camera mounted on a helicopter—the Olympian looking down at a wide map strewn with wriggling mortals and their hungers; I mean by this that Trollope is at heart a cynic. But a cynic is a great deal more than an observer; a cynic is a metaphysical necessity. Trollope is not much concerned with retributive justice: his comeuppances come and go. He accepts and will not judge; or, if he judges, he will not invest his soul in the judgment. He may be a moralist—he certainly responds to the discriminations of the moral life—but he is too dispassionate to jubilate or grieve. Whatever is is exactly what one might expect.

"Cynic" commonly suggests a detached pessimism, a pessimism sans bitterness—but a cynic is acutely alert to an element of strangeness in the way matters fall out. From the Olympian's view, everything is strange—love, hate, religion, skepticism, exultation, apathy, domesticity, class, greed, infatuation, mercilessness, godliness. That may be why, having witnessed in our own century the strangest and the worst, we seem finally to be disconnected from the impersonal though earnest virtues of the photograph. What is a photograph if not a stimulus to the most deliberate attentiveness: time held motionless in a vise of profound concentration, so that every inch of the seized moment can be examined? Bellow, in his own version of James's exhortation, adds it all up as follows: "Writers are naturally attentive; they are trained in attentiveness, and they adduce attentiveness in their readers (without a high degree of attentiveness, aesthetic bliss is an impossibility)." The term "aesthetic bliss" Bellow borrows from Nabokov, linking it to the "recognition or rediscovery of certain essences permanently associated with human life" by "artists who write novels or stories." The notion of the photograph as one likely key to (or recognizer of) human essence is useful enough; though we know the camera can be made to lie, we also know it as reality's aperture. We say we are in earnest about the importance of being earnest, but we frequently choose (it is the way we live now) social superstition over social truth; or the partisan simulacrum over historical reality; or furry pointillism over the unrelenting snapshot; or sentimental distortion over exact measure. All of this is just what Trollope will *not* do; it takes a peculiar literary nerve to admit to the way we live now. And nerve (or call it courage) is the foundation of the aesthetic (or call it, more plainly, art).

Anthony Trollope wrote forty-seven novels. Out of that bottomless inkpot flowed, besides, biographies, histories, travel books, sketches, and five collections of short stories. There is a tradition that Trollope damaged his own reputation by revealing, in his *Autobiography*, how he daily sat with his pocket watch before him on his writing table. This is presumed to be a confession that the Trollopean Muse is mainly and merely mundane diligence (as if diligence were not the only reliable means of securing the Muse's descent); but industry of this kind is itself the artist's portion, indistinguishable from literary passion. There is no question that quantity—added, of course, to genius—is what separates major writers from minor ones. (If only E.M. Forster had written forty-seven—or even fourteen—novels to accompany *A Passage to India*!) Yet Trollope, for all his abundance, is somehow still relegated among the minor.

Restitution is necessary. Trollope's recognition of certain perilous human essences lifts him out of the Victorian minor. Let beginners who have never before read Trollope test this thesis—genuine readers not susceptible to cultism. The cultists, proselytizers all, will usually send novices to *The Warden*, or else to *Barchester Towers*. I would recommend *The Way We Live Now*—Trollope's thirty-third novel, written in 1873 and set in that same year. I would recommend it because it is very long (Trollope's longest) and very contemporary, despite its baronets and squires and rustics, and despite its penniless young women whose chief employment is huband-seeking, and its penniless young lords whose chief employment is heiress-hunting. If all this sounds as far as possible from the way *we* live now, think again; or else wait and see. As for length: *The Way We Live Now* is 952 pages in the orange-framed Penguin softcover edition, and therefore will take longer to disappoint. What disappoints in any novel by Trollope is the visible approach of its end: when more has been read than remains to be read.

The Way We Live Now is best described as a business novel; it is above all about deal-making, and about how power can be nudged to tip, and about taking advantage. It is about all these marketplace things even when what is at issue is romance, or marriage, or religion, or law, or book reviewing, or gambling, or property, or altruism, or running for office. There is almost no character who does not have an eye out for the main chance, whether it is a London millionaire or an American frontierswoman, a raffish solicitor or an unmarried elder sister worried about being left on the shelf.

In the very first chapter, called "Three Editors," we come upon Lady Carbury in the act of insuring a fraudulent reception for work she knows is shoddy; she is a hack writer in urgent need of financial rescue via bestsellerdom. (Nothing dated in that. Ambitious mediocrities nowadays chase after blurbs with equal oil and chutzpah.) Lady Carbury is a widow supporting a reprobate son whom she coddles and a neglected daughter too love-struck, and too recalcitrant, to yield to a sensible marriage. Marriage—or, rather, match-making—is the center, and not only because it is the late nineteenth century, when few women have careers (though Lady Carbury herself surely does, and tends it assiduously), but because a perspicacious match is, then and now, the nexus of every business deal. Exploitation, after all, signifies a contract between two parties: the greed of the exploiter is ideally met by the need of the exploited. Trollope's great theme is people making use of other people, especially in the accumulation of money, and who can doubt the contemporaneity of a novel about money?

The commanding money-man who is, so to speak, the

lubricant of *The Way We Live Now,* greasing its wheelings and dealings with promises and promissory notes, is Augustus Melmotte, a foreigner arrived in London with his daughter and his cowed Bohemian Jewish wife to become the City's most powerful financier. Now and again Trollope will play the game of giveaway names, so we may look into "Melmotte" and see a Latinic glimmer of "honey-word." Melmotte is, in short, a mighty con artist: we are on to him almost instantly. Our interest is not in finding out his scam, but in watching him inveigle and enmesh the gullible. What he has to offer is air—the South Central Pacific and Mexican Railway, "which was to run from the Salt Lake City, thus branching off from the San Francisco and Chicago line, and pass down through the fertile lands of New Mexico and Arizona, into the territory of the Mexican Republic, run by the city of Mexico, and come out on the gulf at the port of Vera Cruz," a distance of more than two thousand miles. As for the probable cost of this grand undertaking, and the actual laying of track, "no computation had or perhaps could be made."

In fact, there will never be a railway to Vera Cruz. Melmotte and his several shady sidekicks (one of whom is named Cohenlupe—ancient priestly honorific joined to the wolfish) are successfully engaged in selling shares in a phantom project. It is a ruse—a Ponzi scheme—to attract investors. Melmotte's prestige and influence are themselves phantoms, seductive constructs in the minds of the ignorant young dupes invited to serve on his board of directors. These are aristocratic wastrels, gamblers and boozers, some goodnatured enough, one or two of them actual louts, many bearing hereditary titles. Lady Carbury's son, Sir Felix, a baronet, is certainly among the louts. The search for respectability is double-edged: Melmotte requires the presence of titles to legitimate and adorn—and Anglicize—his imperfect status, and the raw young nobles, glad to take on the appearance of being seriously occupied, are hoping for quick and lavish returns. The clever business buccaneer may be a commonplace of public ambition (and not only in novels: Melmotte's uncannily exact real-life counterpart is the notorious late tycoon Robert Maxwell), but Trollope's high-flying swindler is one of those masterly figures who break through the membrane of invention to go on electrifying the living imagination ever after.

Melmotte at the pinnacle of his London fame takes everyone's measure, mentally auditing the value of properties, titles, inherited wealth: his aim is to find footholds on an ascent to the loftiest plane of London society. Having himself no claim to English blood, he means to attain it through his only daughter, the unprepossessing Marie Melmotte. Marie is up for sale in a marriage of mutual service: the asking price is the best available title. A bargain is to be struck: the rich foreign intruder with no background (or, as the rumors have it, a soiled and possibly crooked history in far-off places) will negotiate hard for a visibly aristocratic son-in-law. Gold in exchange for the bluest blood.

Sir Felix Carbury, at his mother's urging, is enlisted as suitor; he botches the job through drunkenness and half-hearted dallying with a brash country girl. But Marie is not the only young woman who is buffeted and thwarted by matrimonial opportunism: there is Hetta, Sir Felix's sister, maternally pressed toward marriage with her propertied older cousin Roger; and Georgiana Longestaffe, desperate to marry anyone who can supply a house in London during the high season; and Ruby Ruggles of Sheep's Acre Farm, shoved into taking a husband for the sake of a dry roof over her head. Not all these coercions are conceived in unkindness; some, in fact, are rooted in sense and solicitude; but they *are* coercions.

Still, in the company of Trollope, let no one pity the condition of nineteenth-century women! Trollope's young marriageables are not so vulnerable, and not so easily crushed, as their dependent circumstances would lead us to think. Apart from Melmotte's mammoth grip (both as charmer and as bully), all the sexual force and aggressive scheming are, in this novel, the province of women. The older men, the men of position, are mainly fools and bigots: the younger men are fools, too, and also idle and enervated. But the women are robust, demanding, driven, resolute, erotically insistent.

Even Melmotte's mousy daughter turns dangerously head-strong. And the remarkable Mrs. Hurtle of San Francisco, sophisticated, compassionate, ingratiating, yet a woman who can shoot to kill, is a dozen times sturdier than the wan and useless young lords who exchange empty I.O.U.s and cheat at cards. She is undoubtedly more authoritative than her erstwhile fiancé, the always equivocating Paul Montague, Hetta Carbury's lover, whom Mrs. Hurtle pursues with a torrent of contrivance so single-minded that it nearly exhausts the narrative around her.

Yet nothing can really exhaust any part of this narrative; it is alive and stingingly provocative at every turn. The grotesquely overblown dinner party Melmotte gives for the Emperor of China, an elephantiasis of self-advertisement (Trollope based its braggadocio splendors on the royal visit of the Shah of Persia in June of 1873), is as baleful as it is comic: Melmotte here becomes a parodic Lear of the banquet hall, too much accommodated by unregarded luster. And always Trollope is after the clamor and confusions of temperament. An argument between an Anglican bishop and a Roman Catholic priest reflects their theological differences far less than it does the divide between tractable and intractable spirits. The fanatical priest lives humbly, the tolerant bishop in conspicuous luxury; and it is the recurrent scramble and contradiction of variable traits that seize the novelist's relentless eye.

A trace of that scramble may be in Trollope himself: the inventor of the gaudily offensive Cohenlupe is also a furious satirist of antisemitism—there is no noisier Jew-hater than Trollope's Mr. Longestaffe, and no more telling vindication of ethical nicety than Trollope's Mr. Brehgert, a Jew. Melmotte, forger as well as swindler, is suspected all around of being a Jew, and is revealed in the novel's last pages to be the son of "a noted coiner in New York—an Irishman of the name of Melmody"—i.e., an American adventurer. (A query. Did Melmotte become Melmody only after Trollope's own exposure to the rantings of Mr. Longestaffe? Novels do frequently influence their authors.)

The Way We Live Now ends in four sensible weddings,

the traditional signal that we have been present at a comedy, and one sensible exile. There is in Trollope a clear pull toward reasonableness; toward moderation; toward reason itself, in language precise, exuberant, consummate—in spite of which, the comic cannot suppress the grievous, and a naturalist's brew of so many botches and blotches sends up its tragical fumes. Suicide, malice, stupidity, greed, manipulativeness, fakery, cowardice, dissoluteness, deceit, prejudice without pride, pretension, ambitiousness, even pathological self-abnegation—excess of every kind—dominate Trollope's scrutiny of his "now." If our now departs a little from his, it is only because we have augmented our human matériel with heightened technological debris. All the same, there is the impress of grandeur in Trollope's account—or call it, with James, his photography. What James missed was the peculiarly elusive quality of a poetry akin to his own. Like it or not, Trollope is the poet of anti-poetry. His lens is wide, extraordinarily so: wide enough to let in, finally, a slim ghost of the prophetic.

Isaac Babel and the Identity Question

Identity, at least, is prepared to ask questions.
—*Leon Wieseltier*

A YEAR OR SO before the Soviet Union imploded, S.'s mother, my first cousin—whose existence until then had been no more than a distant legend—telephoned from Moscow. "Save my child!" she cried, in immemorial tones. So when S. arrived in New York, I expected a terrified refugee on the run from the intolerable exactions of popular antisemitism; at that time the press was filled with such dire reports. For months, preparing for her rescue, I had been hurtling from one agency to another, in search of official information on political asylum.

But when S. finally turned up, in black tights, a miniskirt, and the reddest lipstick, it was clear she was indifferent to all that. She didn't want to be saved; what she wanted was an American holiday, a fresh set of boyfriends, and a leather coat. She had brought with her a sizable cosmetics case, amply stocked, and a vast, rattling plastic bag stuffed with hundreds of cheap tin Komsomol medals depicting Lenin as a boy. She was scornful of these; they were worthless, she said; she had paid pennies for the lot. Within two weeks S., a natural entrepreneur, had established romantic relations with the handsome young manager of the local sports store and had got him to set up a table at Christmas in his heaviest traffic location. She sold the tin Lenin medals for three dollars

220

each, made three hundred dollars in a day, and bought the leather coat.

Of course she was a great curiosity. Her English was acutely original, her green eyes gave out ravishing ironic lightnings, her voice was as dark as Garbo's in *Ninotchka*, and none of us had ever seen an actual Soviet citizen up close before. She thought the telephone was bugged. She thought the supermarket was a public exhibition. Any show of household shoddiness—a lamp, say, that came apart—would elicit from her a comical crow: "Like in Soviet!" She was, emphatically, no atheist: she had an affinity for the occult, believed that God could speak in dreams (she owned a dream book, through which Jesus often walked), adored the churches of old Russia, and lamented their destruction by the Bolsheviks. On the subject of current antisemitism she was mute; that was her mother's territory. Back in Moscow, her boyfriend, Gennadi, had picked her up in the subway *because* she was Jewish. He was in a hurry to marry her. "He want get out of Soviet," she explained.

At home she was a *Sportsdoktor:* she traveled with the Soviet teams, roughneck country boys, and daily tested their urine for steroids. (Was this to make sure her athletes were properly dosed?) She announced that *everybody* hated Gorbachev, only the gullible Americans liked him, he was a joke like all the others. A historically-minded friend approached S. with the earnest inquiry of an old-fashioned liberal idealist: "We all know, obviously, about the excesses of Stalinism," she said, "but what of the *beginning?* Wasn't Communism a truly beautiful hope at the start?" S. laughed her cynical laugh; she judged my friend profoundly stupid. "Communism," she scoffed, "what Communism? Naive! Fairy tale, always! No Communism, never! Naive!"

And leaving behind five devastated American-as-apple-pie boyfriends (and wearing her leather coat), S. returned to Moscow. She did not marry Gennadi. Her mother emigrated to Israel. The last I heard of S., she was in business in Sakhalin, buying and selling—and passing off as the real thing—ersatz palaeolithic mammoth tusks.

Well, it is all over now—the Great Experiment, as the old brave voices used to call it—and S. is both symptom and proof of how thoroughly it is over. She represents the Soviet Union's final heave, its last generation. S. is the consummate New Soviet Man: the unfurled future of its seed. If there is an axiom here, it is that idealism squeezed into utopian channels will generate a cynicism so profound that no inch of human life—not youth, not art, not work, not romance, not introspection—is left untainted. The S. I briefly knew trusted nothing; in her world there was nothing to trust. The primal Communist fairy tale had cast its spell: a baba yaga's birth-curse.

In college I read the Communist Manifesto, a rapture-bringing psalm. I ought to have read Isaac Babel's *Red Cavalry* stories—if only as a corrective companion-text. Or antidote. "But what of the beginning?" my friend had asked. S. answered better than any historian, but no one will answer more terrifyingly than Isaac Babel. If S. is the last generation of New Soviet Man, he is the first—the Manifesto's primordial manifestation.

That Babel favored the fall of the Czarist regime is no anomaly. He was a Jew from Odessa, the child of an enlightened family, hungry for a European education; he was subject to the *numerus clausus*, the Czarist quota that kept Jews as a class out of the universities, and Babel in particular out of the University of Odessa. As a very young writer, he put himself at risk when—to be near Maxim Gorky, his literary hero—he went to live illegally in St. Petersburg, a city outside the Pale of Settlement (the area to which Jews were restricted). What Jew would not have welcomed the demise of a hostile and obscurantist polity that, as late as 1911, tried Mendel Beiliss in a Russian court on a fantastic blood libel charge, and what Jew in a time of government-sanctioned pogroms would not have turned with relief to forces promising to topple the oppressors? In attaching himself to the Bolshevik cause, Babel may have been more zealous than many, but far from aberrant. If the choice were either Czar or Bolshevism, what Jew could choose Czar? (A third possibility, which scores of thousands sought, was escape to America.)

But even if one were determined to throw one's lot in with the Revolution, what Jew would go riding with Cossacks?

In 1920 Isaac Babel went riding with Cossacks. It was the third year of the Civil War—revolutionary Reds versus Czarist Whites; he was twenty-six. Babel was not new to the military. Two years earlier, during the First World War, he had been a volunteer—in the Czar's army—on the Romanian front, where he contracted malaria. In 1919 he fought with the Red Army to secure St. Petersburg against advancing government troops. And in 1920 he joined ROSTA, the Soviet wire service, as a war correspondent for the newspaper *Red Cavalryman*. Poland, newly independent, was pressing eastward, hoping to recover its eighteenth-century borders, while the Bolsheviks, moving west, were furiously promoting the Communist salvation of Polish peasants and workers. The Polish-Soviet War appeared to pit territory against ideology; in reality territory—or, more precisely, the conquest of impoverished villages and towns and their wretched inhabitants—was all that was at stake for either side. Though the Great War was over, the Allies, motivated by fear of the spread of Communism, went to the aid of Poland with equipment and volunteers. (Ultimately the Poles prevailed and the Bolsheviks retreated, between them despoiling whole populations.)

In an era of air battles, Babel was assigned to the First Cavalry Army, a Cossack division led by General Semyon Budyonny. The Cossack image—glinting sabers, pounding hooves—is indelibly fused with Czarist power, but the First Cavalry Army was, perversely, Bolshevik. Stalin was in command of the southern front—the region abutting Poland— and Budyonny was in league with Stalin. Ostensibly, then, Babel found himself among men sympathetic to Marxist doctrine; yet Red Cossacks were no different from White Cossacks: untamed riders, generally illiterate, boorish and brutish, suspicious of ideas of any kind, attracted only to horseflesh, rabid looting, and the quick satisfaction of hunger and lust. "This isn't a Marxist revolution," Babel privately noted; "it's a rebellion of Cossack wild men." Polish and Russian cavalrymen clashing in ditches while warplanes streaked overhead was no more incongruous than the raw sight of Isaac Babel—a writer who had already published short stories praised by Gorky—sleeping in mud with Cossacks.

Lionel Trilling, in a highly nuanced (though partially misinformed) landmark introduction to a 1955 edition of *The Collected Stories of Isaac Babel*—which included the *Red Cavalry* stories—speaks of "the joke of a Jew who is a member of a Cossack regiment." A joke, Trilling explains, because

> traditionally the Cossack was the feared and hated
> - enemy of the Jew. . . . The principle of his existence stood
> in total antithesis to the principle of the Jew's existence.
> The Jew conceived of his own ideal character as being
> intellectual, pacific, humane. The Cossack was physical,
> violent, without mind or manners . . . the natural and
> appropriate instrument of ruthless oppression.

Yet Trilling supplies another, more glamorous, portrait of the Cossack, which he terms Tolstoyan: "He was the man as yet untrammeled by civilization, direct, immediate, fierce. He was the man of enviable simplicity, the man of the body— the man who moved with speed and grace." In short, "our fantasy of the noble savage." And he attributes this view to Babel.

As it turns out, Babel's tenure with Budyonny's men was more tangled, and more intricately psychological, than Trilling—for whom the problem was tangled and psychological enough—could have known or surmised. For one thing, Trilling mistakenly believed that Babel's job was that of a supply officer—i.e., that he was actually a member of the regiment. But as a correspondent for a news agency (which meant grinding out propaganda), Babel's position among the troops was from the start defined as an outsider's, Jew or no. He was there as a writer. Worse, in the absence of other sources, Trilling fell into a crucial—and surprisingly naive—second error: he supposed that the "autobiographical" tales were, in fact, autobiographical.

Babel, Trilling inferred from Babel's stories, "was a Jew of the ghetto" who "when he was nine years old had seen his father kneeling before a Cossack captain." He compares this (fictitious) event to Freud's contemplation of his father's "having accepted in a pacific way the insult of having his new fur cap knocked into the mud by a Gentile who shouted at him, 'Jew, get off the pavement' " "We might put it," Trilling concludes, that Babel rode wth Budyonny's troops because he had witnessed his father's humiliation by "a Cossack on a horse, who said, 'At your service,' and touched his fur cap with his yellow-gloved hand and politely paid no heed to the mob looting the Babel store."

There was no Babel store. This scene—the captain with the yellow glove, the Jew pleading on his knees while the pogrom rages—is culled from Babel's story "First Love." But it was reinforced for Trilling by a fragmentary memoir, published in 1924, wherein Babel calls himself "the son of a Jewish shopkeeper." The truth was that Babel was the son of the class enemy: a well-off family. His father sold agricultural machinery and owned a warehouse in a business section of Odessa where numerous import-export firms were located. In the same memoir Babel records that, because he had no permit allowing him residence in St. Petersburg, he hid out "in a cellar on Pushkin Street which was the home of a tormented, drunken waiter." This was pure fabrication: in actuality Babel was taken in by a highly respectable engineer and his wife, with whom he was in correspondence. The first invention was to disavow a bourgeois background in order to satisfy Communist dogma. The second was a romantic imposture.

It did happen, nevertheless, that the young Babel was witness to a pogrom. He was in no way estranged from Jewish suffering or sensibility, or, conversely, from the seductive winds of contemporary Europe. Odessa was modern, bustling, diverse, cosmopolitan; its very capaciousness stimulated a certain worldliness and freedom of outlook. Jewish children were required to study the traditional texts and commentaries, but they were also sent to learn the violin. Babel was early on infatuated with Maupassant and Flaubert, and wrote his first stories in fluent literary French. In his native Russian he lashed himself mercilessly to the discipline of an original style, the credo of which was burnished brevity. At the time of his arrest by the NKVD in 1939—he had failed to conform to Socialist Realism—he was said to be at work on a Russian translation of Sholem Aleichem.

Given these manifold intertwinings, it remains odd that Trilling's phrase for Babel was "a Jew of the ghetto." Trilling himself had characterized Babel's Odessa as "an eastern Marseilles or Naples," observing that "in such cities the transient, heterogeneous population dilutes the force of law and tradition, for good as well as for bad." One may suspect that Trilling's cultural imagination (and perhaps his psyche as well) was circumscribed by a kind of either/or: *either* worldly sophistication *or* the ghetto; and that, in linking Jewish learning solely to the ghetto, he could not conceive of its association with a broad and complex civilization. This partial darkening of mind, it seems to me, limits Trilling's understanding of Babel. An intellectual who had mastered the essentials of rabbinic literature, Babel was an educated Jew not "of the ghetto"; but of the world. And not "of both worlds," as the divisive expression has it, but of the great and variegated map of human thought and experience.

Trilling, after all, in his own youth had judged the world to be rigorously divided. In 1933, coming upon one of Hemingway's letters, he wrote in his notebook:

[A] crazy letter, written when he was drunk—self-revealing, arrogant, scared, trivial, absurd; yet [I] felt from reading it how right such a man is compared to the 'good minds' of my university life—how he will produce and mean something to the world . . . how his life which he could expose without dignity and which is anarchic and 'childish' is a better life than anyone I know could live, and right for his job. And how far-far-far I am going from being a writer.

Trilling envied but could not so much as dream himself into becoming a version of Hemingway—rifle in one hand and pen in the other, intellectual Jew taking on the strenuous life; how much less, then, could he fathom Babel as Cossack.

Looking only to Jewish constriction, what Trilling vitally missed was this: coiled in the bottommost pit of every driven writer is an impersonator—protean, volatile, restless and relentless. Trilling saw only stasis, or, rather, an unalterable consistency of identity: either lucubrations or daring, never both. But Babel imagined for himself an identity so fluid that, having lodged with his civilized friend, the St. Petersburg engineer, it pleased him to invent a tougher Babel consorting underground with a "tormented, drunken waiter." A drunken waiter would have been adventure enough—but ah, that Dostoyevskian "tormented"!

"He loved to confuse and mystify people," his daughter Nathalie wrote of him, after decades spent in search of his character. Born in 1929, she lived with her mother in Paris, where her father was a frequent, if raffish, visitor. In 1935 Babel was barred from leaving the Soviet Union, and never again saw his wife and child. Nathalie Babel was ten when Babel was arrested. In 1961 she went to look for traces of her father in Moscow, "where one can still meet people who loved him and continue to speak of him with notalgia. There, thousands of miles from my own home in Paris, sitting in his living room, in his own chair, drinking from his glass, I felt utterly baffled. Though in a sense I had tracked him down, he still eluded me. The void remained."

In a laudatory reminiscence published in a Soviet literary magazine in 1964—a time when Babel's reputation was undergoing a modicum of "rehabilitation"—Georgy Munblit, a writer who had known Babel as well as anyone, spoke of "this sly, unfaithful, eternally evasive and mysterious Babel"; and though much of this elusiveness was caution in the face of Soviet restriction, a good part of it nevertheless had to do with the thrill of dissimulation and concealment. In a mid-Sixties Moscow speech at a meeting championing Babel's work, Ilya Ehrenburg—the literary Houdini who managed to survive every shift of Stalinist whim—described Babel as liking to "play the fool and put on romantic airs. He liked to create an atmosphere of mystery about himself; he was secretive and never told anybody where he was going."

Other writers (all of whom had themselves escaped the

227

purges) came forward with recollections of Babel's eccentricities in risky times: Babel as intrepid wanderer; as trickster, rapscallion, ironist; penniless, slippery, living on the edge, off the beaten track, down and out; seduced by the underlife of Paris, bars, whores, cabdrivers, jockeys—all this suggests Orwellian experiment and audacity. Babel relished Villon and Kipling, and was delighted to discover that Rimbaud too was an "adventurer." Amusing and mercurial, "he loved to play tricks on people," according to Lev Nikulin, who was at school with Babel and remembered him "as a bespectacled boy in a rather shabby school coat and a battered cap with a green band and badge depicting Mercury's staff."

Trilling, writing in 1955, had of course no access to observations such as these; and we are as much in need now as Trilling was of a valid biography of Babel. Yet it is clear even from such small evidences and quicksilver portraits that Babel's connection with the Cossacks was, if not inevitable, more natural than not; and that Trilling's Freudian notion of the humiliated ghetto child could not have been more off the mark. For Babel lamp-oil and fearlessness were not antithetical. He was a man with the bit of recklessness between his teeth. One might almost ask how a writer so given to disguises and role-playing could *not* have put on a Cossack uniform.

"The Rebbe's Son," one of the *Red Cavalry* tales, is explicit about this fusion of contemplative intellect and physical danger. Ilya, the son of the Zhitomir Rebbe, "the last prince of the dynasty," is a Red Army soldier killed in battle. The remnant of his possessions is laid out before the narrator:

Here everything was dumped together—the warrants of the agitator and the commemorative booklets of the Jewish poet. Portraits of Lenin and Maimonides lay side by side. Lenin's nodulous skull and the tarnished silk of the portraits of Maimonides. A strand of female hair had been placed in a book of the resolutions of the Sixth Party Congress, and in the margins of Communist leaflets swarmed crooked lines of ancient Hebrew verse.

228

In a sad and meager rain they fell on me—pages of the
Song of Songs and revolver cartridges.

Babel was himself drawn to the spaciousness and elasticity
of these unexpected combinations. They held no enigma for
him. But while the Rebbe's son was a kind of double patriot—
loyal to the God of Abraham, Isaac and Jacob, and loyal to
a dream of the betterment of Russia—Babel tended toward
both theological and (soon enough) political skepticism. His
amor patriae was—passionately—for the Russian mother-
tongue. Before the Stalinist prison clanged shut in 1935,
Babel might easily have gone to live permanently in France,
with his wife and daughter. Yet much as he reveled in French
literature and language, he would not suffer exile from his
native Russian. A family can be replaced, or duplicated; but
who can replace or duplicate the syllables of Pushkin and
Tolstoy? And, in fact (though his wife in Paris survived until
1957, and there was no divorce), Babel did take another wife
in the Soviet Union, who gave birth to another daughter; a
second family was possible. A second language was not.
(Only consider what must be the intimate sorrows—even in
the safety of America, even after the demise of Communism—
of Czeslaw Milosz, Joseph Brodksy, Norman Manea, and
countless other less celebrated literary refugees.) By remaining in the Soviet Union, and refusing finally to bend his art
to Soviet directives, Babel sacrificed his life to his language.

It was a language he did not allow to rest. He meant to
put his spurs to it, and run it to unexampled leanness. He
quoted Pushkin: "precision and brevity." "Superior crafts-
manship," Babel told Munblit, "is the art of making your
writing as unobtrusive as possible." Ehrenburg recalled a
conversation in Madrid with Hemingway, who had just discovered Babel. "I find that Babel's style is even more concise
than mine. . . . It shows what can be done," Hemingway
marveled. "Even when you've got all the water out of them,
you can still clot the curds a little more." Such idiosyncratic
experiments in style were hardly congruent with official pressure to honor the ascent of socialism through prescriptive
prose about the beauty of collective farming. Babel did not

dissent from Party demands; instead he fell mainly into silence, writing in private and publishing almost nothing. His attempts at a play and a filmscript met convulsive Party criticism; the director of the film, an adaptation of a story by Turgenev, was forced into a public apology.

The *Red Cavalry* stories saw print, individually, before 1924. Soviet cultural policies in those years were not yet consolidated; it was a period of postrevolutionary leniency and ferment. Russian modernism was sprouting in the shape of formalism, acmeism, imagism, symbolism; an intellectual and artistic avant-garde flourished. Censorship, which had been endemic to the Czarist regime, was reintroduced in 1922, but the restraints were loose. Despite a program condemning elitism, the early Soviet leadership, comprising a number of intellectuals—Lenin, Bukharin, Trotsky—recognized that serious literature could not be wholly entrusted to the sensibilities of Party bureaucrats. By 1924, then, Babel found himself not only famous, but eligible eventually for Soviet rewards: an apartment in Moscow, a dacha in the country, a car and chauffeur.

Yet he was increasingly called on to perform (and conform) by the blunter rulers of a darkening repression: why was he not writing in praise of New Soviet Man? Little by little a perilous mist gathered around Babel's person: though his privileges were not revoked (he was at his dacha on the day of his arrest), he began to take on a certain pariah status. When a leftist Congress for the Defense of Culture and Peace met in Paris, for example, Babel was deliberately omitted from the Soviet delegation, and was grudgingly allowed to attend only after the French organizers brought their protests to the Soviet Embassy.

Certain manuscripts he was careful not to expose to anyone. Among these was the remarkable journal he had kept, from June to September 1920, of the actions of Budyonny's First Cavalry Army in eastern Poland. Because it was missing from the papers seized by the secret police at the dacha and in his Moscow flat, the manuscript escaped destruction, and came clandestinely into the possession of Babel's (second) wife only in the 1950's. Ehrenburg was apparently the journal's first influential reader, though very likely he did not see it until the 1960's, when he mentioned it publicly, and evidently spontaneously, in his rehabilitation speech:

> I have been comparing the diary of the Red Cavalry with the stories. He scarcely changed any names, the events are all practically the same, but everything is illuminated with a kind of wisdom. He is saying: this is how it was. This is how the people were—they did terrible things and they suffered, they played tricks on others and they died. He made his stories out of the facts and phrases hastily jotted down in his notebook.

It goes without saying that the flatness of this essentially evasive summary does almost no justice to an astonishing historical record set down with godlike prowess in a prose of frightening clarity. In Russia the complete text of the journal finally appeared in 1990. Yale University Press brings it to us now under the title *Isaac Babel: 1920 Diary*, in an electrifying translation, accompanied by a first-rate (and indispensable) introduction. (It ought to be added that an informative introduction can be found also in the Penguin *Collected Stories*; but the reader's dependence on such piece-meal discussions only underscores the irritating absence of a formal biography.) In 1975 Ardis Publishers, specialists in Russian studies, made available the first English translation of excerpts from the journal (*Isaac Babel: Forgotten Prose*). That such a manuscript existed had long been known in the Soviet Union, but there was plainly no chance of publication; Ehrenburg, in referring to it, was discreet about its contents.

The *Diary* may count, then, as a kind of secret document; certainly as a suppressed one. But it is "secret" in another sense as well. Though it served as raw material for the *Red Cavalry* stories, Babel himself, in transforming private notes into daring fiction, was less daring than he might have been. He was, in fact, circumspect and selective. One can move from the notes to the stories without surprise—or put it that the surprise is in the masterliness and shock of a ripe and radical style. Still, as Ehrenburg reported, "the events are all

231

practically the same," and what is in the *Diary* is in the stories.

But one cannot begin with the stories and then move to the journal without the most acute recognition of what has been, substantively and for the most part, shut out of the fiction. And what has been shut out is the calamity (to say it in the most general way) of Jewish fate in Eastern Europe. The *Diary* records how the First Cavalry Army, and Babel with it, went storming through the little Jewish towns of Galicia, in Poland—towns that had endured the Great War, with many of their young men serving in the Polish army, only to be decimated by pogroms immediately afterward, at the hands of the Poles themselves. And immediately after *that*, the invasion of the Red Cossacks. The Yale edition of the *Diary* supplies maps showing the route of Budyonny's troops; the resonant names of these places, rendered half-romantic through the mystical tales of their legendary hasidic saints, rise up with the nauseous familiarity of their deaths: Brody, Dubno, Zhitomir, Belz, Chelm, Zamosc, etc. Only two decades after the Red Cossacks stampeded through them, their Jewish populations fell prey to the Germans and were destroyed. Riding and writing, writing and riding, Babel saw it all: saw it like a seer. "Ill-fated Galicia, ill-fated Jews," he wrote. "Can it be," he wrote, "that ours is the century in which they perish?"

True: everything that is in the stories is in the *Diary*—priest, painter, widow, guncart, soldier, prisoner; but the heart of the *Diary* remains secreted in the *Diary*. When all is said and done—and much is said and done in these blistering pages: pillaged churches, ruined synagogues, wild Russians, beaten Poles, mud, horses, hunger, looting, shooting—Babel's journal is a Jewish lamentation: a thing the Soviet system could not tolerate, and Ehrenburg was too prudent to reveal. The merciless minds that snuffed the identities of the murdered at Babi Yar would hardly sanction Babel's whole and bloody truths.

Nor did Babel himself publicly sanction them. The *Red Cavalry* narratives include six stories (out of thirty-five) that touch on the suffering of Jews; the headlong *Diary* contains hundreds. An act of authorial self-censorship, and not only because Babel was determined to be guarded. Impersonation, or call it reckless play, propelled him at all points. The *Diary* can muse: "The Slavs—the manure of history?"—but Babel came to the Cossacks disguised as a Slav, having assumed the name K.L. Lyutov, the name he assigns also to his narrator. And in the *Diary* itself, encountering terrified Polish Jews, he again and again steers them away from the knowledge that rides in his marrow, and fabricates deliberate Revolutionary fairy tales (his word): he tells his trembling listeners how "everything's changing for the better—my usual system—miraculous things are happening in Russia—express trains, free food for children, theaters, the International. They listen with delight and disbelief. I think—you'll have your diamond-studded sky, everything and everyone will be turned upside down and inside out for the umpteenth time, and [I] feel sorry for them."

"My usual system": perhaps it is kind to scatter false consolations among the doomed. Or else it is not kindness at all, merely a writer's mischief or a rider's diversion—the tormented mice of Galicia entertained by a cat in Cossack dress. Sometimes he is recognized as a Jew (once by a child), and then he half-lies and explains that he has a Jewish mother. But mainly he is steadfast in the pretense of being Lyutov. And nervy: the *Diary* begins on June 3, in Zhitomir, and on July 12, one day before Babel's twenty-sixth birthday, he notes: "My first ride on horseback." In no time at all he is, at least on horseback, like all the others: a skilled and dauntless trooper. "The horse galloped well," he says on that first day. Enchanted, proud, he looks around at his companions: "red flags, a powerful, well-knit body of men, confident commanders, calm and experienced eyes of top-knotted Cossack fighting men, dust, silence, order, brass band." But moments later the calm and experienced eyes are searching out plunder in the neat cottage of an immigrant Czech family, "all good people." "I took nothing, although I could have," the new horseman comments. "I'll never be a real Budyonny man."

The real Budyonny men are comely, striking, stalwart.

Turning off a highway, Babel catches sight of "the brigades suddenly appear[ing], inexplicable beauty, an awesome force advancing." Another glimpse: "Night ... horses are quietly snorting, they're all Kuban Cossacks here, they eat together, sleep together, a splendid silent comradeship ... they sing songs that sound like church music in lusty voices, their devotion to horses, beside each man a little heap-saddle, bridle, ornamental saber, greatcoat, I sleep in the midst of them."

Babel is small, his glasses are small and round, he sets down secret sentences. And meanwhile his dispatches, propaganda screeches regularly published in *Red Cavalryman*, have a different tone: "Soldiers of the Red Army, finish them off! Beat down harder on the opening covers of their stinking graves!" And: "That is what they are like, our heroic nurses! Caps off to the nurses! Soldiers and commanders, show respect to the nurses!" (In the *Diary* the dubious propagandist writes satirically, "Opening of the Second Congress of the Third International, unification of the peoples finally realized, now all is clear ... We shall advance into Europe and conquer the world.")

And always there is cruelty, and always there are the Jews. "Most of the rabbis have been exterminated." "The Jewish cemetery ... hundreds of years old, gravestones have toppled over ... overgrown with grass, it has seen Khmelnitsky, now Budyonny ... everything repeats itself, now that whole story—Poles, Cossacks, Jews—is repeating itself with stunning exactitude, the only new element is Communism." "They all say they're fighting for justice and they all loot." "Life is loathsome, murderers, it's unbearable, baseness and crime." "I ride along with them, begging the men not to massacre prisoners ... I couldn't look at their faces, they bayoneted some, shot others, bodies covered by corpses, they strip one man while they're shooting another, groans, screams, death rattles." "We are destroyers ... we move like a whirlwind, like a stream of lava, hated by everyone, life shatters, I am at a huge, never-ending service for the dead ... the sad senselessness of my life."

The Jews: "The Poles ransacked the place, then the

Cossacks." "Hatred for the Poles is unanimous. they have looted, tortured, branded the pharmacist with a red-hot iron, put needles under his nails, pulled out his hair, all because somebody shot at a Polish officer." "The Jews ask me to use my influence to save them from ruin, they are being robbed of food and goods ... The cobbler had looked forward to Soviet rule—and what he sees are Jew-baiters and looters .. Organized looting of a stationer's shop, the proprietor in tears, they tear up everything ... When night comes the whole town will be looted—everyone knows it."

The Jews at the hands of the Poles: "A pogrom ... a naked, barely breathing prophet of an old man, an old woman butchered, a child with fingers chopped off, many people still breathing, stench of blood, everything turned upside down, chaos, a mother sitting over her sabered son, an old woman lying twisted up like a pretzel, four people in one hovel, filth, blood under a black beard, just lying there in the blood."

The Jews at the hands of the Bolsheviks: "Our men nonchalantly walking around looting whenever possible, stripping mangled corpses. The hatred is the same, the Cossacks just the same, it's nonsense to think one army is different from another. The life of these little towns. There's no salvation. Everyone destroys them." "Our men were looting last night, tossed out the Torah scrolls in the synagogue and took the velvet covers for saddlecloths. The military commissar's dispatch rider examines phylacteries, wants to take the straps." The *Diary* mourns, "What a mighty and marvelous life of a nation existed here. The fate of Jewry."

And then: "I am an outsider." And again: "I don't belong, I'm all alone, we ride on ... five minutes after our arrival the looting starts, women struggling, weeping and wailing, it's unbearable, I can't stand these never-ending horrors ... [I] snatch a flatcake out of the hands of a peasant woman's little boy." He does this mechanically, and without compunction.

"How we eat," he explains. "Red troops arrive in a village, ransack the place, cook, stoves crackling all night, the householders' daughters have a hard time" (a comment we will know how to interpret). Babel grabs the child's flatcake—a snack on the fly, as it were—on August 3. On July 25, nine days earlier, he and a riding companion, Prishchepa, a loutish syphilitic illiterate, have burst into a pious Jewish house in a town called Demidovka. It is the Sabbath, when lighting a fire is forbidden; it is also the eve of the Ninth of Av, a somber fast day commemorating the destruction of the Temple in Jerusalem. Prishchepa demands fried potatoes. The dignified mother, a flock of daughters in white stockings, a scholarly son, are all petrified; on the Sabbath, they protest, they cannot dig potatoes, and besides, the fast begins at sundown. "Fucking Yids," Prischepa yells; so the potatoes are dug, the fire to cook them is lit.

Babel, a witness to this anguish, says nothing. "I keep quiet, because I'm a Russian"—will Prishchepa discover that Lyutov is only another Yid? "We eat like oxen, fried potatoes and five tumblersful of coffee each. We sweat, they keep serving us, all this is terrible, I tell them fairy tales about Bolshevism." Night comes, the mother sits on the floor and sobs, the son chants the liturgy for the Ninth of Av—Jeremiah's Lamentations: "they eat dung, their maidens are ravished, their menfolk killed, Israel subjugated." Babel hears and understands every Hebrew word. "Demidovka, night, Cossacks," he sums it up, "all just as it was when the Temple was destroyed. I go out to sleep in the yard, stinking and damp."

And there he is, New Soviet Man: stinking, a sewer of fairy tales, an unbeliever—and all the same complicit. Nathalie Babel said of her father that nothing "could shatter his feeling that he belonged to Russia and that he had to share the fate of his countrymen. What in so many people would have produced only fear and terror, awakened in him a sense of duty and a kind of blind heroism." In the brutal light of the *Diary*—violation upon violation—it is hard not to resist this point of view. Despair and an abyss of cynicism do not readily accord with a sense of duty; and whether or not Babel's travels with the Cossacks—and with Bolshevism altogether—deserve to be termed heroic, he was anything but blind. He saw, he saw, and he saw.

It may be that the habit of impersonation, the habit of deception, the habit of the mask, will in the end lead a man to become what he impersonates. Or it may be that the force of "I am an outsider" overwhelms the secret gratification of having got rid of a fixed identity. In any case, the *Diary* tells no lies. These scenes in a journal, linked by commas quicker than human breath, run like rapids through a gorge—on one side the unrestraint of violent men, on the other the bleaker freedom of unbelonging. Each side is subversive of the other; and still they embrace the selfsame river.

To venture yet another image, Babel's *Diary* stands as a tragic masterwork of breakneck cinematic "dailies"—those raw, unedited rushes that expose the director to himself. If Trilling, who admitted to envy of the milder wilderness that was Hemingway, had read Babel's *Diary*—what then? And who, in our generation, should read the *Diary*? Novelists and poets, of course; specialists in Russian literature, obviously; American innocents who define the world of the Twenties by jazz, flappers, and Fitzgerald. And also: all those who protested Claude Lanzmann's film *Shoah* as unfair to the psyche of the Polish countryside; but, most of all, the cruelly ignorant children of the Left who still believe that the Marxist utopia requires for its realization only a more favorable venue, and another go.

No one knows when or exactly how Babel perished. Some suppose he was shot immediately after the NKVD picked him up and brought him to Moscow's Lyubanka prison, on May 15, 1939. Others place the date of his murder in 1941, following months of torture. More than fifty years later, as if the writer were sending forth phantoms of his first and last furies, Babel's youthful *Diary* emerges. What it attests to above all is not simply that fairy tales can kill—who doesn't understand this?—but that Bolshevism was lethal in its very cradle.

Which is just what S., my ironical Muscovite cousin, found so pathetically funny when, laughing at our American stupidity, she went home to Communism's graveyard.

THE QUESTION OF OUR SPEECH: THE RETURN TO AURAL CULTURE

WHEN I WAS a thirteen-year-old New Yorker, a trio of women from the provinces took up, relentlessly and extravagantly, the question of my speech. Their names were Miss Evangeline Trolander, Mrs. Olive Birch Davis, and Mrs. Ruby S. Papp (pronounced *pop*). It was Mrs. Papp's speciality to explain how to "breathe from the diaphragm." She would place her fingers tip-to-tip on the unyielding hard shell of her midriff, hugely inhaling: how astonishing then to see how the mighty action of her lungs caused her fingertips to spring apart! This demonstration was for the repair of the New York voice. What the New York voice, situated notoriously "in the throat," required above everything was to descend, pumping air, to this nether site, so that "Young Lochinvar came out of the WEST" might come bellowing out of the pubescent breast.

The New York palate, meanwhile, was consonantally in neglect. *T*'s, *d*'s, and *l*'s were being beaten out against the teeth, European-fashion—this was called "dentalization"—while the homeless *r* and *n* went wandering in the perilous trough behind the front incisors. There were corrective exercises for these transgressions, the chief one being a liturgical recitation of "Tillie the Toiler took Tommy Tucker to tea," with the tongue anxiously flying up above the teeth to strike precisely on the lower ridge of the upper palate.

The diaphragm; the upper palate; and finally the arena in the cave of the mouth where the vowels were prepared. A New Yorker could not say a proper *a*, as in "paper"—this indispensable vibration was manufactured somewhere back near the nasal passage, whereas civility demanded the *a* to emerge frontally, directly from the lips' vestibule. The New York *i* was worst of all: how Mrs. Davis, Mrs. Papp, and Miss Trolander mimicked and ridiculed the New York *i*! "Oi loik oice cream," they mocked.

All these emendations, as it happened, were being applied to the entire population of a high school for girls in a modest Gothic pile on East Sixty-eighth Street in the 1940s, and no one who emerged from that pile after four years of daily speech training ever sounded the same again. On the eve of graduation, Mrs. Olive Birch Davis turned to Mrs. Ruby S. Papp and said: "Do you remember the *ugliness* of her *diction* when she came to us?" She meant me; I was about to deliver the Class Speech. I had not yet encountered Shaw's *Pygmalion*, and its popular recrudescence in the form of *My Fair Lady* was still to occur; all the same, that night, rehearsing for commencement, I caught in Mrs. Davis and Mrs. Papp something of Professor Higgins's victory, and in myself something of Eliza's humiliation.

Our teachers had, like young Lochinvar, come out of the West, but I had come out of the northeast Bronx. Called on to enunciate publicly for the first time, I responded with the diffidence of secret pleasure; I liked to read out loud, and thought myself not bad at it. Instead, I was marked down as a malfeasance in need of overhaul. The revisions and transformations that followed were not unlike an evangelical conversion. One had to be willing to be born again; one had to be willing to repudiate wholesale one's former defective self. It could not be accomplished without faith and shame: faith in what one might newly become, shame in the degrading process itself—the dedicated repetition of mantras. "Tillie the Toiler took Tommy Tucker to tea," "Oh! young LOCHinvar has come out of the WEST, Through all the wide BORDer HIS steed was the BEST." All the while pneumatically shooting out one's diaphragm, and keeping one's eye (never one's *oi*) peeled for the niggardly approval of Miss Evangeline Trolander.

In this way I was, at an early age, effectively made over.

Like a multitude of other graduates of my high school, I now own a sort of robot's speech—it has no obvious native country. At least not to most ears, though a well-tutored listener will hear that the vowels hang on, and the cadence of every sentence has a certain laggardly northeast Bronx drag. Brooklyn, by contrast, is divided between very fast and very slow. Irish New York has its own sound, Italian New York another; and a refined ear can distinguish between Bronx and Brooklyn Irish and Bronx and Brooklyn Jewish: four separate accents, with the differences to be found not simply in vowels and consonants, but in speed and inflection. Nor is it so much a matter of ancestry as of neighborhood. If, instead of clinging to the green-fronded edge of Pelham Bay Park, my family had settled three miles west, in a denser "section" called Pelham Parkway, I would have spoken Bronx Jewish. Encountering City Island, Bronx Jewish said Ciddy Oilen. In Pelham Bay, where Bronx Irish was almost exclusively spoken in those days, it was Ciddy Allen. When Terence Cooke became cardinal of New York, my heart leaped up: Throggs Neck! I had assimilated those sounds long ago on a pebbly beach. No one had ever put the cardinal into the wringer of speech repair. I knew him through and through. He was my childhood's brother, and restored my orphaned ear.

Effectively made over: these noises that come out of me are not an overlay. They do not vanish during the free play of dreams or screams. I do not, cannot, "revert." This may be because Trolander, Davis, and Papp caught me early; or because I was so passionate a devotee of their dogma.

Years later I tried to figure it all out. What did these women have up their sleeves? An aesthetic ideal, perhaps: Standard American English. But behind the Ideal—and Trolander, Davis, and Papp were the strictest and most indefatigable idealists—there must have been an ideology; and behind the ideology, whatever form it might take, a repugnance. The speech of New York streets and households soiled them: you could see it in their proud pained meticulous frowns. They were intent on our elevation. Though they were dead set on annihilating Yiddish-derived "dentalization," they could not be said to be anti-Semites, since they were just as set on erasing the tumbling consonants of Virginia Greene's Alexander Avenue Irish Bronx; and besides, in our different styles, we *all* dentalized. Was it, then, the Melting Pot that inspired Trolander, Davis, and Papp? But not one of us was an "immigrant"; we were all fully Americanized, and our parents before us, except for the handful of foreign-born "German refugees." These were marched off to a special Speech Clinic for segregated training; their *r*'s drew Mrs. Davis's eyes toward heaven, and I privately recognized that the refugees were almost all of them hopeless cases. A girl named Hedwig said she *didn't care*, which made me conclude that she was frivolous, trivialized, not serious; wasn't it ignominious enough (like a kind of cheese) to be called "Hedwig"?

Only the refugees were bona fide foreigners. The rest of us were garden-variety subway-riding New Yorkers. Trolander, Davis, and Papp saw us nevertheless as tainted with foreignness, and it was the remnants of that foreignness they meant to wipe away: the last stages of the great turn-of-the-century alien flood. Or perhaps they intended that, like Shaw's Eliza, we should have the wherewithal to rise to a higher station. Yet, looking back on their dress and manner, I do not think Trolander, Davis, and Papp at all sought out or even understood "class"; they were reliably American, and class was nothing they were capable of believing in.

What, then, did these ferrywomen imagine we would find on the farther shore, once we left behind, through artifice and practice, our native speech? Was it a kind of "manners," was it what they might have called "breeding"? They thought of themselves as democratic noblewomen (nor did they suppose this to be a contradiction in terms), and they expected of us, if not the same, then at least a recognition of the category. They trusted in the power of models. They gave us the astonishing maneuvers of their teeth, their tongues, their lungs, and drilled us in imitation of those maneuvers. In the process, they managed—this was their highest feat—to break down embarrassment, to deny the shaming theatricality of the ludicrous. We lost every delicacy and dignity in acting like freaks or fools while trying out the new accent. Contrived consonants began freely to address feigned vowels: a world of parroting and parody. And what came of it all?

What came of it was that they caused us—and here was a category *they* had no recognition of—they caused us to exchange one regionalism for another. New York gave way to Midwest. We were cured of Atlantic Seaboard, a disease that encompassed north, middle, and south; and yet only the middle, and of that middle only New York, was considered to be on the critical list. It was New York that carried the hottest and sickest inflammation. In no other hollow of the country was such an effort mounted, on such a scale, to eliminate regionalism. The South might have specialized in Elocution, but the South was not ashamed of its idiosyncratic vowels; neither was New England; and no one sent missionaries.

Of course this was exactly what our democratic noble-women were: missionaries. They restored, if not our souls, then surely and emphatically our *r*'s—those *r*'s that are missing in the end syllables of New Yorkers, who call themselves Noo Yawkizz and nowadays worry about muggizz. From Boston to New York to Atlanta, the Easterner is an Eastinna, his mother is a mutha, his father a fahtha, and the most difficult stretch of anything is the hahd paht; and so fawth. But only in New York is the absent *r*—i.e., the absent *aw*—an offense to good mannizz. To be sure, our missionaries did not dream that they imposed a parochialism of their own. And perhaps they were right not to dream it, since by the forties of this century the radio was having its leveling effect, and Midwest speech, colonizing by means of "announcers," had ascended to the rank of standard speech.

Still, only forty years earlier, Henry James, visiting from England after a considerable period away, was freshly noticing and acidly deploring the pervasively conquering *r*:

> . . . the letter, I grant, gets terribly little rest among those great masses of our population that strike us, in the boundless West especially, as, under some strange impulse received toward consonantal recovery of balance, making it present even in words from which it is

absent, bringing it in everywhere as with the small vulgar effect of a sort of morose grinding of the back teeth. There are, you see, sounds of a mysterious intrinsic meanness, and there are sounds of a mysterious intrinsic frankness and sweetness; and I think the recurrent note I have indicated—fartherr and motherr and otherr, waterr and matterr and scatterr, harrd and barrd, parrt, starrt, and (dreadful to say) arrt (the repetition it is that drives home the ugliness), are signal specimens of what becomes of a custom of utterance out of which the principle of taste has dropped.

In 1905, to drop the *r* was to drop, for the cultivated ear, a principle of taste; but for our democratic noblewomen four decades on, exactly the reverse was true. James's New York/ Boston expectations, reinforced by southern England, assumed that Eastern American speech, tied as it was to the cultural reign of London, had a right to rule and to rule out. The history and sociolinguistics governing this reversal is less pressing to examine than the question of "standard speech" itself. James thought that "the voice *plus* the way it is employed" determined "positively the history of the national character, almost the history of the people." His views on all this, his alarms and anxieties, he compressed into a fluid little talk ("The Question of Our Speech") he gave at the Bryn Mawr College commencement of June 8, 1905—exactly one year and two days before my mother, nine years old, having passed through Castle Garden, stood on the corner of Battery Park, waiting to board the horsecar for Madison Street on the Lower East Side.

James was in great fear of the child waiting for the horsecar. "Keep in sight," he warned, "the so interesting historical truth that no language, so far back as our acquaintance with history goes, has known any such ordeal, any such stress or strain, as was to await the English in this huge new community it was to help, at first, to gather and mother. It came *over*, as the phrase is, came over originally without fear and without guile—but to find itself transplanted to spaces it had never dreamed, in its comparative humility, of covering, to

conditions it had never dreamed, in its comparative innocence, of meeting." He spoke of English as an "unfriended
heroine," "our transported medium, our unrescued Andro-
meda, our medium of utterance, . . . disjoined from all the
associations, the other presences, that had attended her, that
had watched for her and with her, that had helped to form
her manners and her voice, her taste and her genius."

And if English, orphaned as it was and cut off from its
"ancestral circle," did not have enough to contend with in
its own immigrant situation, arriving "without fear and without guile" only to be ambushed by "a social and political
order that was both without previous precedent and example
and incalculably expansive," including also the expansiveness
of a diligent public school network and "the mighty
maniac" of journalism—if all this was not threatening
enough, there was the special danger my nine-year-old
mother posed. She represented an unstable new ingredient.
She represented violation, a kind of linguistic Armageddon.
She stood for disorder and promiscuity. "I am perfectly
aware," James said at Bryn Mawr,

> that the common school and the newspaper are influ-
> ences that shall often have been named to you, exactly,
> as favorable, as positively and actively contributive, to
> the prosperity of our idiom; the answer to which is
> that the matter depends, distinctively, on what is meant
> by prosperity. It is prosperity, of a sort, that a hundred
> million people, a few years hence, will be unanimously,
> loudly—above all loudly, I think!—speaking it, and that,
> moreover, many of these millions will have been artfully
> wooed and weaned from the Dutch, from the Spanish,
> from the German, from the Italian, from the Norse, from
> the Finnish, from the Yiddish even, strange to say, and
> (stranger still to say), even from the English, for the
> sweet sake, or the sublime consciousness, as we may
> perhaps put it, of speaking, of talking, for the first time
> in their lives, *really* at their ease. There are many things
> our now so profusely important and, as is claimed,
> quickly assimilated foreign brothers and sisters may do

at their ease in this country, and at two minutes' notice, and without asking any one else's leave or taking any circumstance whatever into account—any save an infinite uplifting sense of freedom and facility; but the thing they may best do is play, to their heart's content, with the English language, or, in other words, dump their mountain of promiscuous material into the foundation of the American.

"All the while we sleep," he continued, "the vast contingent of aliens whom we make welcome, and whose main contention, as I say, is that, from the moment of their arrival, they have just as much property in our speech as we have, and just as good a right to do what they choose with it . . . all the while we sleep the innumerable aliens are sitting up (*they* don't sleep!) to work their will on their new inheritance." And he compared the immigrants' use of English to oilcloth—"highly convenient . . . durable, tough, cheap."

James's thesis in his address to his audience of young aristocrats was not precisely focused. On the one hand, in describing the depredations of the innumerable sleepless aliens, in protesting "the common schools and the 'daily paper,' " he appeared to admit defeat—"the forces of looseness are in possession of the field." Yet in asking the graduates to see to the perfection of their own speech, he had, he confessed, no models to offer them. Imitate, he advised—but whom? Parents and teachers were themselves not watchful. "I am at a loss to name you particular and unmistakable, edifying and illuminating groups or classes," he said, and recommended, in the most general way, the hope of "encountering, blessedly, here and there, articulate individuals, torch-bearers, as we may rightly describe them, guardians of the sacred flame."

As it turned out, James not only had no solution; he had not even put the right question. These young women of good family whom he was exhorting to excellence were well situated in society to do exactly what James had described the immigrants as doing: speaking "*really* at their ease," playing, "to their heart's content, with the English language" in "an infinite uplifting sense of freedom and facility."

245

Whereas the "aliens," hard-pressed by the scramblings of poverty and cultural confusions, had no notion at all of linguistic "freedom and facility," took no witting license with the English tongue, and felt no remotest ownership in the language they hoped merely to earn their wretched bread by. If they did not sleep, it was because of long hours in the sweatshops and similar places of employment; they were no more in a position to "play" with English than they were to acquire bona fide *Mayflower* ancestry. Ease, content, facility—these were not the lot of the unsleeping aliens.

To the young people of Bryn Mawr James could offer nothing more sanguine, nothing less gossamer, than the merest metaphor—"guardians of the sacred flame." Whom then should they imitate but himself, the most "articulate individual" of them all? We have no record of the graduates' response to James's extravagant "later style" as profusely exhibited in this address: whatever it was, they could not have accepted it for standard American. James's English had become, by this time, an invention of his own fashioning, so shaded, so leafy, so imbricated, so brachiate, so filigreed, as to cast a thousand momentary ornamental obscurities, like the effect of the drill-holes in the spiraled stone hair of an imperial Roman portrait bust. He was the most eminent torchbearer in sight, the purest of all possible guardians of the flame—but a model he could not have been for anyone's everyday speech, no more than the Romans talked like the Odes of Horace. Not that he failed to recognize the exigencies of an active language, "a living organism, fed by the very breath of those who employ it, whoever these may happen to be," a language able "to respond, from its core, to the constant appeal of time, perpetually demanding new tricks, new experiments, new amusements." He saw American English as the flexible servant "of those who carry it with them, on their long road, as their specific experience grows larger and more complex, and who need it to help them to meet this expansion." And at the same time he excluded from these widened possibilities its slangy young native speakers and the very immigrants whose educated children would enrich and reanimate the American language (eight decades later we may judge how vividly), as well as master and augment its literature.

Its literature. It is striking beyond anything that James left out, in the course of this lecture, any reference to reading. Certainly it was not overtly his subject. He was concerned with enunciation and with idiom, with syllables, with vowels and consonants, with tone and inflection, with *sound*—but he linked the American voice to such "underlying things" as "properties and values, perfect possessions of the educated spirit, clear humanities," as well as "the imparting of a coherent culture." Implicit was his conviction that speech affects literature, as, in the case of native speakers, it inevitably does: naturalism in the dialogue of a novel, say, is itself always a kind of dialect of a particular place and time. But in a newly roiling society of immigrant speakers, James could not see ahead (and why should he have seen ahead? Castle Garden was unprecedented in all of human history) to the idea that a national literature can create a national speech. The immigrants who learned to read learned to speak. Those who only learned to speak did not, in effect, learn to speak.

In supposing the overriding opposite—that quality of speech creates culture, rather than culture quality of speech—James in "The Question of Our Speech" slighted the one formulation most pertinent to his complaints: the uses of literature. Pressing for "civility of utterance," warning against "influences round about us that make for . . . the confused, the ugly, the flat, the thin, the mean, the helpless, that reduce articulation to an easy and ignoble minimum, and so keep it as little distinct as possible from the grunting, the squealing, the barking or roaring of animals," James thought it overwhelmingly an issue of the imitation of oral models, an issue of "the influence of *observation*," above all an issue of manners—"for that," he insisted, "is indissolubly involved." How like Mrs. Olive Birch Davis he is when, at Bryn Mawr, he hopes to inflame his listeners to aspiration! "At first dimly, but then more and more distinctly, you will find yourselves noting, comparing, preferring, at last positively emulating and imitating." Bryn Mawr, of course, was the knowing occasion, not the guilty target, of this admonition—he was speaking of the young voices he had been hearing in the street and in the parlors of friends, and he ended with a sacred charge for the graduates themselves: "you may, sounding the clearer note of intercourse as only women can, become yourselves models and missionaries [sic], perhaps even a little martyrs, of the good cause."

But why did he address himself to this thesis exclusively in America? Could he not, even more emphatically, have made the same declarations, uttered the same dooms, in his adopted England? No doubt it would not have been seemly; no doubt he would have condemned any appearance of ingratitude toward his welcoming hosts. All true, but this was hardly the reason the lecture at Bryn Mawr would not have done for Girton College. In Britain, regionalisms are the soul of ordinary English speech, and in James's time more than in our own. Even now one can move from hamlet to hamlet and hear the vowels chime charmingly with a different tone in each village. Hull, England, is a city farther from London in speech—though in distance only 140 miles to the north—than Hull, Massachusetts, is from San Francisco, 3,000 miles to the west. Of England, it is clear, James had only the expectations of class, and a single class set the standard for cultivated speech. Back home in America, diversity was without enchantment, and James demanded a uniform sound. He would not have dreamed of requiring a uniform British sound: English diversity was *English* diversity, earned, native, beaten out over generations of the "ancestral circle"—while American diversity meant a proliferating concatenation of the innumerable sleepless aliens and the half-educated slangy young. With regard to England, James knew whence the standard derived. It was a quality—an emanation, even—of those who, for generations, had been privileged in their education. As Virginia Woolf acknowledged in connection with another complaint, the standard was Oxbridge. To raise the question of "our" speech in England would have been a superfluity: both the question and the answer were self-evident. In England the question, if anyone bothered to put it at all, was: Who sets the standard? And the answer, if anyone bothered to give it at all, was:

Those who have been through the great public schools, those who have been through either of the great pair of ancient universities—in short, those who run things.

This was perhaps what led James, in his American reflections, to trip over the issues, and to miss getting at the better question, the right and pertinent question: *the* question, in fact, concerning American speech. In Britain, and in the smaller America of his boyhood that strained to be a mirror of the cousinly English culture, it remained to the point to ask who sets the standard. And the rejoinder was simple enough: the people at the top. To risk the identical question in the America of 1905, with my mother about to emerge from Castle Garden to stand waiting for the horsecar on the corner of Battery Park, was unavoidably to hurtle to the very answer James most dreaded and then desperately conceded: the people at the bottom.

The right and pertinent question for America was something else. If, in politics, America's Enlightenment cry before the world was to be "a nation of laws, not of men," then it was natural for culture to apply in its own jurisdiction the same measure: unassailable institutions are preferable to models or heroes. To look for aristocratic models for common speech in the America of 1905 was to end exactly where James *did* end: "I am at a loss to name you particular and unmistakably edifying illuminating groups or classes." It could not be done. As long as James believed—together with Trolander, Davis, and Papp, his immediate though paradoxical heirs: paradoxical because their ideal was democratic and his was the people-at-the-top—as long as he believed in the premise of "edifying and illuminating" models, his analysis could go nowhere. Or, rather, it could go only into the rhapsody of vaporous hope that is the conclusion of "The Question of Our Speech"—"become yourselves models and missionaries, even a little martyrs, of the good cause." Holy and resplendent words I recognize on the instant, having learned them—especially the injunction to martyrdom—at the feet of Trolander, Davis, and Papp.

No, it was the wrong question for America, this emphasis on *who*; the wrong note for a campus (however homogeneous, however elite) just outside Philadelphia, that Enlightenment citadel, whose cracked though mighty Bell was engraved with a rendering of the majestic Hebrew word *dror*: a word my nine-year-old mother, on her way to Madison Street, would have been able to read in the original, though presumably James could not—a deprivation of literacy my mother might have marked him down for. "All life," James asserted on that brilliant June day (my mother's life was that day still under the yoke of the Czar; the Kishinev pogrom, with its massacre and its maimings, had occurred only two years earlier), "all life comes back to the question of our speech, the medium through which we communicate with each other; for all life comes back to the question of our relations with each other." And: "A care for tone is part of a care for many things besides; for the fact, for the value, of good breeding, above all, as to which tone unites with various other personal, social signs to be testimony. The idea of good breeding . . . is one of the most precious conquests of civilization, the very core of our social heritage."

Speech, then, was *who*; it was breeding; it was "relations"; it was manners; and manners, in this view, make culture. As a novelist, and particularly as a celebrated practitioner of the "novel of manners" (though to reduce James merely to this is to diminish him radically as a recorder of evil and to silence his full moral genius), it was requisite, it was the soul of vitality itself, for James to analyze in the mode of *who*. But for a social theorist—and in his lecture social theory was what James was pressing toward—it was a failing and an error. The absence of models was not simply an embarrassment; it should have been a hint. It should have hinted at the necessary relinquishment of *who* in favor of *what*: not who appoints the national speech, but what creates the standard.

If, still sticking to his formulation, James had dared to give his private answer, he might have announced: "Young women, I, Henry James, am that august Who who fixes the firmament of our national speech. Follow me, and you follow excellence." But how had this vast substantial Who that was Henry James come to be fashioned? It was no Who *he* followed. It was instead a great cumulative corporeal What, the voluminous and manifold heritage of Literature he had been saturated in since childhood. In short, he *read*: he was a reader, he had always read, reading was not so much his passion or his possession as it was his bread, and not so much his bread as it was the primordial fountain of his life. Ludicrous it is to say of Henry James that he read, he was a reader! As much say of Vesuvius that it erupted, or of Olympus that it kept the gods. But reading—just that, *what is read*—is the whole, the intricate, secret of his exemplum.

The vulgarity of the low press James could see for himself. On the other hand, he had never set foot in an American public school (his education was, to say the least, Americanly untypical), and he had no inkling of any representative curriculum. Nevertheless it was this public but meticulous curriculum that was to set the standard; and it was a curriculum not far different from what James might have found for himself, exploring on his own among his father's shelves.

A year or so after my mother stepped off the horsecar into Madison Street, she was given Sir Walter Scott's "The Lady of the Lake" to read as a school assignment. She never forgot it. She spoke of it all her life. Mastering it was the triumph of her childhood, and though, like every little girl of her generation, she read *Pollyanna*, and in the last months of her eighty-third year every word of Willa Cather, it was "The Lady of the Lake" that enduringly typified achievement, education, culture.

Some seventy-odd years after my mother studied it at P.S. 131 on the Lower East Side, I open "The Lady of the Lake" and take in lines I have never looked on before:

Not thus, in ancient days of Caledon,
　　Was thy voice mute amid the festal crowd,
When lay of hopeless love, or glory won,
　　Aroused the fearful, or subdued the proud.
At each according pause was heard aloud
　　Thine ardent symphony sublime and high!
Fair dames and crested chiefs attention bowed;
　　For still the burden of thy minstrelsy

251

Was Knighthood's dauntless deed, and Beauty's
matchless eye.

O wake once more! how rude soe'er the hand
That ventures o'er thy magic maze to stray;
O wake once more! though scarce my skill command
Some feeble echoing of thine earlier lay;
Though harsh and faint, and soon to die away,
And all unworthy of thy nobler strain,
Yet if one heart throb higher at its sway,
The wizard note has not been touched in vain.
Then silent be no more! Enchantress, wake again!

My mother was an immigrant child, the poorest of the
poor. She had come in steerage; she knew not a word of
English when she stepped off the horsecar in Madison Street;
she was one of the innumerable unsleeping aliens. Her
teachers were the entirely ordinary daughters of the Irish
immigration (as my own teachers still were, a generation on),
and had no special genius, and assuredly no special training
(a certain Miss Walsh was in fact ferociously hostile), for the
initiation of a Russian Jewish child into the astoundingly
distant and incomprehensible premises of such poetry. And
yet it was accomplished, and within the briefest period after
the voyage in steerage.

What was accomplished was not merely that my mother
"learned" this sort of poetry—i.e., could read and understand
it. She learned what it represented in the widest sense—not
only the legendary heritage implicit in each and every word
and phrase (to a child from Hlusk, where the wooden side-
walks sank into the mud and the peasants carried water
buckets dangling from shoulder yokes, what was "minstrelsy," what was "Knighthood's dauntless deed," what on
earth was a "wizard note"?), but what is represented in
the American social and tribal code. The quickest means of
stitching all this down is to say that what "The Lady of the
Lake" stood for, in the robes and tapestries of its particular
English, was the received tradition exemplified by Bryn Mawr

in 1905, including James's presence there as commencement speaker.

The American standard derived from an American institution: the public school, free, democratic, open, urgent, pressing on the young a program of reading not so much for its "literary value," though this counted too, as for the stamp of Heritage. All this James overlooked. He had no firsthand sense of it. He was himself the grandson of an ambitiously money-making Irish immigrant; but his father, arranging his affluent life as a metaphysician, had separated himself from public institutions—from any practical idea, in fact, of institutions *per se*—and dunked his numerous children in and out of school on two continents, like a nomad in search of the wettest oasis of all. It was hardly a wonder that James, raised in a self-enclosed clan, asserted the ascendancy of manners over institutions, or that he ascribed to personal speech "positively the history of the national character, almost the history of the people," or that he spoke of the "ancestral circle" as if kinship were the only means to transmit that national character and history.

It was as if James, who could imagine nearly everything, had in this instance neglected imagination itself: kinship as construct and covenant, kinship imagined—and what are institutions if not invented kinship circles: society as contract? In the self-generating Enlightenment society of the American founding philosophers, it was uniquely the power of institutions to imagine, to create, kinship and community. The Constitution, itself a kind of covenant or imaginatively established "ancestral circle," created peoplehood out of an idea, and the public schools, begotten and proliferated by that idea, implemented the Constitution; and more than the Constitution. They implemented and transmitted the old cultural mesh. Where there was so much diversity, the institution substituted for the clan, and discovered—through a kind of civic magnetism—that it could transmit, almost as effectively as the kinship clan itself, "the very core of our social heritage."

To name all this the principle of the Melting Pot is not quite right, and overwhelmingly insufficient. The Melting Pot called for imitation. Imagination, which is at the heart of institutionalized covenants, promotes what is intrinsic. I find on my shelves two old textbooks used widely in the "common schools" James deplored. The first is *A Practical English Grammar*, dated 1880, the work of one Albert N. Raub, A.M., Ph.D. ("Author of 'Raub's Readers,' 'Raub's Arithmetics,' 'Plain Educational Talks, Etc.'"). It is a relentless volume, thorough, determined, with no loopholes; every permutation of the language is scrutinized, analyzed, accounted for. It is also a commonplace book replete with morally instructive quotations, some splendidly familiar. Every explanatory chapter is followed by "Remarks," "Cautions," and "Exercises," and every Exercise includes a high-minded hoard of literary Remarks and Cautions. For instance, under Personal Pronouns:

> Though the mills of God grind slowly,
>   yet they grind exceedingly small;
> Though with patience He stands waiting,
>   with exactness grinds He all.

> This above all, to thine own self be true,
> And it must follow, as the night the day,
> Thou canst not then be false to any man.

> These are thy glorious works, Parent of good,
>   Almighty! Thine this universal frame.

> Alas! they had been friends in youth,
> But whispering tongues can poison truth;
> And constancy lives in realms above,
>   And life is thorny, and youth is vain;
> And to be wroth with one we love
>   Doth work like madness on the brain.

So much for Longfellow, Shakespeare, Milton, and Coleridge. But also Addison, Cowper, Pope, Ossian, Scott, Ruskin, Thomson, Wordsworth, Trollope, Gray, Byron, Whittier, Lowell, Holmes, Moore, Collins, Hood, Goldsmith, Byrant, Dickens, Bacon, Franklin, Locke, the Bible—these appear throughout, in the form of addenda to Participles, Parsing,

Irregular Verbs, and the rule of the Nominative Independent; in addition, a handful of lost presences: Bushnell, H. Wise, Wayland, Dwight, Blair, Mrs. Welby (nearly the only woman in the lot), and Anon. The *content* of this volume is not its subject matter, neither its syntactic lesson nor its poetic maxims. It is the voice of a language; rather, of language itself, language as texture, gesture, innateness. To read from beginning to end of a schoolbook of this sort is to recognize at once that James had it backwards and upside down: it is not that manners lead culture; it is culture that leads manners. What shapes culture—this is not a tautology or a redundancy—is culture. "Who makes the country?" was the latent question James was prodding and poking, all gingerly; and it was the wrong—because unanswerable—one. "What kind of country shall we have?" was Albert N. Raub's question, and it *was* answerable. The answer lay in the reading given to the children in the schoolhouses: the institutionalization, so to say, of our common speech at its noblest.

My second text is even more striking: *The Etymological Reader*, edited by Epes Sargent and Amasa May, dated 1872. "We here offer to the schools of the United States," begins the Preface, "the first systematic attempt to associate the study of etymology with exercises in reading." What follows is a blitz of "vocabulary," Latin roots, Saxon roots, prefixes, and suffixes, but these quickly subside, and nine tenths of this inventive book is an anthology engaging in its richness, range, and ambition. "Lochinvar" is here; so are the Declaration of Independence and selections from Shakespeare; so is Shelley's "To a Skylark"; so is the whole "Star-Spangled Banner." But also: "Description of a Bee Hunt," "Creation of a Continuous Work," "The Sahara," "Anglo-Saxon and Norman French," "Conversation," "Progress of Civilization," "Effects of Machinery," "On the Choice of Books," "Our Indebtedness to the Greeks," "Animal Heat," "Corruptions of Language," "Jerusalem from the Mount of Olives," "On the Act of Habeas Corpus," "Individual Character," "Going Up in a Balloon," and dozens of other essays. Among the writers: Dickens, Macaulay, Wordsworth, Irving, Mark

Twain, Emerson, Channing, John Stuart Mill, Carlyle, De Quincey, Tennyson, Mirabeau, and so on and so on.

It would be foolish to consider *The Etymological Reader* merely charming, a period piece, "Americana"—it is too immediately useful, too uncompromising, and, for the most part, too enduring to be dismissed with condescension.

> It was one of those heads which Guido has often painted—mild, pale, penetrating, free from all common-place ideas of fat, contented ignorance, looking down-ward upon the earth; it looked forward, but looked as if it looked at something beyond this world. How one of his order came by it, Heaven above, who let it fall upon a monk's shoulders, best knows; but it would have suited a Brahmin, and had I met it upon the plains of Hindostan, I had reverenced it.

To come upon Sterne, just like this, all of a sudden, for the first time, pressed between Southey's sigh ("How beautiful is night!") and Byron's "And the might of the Gentile, unsmote by the sword,/Hath melted like snow in the glance of the Lord"—to come upon Sterne, just like that, is to come upon an unexpected human fact. Such textbooks filled vessels more fundamental than the Melting Pot—blood vessels, one might venture. Virtuous, elevated, striving and stirring, the best that has been thought and said: thus the voice of the common schools. A fraction of their offerings had a heroic, or monu-mental, quality, on the style perhaps of George Washington's head. They stood for the power of civics. But the rest were the purest belles-lettres: and it was belles-lettres that were expected to be the fountainhead of American civilization, including civility. Belles-lettres provided style, vocabulary, speech itself; and also the themes of Victorian seriousness: conscience and work. Elevated literature was the model for an educated tongue. Sentences, like conscience and work, were demanding.

What did these demanding sentences do in and for society? First, they demanded to be studied. Second, they demanded sharpness and cadence in writing. They promoted, in short, literacy—and not merely literacy, but a vigorous and manifold recognition of literature as a *force*. They promoted an educated class. Not a hereditarily educated class, but one that had been introduced to the initiating and shaping texts early in life, almost like the hereditarily educated class itself.

All that, we know, is gone. Where once the *Odyssey* was read in the schools, in a jeweled and mandarin translation, Holden Caulfield takes his stand. He is winning and truthful, but he is not demanding. His sentences reach no higher than his gaze. The idea of belles-lettres, when we knock our unaccustomed knees against it, looks archaic and bizarre: rusted away, like an old car chassis. The content of belles-lettres is the property of a segregated caste or the dissipated recollections of the very old.

Belles-lettres in the schools fashioned both speech and the art of punctuation—the sound and the look of nuance. Who spoke well pointed well; who pointed well spoke well. One was the skill of the other. No one now punctuates for nuance—or, rather, whoever punctuates for nuance is "corrected." Copy editors do not know the whole stippled range of the colon or the semicolon, do not know that "O" is not "oh," do not know that not all juxtaposed adjectives are coordinate adjectives; and so forth. The denigration of punctuation and word-by-word literacy is pandemic among English speakers: this includes most poets and novelists. To glimpse a typical original manuscript undoctored by a copy editor is to suffer a shock at the sight of ignorant imprecision; and to examine a densely literate manuscript after it has passed through the leveling hands of a copy editor is again to suffer a shock at the sight of ignorant imprecision.

In 1930 none of this was so. The relentlessly gradual return of aural culture, beginning with the telephone (a farewell to letter-writing), the radio, the motion picture, and the phonograph, speeded up by the television set, the tape recorder, and lately the video recorder, has by now, after half a century's worth of technology, restored us to the pre-literate status of face-to-face speech. And mass literacy itself is the fixity of no more than a century, starting with the advancing reforms following the industrial revolution—reforms introducing, in England, the notion of severely limited leisure to the classes that formerly had labored with no leisure at all. Into that small new recreational space fell what we now call the "nineteenth-century novel," in both its supreme and its lesser versions. The act of reading—the *work*, in fact, of the act of reading—appeared to complicate and intensify the most ordinary intelligence. The silent physiological translation of letters into sounds, the leaping eye encoding, the transmigration of blotches on a page into the story of, say, Dorothea Brooke, must surely count among the most intricate of biological and transcendent designs. In 1930 the so-called shopgirl, with her pulp romance, is habitually engaged in this electrifying webwork of eye and mind. In 1980 she reverts, via electronics, to the simple speaking face. And then it is all over, by and large, for mass literacy. High literacy has been the province of an elite class since Sumer; there is nothing novel in having a caste of princely readers. But the culture of mass literacy, in its narrow period from 1830 to 1930, was something else: Gutenberg's revolution did not take effect in a popular sense—did not properly begin—until the rise of the middle class at the time, approximately, of the English Reform Act of 1832. Addison's *Spectator*, with its Latin epigraphs, was read by gentlemen, but Dickens was read by nearly everyone. The almost universal habit of reading for recreation or excitement conferred the greatest complexity on the greatest number, and the thinnest sliver of history expressed it: no more than a single century. It flashed by between aural culture and aural culture, no longer-lived than a lightning bug. The world of the VCR is closer to the pre-literate society of traveling mummers than it is to that of the young Scott Fitzgerald's readership in 1920.

When James read out "The Question of Our Speech" in 1905, the era of print supremacy was still in force, unquestioned; the typewriter and the electric light had arrived to strengthen it, and the telephone was greeted only as a convenience, not a substitute. The telephone was particularly welcome—not much was lost that ought not to have been lost in the omission of letters agreeing to meet the 8:42 on Tuesday night on the east platform. Since then, the telephone has abetted more serious losses: exchanges between artists and thinkers; documents of family and business relations; quarrels and cabals among politicians; everything that in the past tended to be preserved for biographers and cultural historians. The advent of the computer used as word processor similarly points toward the wiping out of any *progressive* record of thought; the grain of a life can lie in the illumination of the crossed-out word.

But James, in the remoteness of post-Victorian technology, spoke unshadowed by these threatened disintegrations among the community of the literate; he spoke in the very interior of what seemed then to be a permanently post-aural culture. He read from a manuscript; later that year, Houghton, Mifflin published it together with another lecture, this one far more famous, "The Lesson of Balzac." We cannot hear his voice on a phonograph record, as we can hear his fellow self-exile T. S. Eliot's; and this, it might be said, is another kind of loss. If we cherish photographs of Henry James's extraordinarily striking head with its lantern eyes, we can regret the loss of a filmed interview or the kind that nowadays captures and delivers into the future Norman Mailer and John Updike. The return to an aural culture is, obviously, not *all* a question of loss; only of the most significant loss of all: the widespread nurture by portable print; print as water, and sometimes wine. It was, in its small heyday (we must now begin to say *was*), the most glorious work of the eye-linked brain.

And in the heyday of that glorious work, James made a false analysis. In asking for living models, his analysis belonged to the old aural culture, and he did not imagine its risks. In the old aural culture, speech *was* manner, manner *was* manners, manners *did* teach the tone of the civilized world. In the new aural culture, speech remains manner, manner becomes manners, manners go on teaching the tone of the world. The difference is that the new aural culture, based, as James urged, on emulation, is governed from below. Emulation as a principle cannot control its sources. To seize on only two blatancies: the guerrilla toy of the urban underclass, the huge and hugely loud portable radio—the "ghetto blaster"—is adopted by affluent middle-class white adolescents; so is the locution "Hey, man," which now crosses both class and gender. James worried about the replacement in America of "Yes" by "Yeah" (and further by the comedic "Yep"), but its source was the drawl endemic to the gilt-and-plush parlors of the upper middle class. "Yeah" did not come out of the street; it went into the street. But it is also fairly certain that the "Yeah"-sayers, whatever their place in society, could not have been strong readers, even given the fissure that lies between reading and the style of one's talk. The more attached one is to the community of readers, the narrower the fissure. In a society where belles-lettres are central to education of the young, what controls speech is the degree of absorption in print. Reading governs speech, governs tone, governs manner and manners and civilization. "It is easier to overlook any question of speech than to trouble about it," James complained, "but then it is also easier to snort or neigh, to growl or 'meaow,' than to articulate and intonate."

And yet he overlooked the primacy of the high act of reading. No one who, in the age of conscience and work, submitted to "The Lady of the Lake," or parsed under the aegis of Albert N. Raub, or sent down a bucket into *The Etymological Reader,* was likely to snort or neigh or emit the cry of the tabby. Agreed, it was a more publicly formal and socially encrusted age than ours, and James was more publicly formal and socially encrusted than many of his contemporaries: he was an old-fashioned gentleman. He had come of age during the Civil War. His clothes were laid out by a manservant. His standard was uncompromising. All the same, he missed how and where his own standard ruled. He failed to discover it in the schoolhouses, to which it had migrated after the attenuation of the old aural culture. To be sure, the school texts, however aspiring, could not promise to the children of the poor, or to the children of the immigrants, or to the children of working men, any hope of a manservant; but they *did* promise a habit of speech, more mobilizing and organizing, even, than a valet. The key to American speech was under James's nose. It was at that very moment being turned in a thousand locks. It was opening gate after gate. Those who could read according to an elevated standard could write sufficiently accomplished sentences, and those who could write such sentences could "articulate and intonate."

"Read, read! Read yourself through all the stages of the masters of the language," James might have exhorted the graduates. Instead, he told them to seek "contact and communication, a beneficent contagion," in order to "bring about the happy state—the state of sensibility to tone." It offended him, he confessed, that there were "forces assembled to make you believe that no form of speech is provably better than another." Forty years on, Trolander, Davis, and Papp set their own formidable forces against the forces of relativism in enunciation. Like James, they were zealous to impose their own parochialisms. James did not pronounce the *r* in "mother"; it was, therefore, vulgar to let it be heard. Our Midwestern teachers did pronounce the *r*; it was, therefore, vulgar *not* to let it be heard. How, then, one concludes, *is* any form of speech "provably better than another"? In a relativist era, the forces representing relativism in enunciation have for the moment won the argument, it seems; yet James has had his way all the same. With the exception of the South and parts of the East Coast, there is very nearly a uniform *vox Americana*. And we have everywhere a uniform "tone." It is in the streets and in the supermarkets, on the radio and on television; and it is low, low, low. In music, in speech, in manner, the upper has learned to imitate the lower. Cheapened imprecise speech is the triumph of James's tribute to emulation; it is the only possible legacy that could have come of the principle of emulation.

Then why did James plead for vocal imitation instead of reading? He lived in a sea of reading, at the highest tide of literacy, in the time of the crashing of its billows. He did not dream that the sea would shrink, that it was impermanent, that we would return, through the most refined technologies, to the aural culture. He had had his own dealings with a continuing branch of the aural culture—the theater. He had written for it as if for a body of accomplished readers, and it turned on him with contempt. "Forget not," he warned in the wake of his humiliation as a playwright, "that you must write for the stupid—that is, your maximum of refinement must meet the minimum of intelligence of the audience—the intelligence, in other words, of the biggest ass it may conceivably contain. It is a most unholy trade!" He was judging, in this outcry, all those forms that arrange for the verbal to bypass the eye and enter solely through the ear. The ear is, for subtlety of interpretation, a coarser organ than the eye; it follows that nearly all verbal culture designed for the ear is broader, brighter, larger, louder, simpler, less intimate, more insistent—more *theatrical*— than any page of any book.

For the population in general, the unholy trades—they are now tremendously in the plural, having proliferated—have rendered reading nearly obsolete, except as a source of data and as a means of record-keeping—"warehousing information." For this the computer is an admittedly startling advance over Pharaoh's indefatigably meticulous scribes, notwithstanding the lofty liturgical poetry that adorned the ancient records, offering a tendril of beauty among the granary lists. Pragmatic reading cannot die, of course, but as the experience that feeds *Homo ridens*, reading is already close to moribund. In the new aural culture of America, intellectuals habitually define "film" as "art" in the most solemn sense, as a counterpart of the literary novel, and ridicule survivors of the age of "movies" as naïfs incapable of making the transition from an old form of popular entertainment to a new form of serious expression meriting a sober equation with written art—as if the issue had anything to do with what is inherently complex in the medium, rather than with what is inherently complex in the recipient of the medium. Undoubtedly any movie is more "complicated' than any book; and also more limited by the apparatus of the "real." As James noted, the maker of aural culture brings to his medium a "maximum of refinement"—i.e., he does the best he can with what he has to work with; sometimes he is even Shakespeare. But the job of sitting in a theater or in a movie house or at home in front of a television set is not so reciprocally complex as the wheels-within-wheels job of reading almost anything at all (including the comics). Reading is an

262

act of imaginative conversion. That specks on a paper can turn into tale or philosophy is as deep a marvel as alchemy or wizardry. A secret brush construes phantom portraits. In the proscenium or the VCR everything is imagined *for* one: there is nothing to do but see and hear, and what's there is what is literally there. When film is "poetic," it is almost never because of language, but rather because of the resemblance to paintings or engravings—one thinks of the knight on a horse in a field of flowers in Bergman's *The Virgin Spring*. Where film is most art, it is least a novelty.

The new aural culture is prone to appliance-novelty—a while ago who could have predicted the video recorder or the hand-held miniature television set, and who now knows what variations and inventions lie ahead? At the same time there is a rigidity to the products of the aural culture—like those static Egyptian sculptures, stylistically unaltered for three millennia, that are brilliantly executed but limited in imaginative intent.

In the new aural culture there is no prevalent belles-lettres curriculum to stimulate novel imaginative intent, that "wizard note" of the awakened Enchantress; what there is is replication—not a reverberation or an echo, but a copy. The Back to Basics movement in education, which on the surface looks as if it is calling for revivification of a belles-lettres syllabus, is not so much reactionary as lost in literalism, or *trompe l'oeil*: another example of the replication impulse of the new aural culture, the culture of theater. Only in a *trompe l'oeil* society would it occur to anyone to "bring back the old values" through bringing back the McGuffey Reader—a scenic designer's idea, and still another instance of the muddle encouraged by the notion of "emulation." The celebration of the McGuffey Reader can happen only in an atmosphere where "film," a copyist's medium, is taken as seriously as a book.

A book is not a "medium" at all; it is far spookier than that, one of the few things-in-themselves that we can be sure of, a Platonic form that can inhabit a virtual infinity of experimental incarnations: any idea, any story, any body of poetry, any incantation, in any language. Above all, a book is the riverbank for the river of language. Language without the riverbank is only television talk—a free fall, a loose splash, a spill. And that is what an aural society, following a time of complex literacy, finally admits to: spill and more spill. James had nothing to complain of: he flourished in a period when whoever read well could speak well; the rest was provincialism—or call it, in kindness, regional exclusiveness. Still, the river of language—to cling to the old metaphor—ran most forcefully when confined to the banks that governed its course. But we who come after the hundred-year hegemony of the ordinary reader, we who see around us, in all these heaps of appliances (each one a plausible "electronic miracle"), the dying heaves of the caste-free passion for letters, should know how profoundly—and possibly how irreversibly—the mummers have claimed us.

ANNALS OF THE TEMPLE
1918–1927

A CENTURY, LIKE any entrenched institution, runs on inertia and is inherently laggard. Even when commanded by the calendar, it will not easily give up the ghost. The turn of the century, as the wistful phrase has it, hardly signifies the brisk swing of a gate on its hinge: a century turns, rather, like a rivulet – a silky, lazy, unwitting flow around a silent bend. Whatever the twenty-first century (seemingly only minutes away) may bring, we, entering it, will go on being what we are: creatures born into, and molded and muddied by, the twentieth.

And the twentieth, too, did not properly begin with the demise of the nineteenth. When the fabled Armory Show introduced modern art to New York in 1913, the American cultural establishment (to use a term typically ours, not theirs) was in the governing hands of men born before the Civil War—men who were marked by what Santayana, as early as 1911, had already condemned as "the genteel tradition." Apart from the unjust condescensions of hindsight, and viewed in the not-so-easily scorned light of its own standards, what *was* the genteel tradition? Its adherents, after all, did not know themselves to be pre-modernist; they did not know that a volcanic alteration of taste and expression was about to consume the century; they did not know that irony and pastiche and parody and a conscious fever of innovation-through-rupture would overcome notions of nobility, spirituality, continuity, harmony, uncomplicated patriotism, romanticized classicism. It did not occur to them

265

that the old patterns were threadbare, or could be repudiated on grounds of exhaustion.

To be able to say what the men of the genteel tradition (its constituents were nearly all men) did know, and what they saw themselves as, and what they in fact were, would lead us directly to the sublimely conceived fellowship they established to embody their ideals—a kind of latterday temple to the Muses. And the word "temple" is apt: it calls up an alabaster palace on a hill; an elite priesthood; ceremonial devotions pursued in a serious though lyrical frame of mind— a resolute thoughtfulness saturated in notions of beauty and virtue, and turned from the trivial, the frivolous, the ephemeral. The name these aspirants gave to their visionary society—a working organization, finally, with a flesh-and-blood membership and headquarters in New York—was the American Academy of Arts and Letters.

The cornerstone of what was to become the Academy's permanent home, a resplendent Venetian Renaissance edifice just off Riverside Drive on West 155th Street, was laid on November 19, 1921, by Marshal Ferdinand Foch of France. The commander-in-chief of the Allied forces in the First World War, Foch was summoned to wield a ritual trowel not only as the hero of the recent victory over the Kaiser, but— more gloriously still—as an emissary of French cultural prestige. The nimbus of power that followed him from Paris to this plot of freshly broken ground along the remote northern margins of Manhattan was kindled as much by his membership in the French Academy as by his battlefield triumphs.

The venerable French Academy, founded by Cardinal Richelieu to maintain the purity of the French language, and limited to forty "Immortals," had preceded its New World counterpart (or would-be counterpart) by some two and a half centuries. Though this august company of scholars and men of letters was to serve as inspiration and aristocratic model, American democratic principles demanded a wider roster based on a bicameral system: hence membership in the American Academy was open to as many as fifty, and these fifty were selected by ballot from the two hundred and fifty distinguished authors, painters, sculptors, architects, and composers of the National Institute of Arts and Letters, the lower (and older) body. And while the "chairs" of the French Academy were phantom chairs—metaphoric, platonic— American pragmatism (and one Mrs. Cochran Bowen, who donated the requisite five thousand dollars) supplied *real* chairs, with arms and backs of dark polished wood, each with a plaque for its occupant's name.

The homegrown Richelieu of this grand structure of mind and marble was Robert Underwood Johnson, a powerful magazine editor and tireless poet who, though not precisely the organization's founder, was present at the Academy's earliest meetings, and as Permanent Secretary was its dominating spirit for the first three decades. In 1920 he disappeared, temporarily, having been appointed United States Ambassador to Italy. A 1922 newspaper photograph of Johnson— occasioned by a dispute with the Internal Revenue Department over unpaid taxes on ambassadorial meals and lodgings—shows a determined elderly gentleman with a steady yet relentless eye and a rather fierce pince-nez, the ribbon of which flows down over a full white beard and high collar. Unfortunately, no mouth is visible; it would be instructive to see the lips that so often speechified at Academy events, or adorned the hour with original verse. In still another portrait—a wood engraving by Timothy Cole, artist and Academy member—the Johnsonian mouth is again concealed under a cloud of furry whiskers, but the stiff cravat, scimitar nose, straight spine, and erect head are eloquent enough. They declare a fine facsimile of a Roman bust, attentive to what is noble and what is not—the face and figure of a man of established importance, a man who knows his worth: editor of *The Century*, Ambassador to Italy, Director of the Hall of Fame, Secretary of the American Academy of Arts and Letters.

Above all it is the face and figure of the nineteenth century, when the ideal of the publicly Noble could still stir the Western world. Together with the Harmonious, the Noble spoke in lofty statuary, in the balanced configurations of painting and music, in the white pilasters of heirloom architecture—but nowhere more melodiously than in the poetry that descended (though somewhat frayed by over-handling) from Keats.

The cornerstone affixed by Marshal Foch—in high-laced boots and full uniform—on that rainy November afternoon in 1921 was a hollow repository. In it Brander Matthews, Chancellor of the Academy and a professor of literature at Columbia University, placed numerous historic articles and documents—congratulatory messages from the President of the United States, from the Governor of New York, from the Academies of Belgium, Rome, Spain, and Brazil; papers recording the Special Symposium on Diction; "Utterances by Members of the Academy Concerning the War of 1914–1918," bound in purple; replicas and photographs of medals, including one presented to Marshal Foch by the American Numismatic Society (located next door); minutes of meetings; commemorative addresses; and a holographic copy of a dedicatory poem by Robert Underwood Johnson:

The Temple

If this be but a house, whose stone we place,
   Better the prayer unbreathed, the music mute
   Ere it be stifled in the rifted lute;
Better had been withheld those hands of grace,
Undreamed the dream that was this moment's base
   Through nights that did the empty days refute.
   Accurs'd the fig-tree if it bear no fruit;
Only the flower sanctifies the vase.
No, 'tis a temple—where the mind may kneel
   And worship Beauty changeless and divine;
     Where the sage Past may consecrate the stole
Of Truth's new priest, the Future; where the peal
   Of organ voices down the human line
   Shall sound the diapason of the soul.

And there it was: the echoing legacy of Keats. But Keats's season of mists and mellow fruitfulness had long since passed into fog and desiccation; the Romantic exhalations of the last century—a century more than twenty years gone—could not be kept going by pumping up a useless bellows that had run out of breath. The cornerstone may have received the pious mimicry of "The Temple" as its chief treasure, but modernism (one of its names was Ezra Pound) was pounding at the Temple's gates, shattering the sage Past and slighting the old forms of Beauty.

The Temple was not unaware of these shocking new vibrations: it derided and dismissed them. In 1925, in an address before the Academy-Institute (as the two closely allied bodies came to be called), three years after the publication of "The Waste Land," Robert Underwood Johnson pointed to T. S. Eliot as one of the "prominent apostles" of "this so-called modern American poetry," and scolded him for prosiness and lack of taste and humor, while praising "the dignity and beauty of Landor's invocation to an English brook." (Walter Savage Landor, it might be noted, was born in 1775 and died in 1864, when Johnson was eleven years old.) Quoting lines from Marianne Moore, Johnson asked, "What is the remedy for this disease?" "The Academy's chief influence," he concluded, "will come from what and whom it recognizes, what and whom it praises, and what and whom it puts forth."

In the extraordinary literary decade that followed the Great War, the Academy neither recognized nor praised nor put forth nor took in T. S. Eliot, Ezra Pound, Marianne Moore, William Carlos Williams, Hart Crane, Wallace Stevens, Conrad Aiken, H. D., Louise Bogan, John Crowe Ransom, or E. E. Cummings—revolutionaries, in their varying degrees, of voice, theme, and line. Not since Whitman had there been such a configuration of fresh sound in American verse; it engulfed the poets of the Harlem Renaissance, Langston Hughes and Jean Toomer among them, and burned brilliantly, though in another language, among the American Yiddish imagists of the *In Zikh* movement farther downtown. Beauty, it seemed, was turning out to be neither changeless nor divine: it could take the form of the Brooklyn Bridge, and manifest itself in idioms and accents that an unreceptive Temple, immaculately devoted to the difference between "can" and "may" (the Academy's task, Johnson said, was to preserve this distinction), might be oblivious to at best, or at worst recoil from.

Established in 1898 as an outgrowth of the American Social Science Association, the National Institute of Arts and Letters flourished alone until 1904, when it gave birth to the American Academy of Arts and Letters, its hierarchical superior. The Academy was incorporated by an Act of Congress on April 17, 1916; its first president, who served from 1908 to 1920, was William Dean Howells, one of the few early Academicians whose names are recognizable to later generations. *The Rise of Silas Lapham* may not be much read today—not, say, as *The Great Gatsby* is read, zealously and regularly—but Howells (who was long ago dropped from routine high school curricula) is nevertheless permanently lodged in American history. He was succeeded as president (from his death in 1920 to Sloane's death in 1928) by William Milligan Sloane, a professor of history at Columbia University, the author of a mammoth four-volume *Life of Napoleon Bonaparte* and of seven other equally ambitious works. A public presence—an eminence—in his time, Sloane must now be researched in the *Dictionary of American Biography*.

And so it is with numerous others. The cycle of generations dims if not eclipses even the most illustrious, and if an examination of the Academy-Institute's membership reveals nothing else, it surely affirms the melancholy wisdom of Ecclesiastes. Yet one need not go to the Preacher to learn how there is "no remembrance of former things"; sometimes biblical perspective comes without waiting so much as a day. In 1923—the very year the Academy moved into its just-completed Renaissance palace—Burton Roscoe, a journalist with the *New York Tribune*, targeted the Temple's newest anointed: "[W]hen Mr. Johnson handed me a list of the fledglings upon whom the organization had just conferred harps and wings and other eternal impediments, I was even more startled to observe that scarcely one of the twenty outstanding literary personages of America was included, but a whole roster of nobodies whose careers were so limited and obscure that I had to spend an hour or so in the morgue after I got back to the office to find out what they had done or written." Roscoe's literary nobodies of 1923 included John Spencer Bassett, James Bucklin Bishop, Owen David, Burton

J. Hendrick, Rollo Ogden—names that, if they meant nothing to Roscoe, are merest dust to us. But Eugene O'Neill was on that same list, and Don Marquis (the celebrated progenitor of Archie the Cockroach); and if Roscoe—himself reduced now to one of the nobodies—had looked back a few years, from 1918 on (i.e., from the end of the war), he would have encountered literary somebodies we still remember, and sometimes even read: James Gibbon Huneker, Edgar Lee Masters, Irving Babbitt, John Erskine, Joseph Hergesheimer, and Bernard Berenson.

Still, the forgotten Burton Roscoe is not mistaken about the forgettable among his own contemporaries, or about the deadly absence of "outstanding literary personages." During the Academy's third decade of life—the vital cultural period between 1918 and 1927—the single major American writer to attain membership was Edith Wharton. (A belated elevation that took place in 1926, after an effort toward securing the admission of women finally prevailed over an acrimonious opposition.) Whereas in the world beyond the Temple—to confine our inquiry at this moment to literature only—there was an innovative ferment so astounding (and exhilarating) that no other segment of the twentieth century can match it. Consider: 1918 saw the publication of Willa Cather's *My Antonia*, Lytton Strachey's *Eminent Victorians*, the first installments of James Joyce's Ulysses, volumes by Rebecca West and H. L. Mencken; *The Education of Henry Adams* won the Pulitzer Prize; the Theater Guild was founded in New York; in Germany, the Dada movement began; in Russia, Aleksandr Blok was writing poetry in praise of the Bolshevik Revolution (without suspecting that its dissolution eight decades later would draw equal praise).

The following year brought *Winesburg, Ohio*, by Sherwood Anderson: *Jurgen*, by James Branch Cabell; *The Arrow of Gold*, by Joseph Conrad; *La Symphonie pastorale*, by André Gide; *Damian*, by Hermann Hesse; *The Moon and Sixpence*, by Somerset Maugham—and Carl Sandburg won the Pulitzer. Finally, the next eight years—1920 to 1927—introduced a torrent of works by F. Scott Fitzgerald, John Galsworthy, Katherine Mansfield, Max Beerbohm, H. G.

Wells, Sigrid Undset, John Dos Passos, Aldous Huxley, D. H. Lawrence, George Bernard Shaw, Luigi Pirandello, Bertolt Brecht, T. S. Eliot, Sinclair Lewis, François Mauriac, Virginia Woolf, Stefan Zweig, Rainer Maria Rilke, Italo Svevo, Robert Frost, Colette, S. Ansky, E. M. Forster, Edna Ferber, Thomas Mann, Maxwell Anderson, Michael Arlen, Theodore Dreiser, Maxim Gorky, Franz Kafka, Gertrude Stein, Edward Arlington Robinson, Ernest Hemingway, W. E. B. DuBois, T. E. Lawrence, Sean O'Casey, William Faulkner, Jean Cocteau, William Butler Yeats, Thornton Wilder, Henri Bergson. Mixed though these writers are in theme, genre, nationality, and degree of achievement, they represent, on the literary side, what we mean when we speak of the Twenties—an era staggering in its deliverance from outworn voices and overly familiar modes and moods. Not all were "experimental"; indeed, most were not; but all claimed an idiosyncratic distinction between their own expectations of language and art and the expectations of the author of "The Temple."

Some of the Americans among them did finally gain admission to the Academy-Institute, but not without opposition. To combat the new streams of expression, Harrison Smith Morris—a writer elected to the Institute in 1908—proposed a Resolution:

> The National Institute of Arts and Letters in its long established office of upholder of Taste and Beauty in Arts and Letters in America, welcomes the approach of a return to the standards made sacred by tradition and by the genius of the great periods of the past.
>
> The National Institute feels that the time has arrived to distinguish the good from the bad in the Arts, and to urge those who have loved the literature and painting that are accepted by the winnowing hand of time to turn away from the Falsehoods of this period and again to embrace only the genuine expressions of man's genius.
>
> And the National Institute calls upon all those who write or speak on this essential subject of our culture as a

nation, to ask their hearers to join in abhorrence of the offences, and to insist on the integrity of our arts.

Though the archives of the Academy do not yield information on how the members voted (or at least I have been unable to uncover the results), the Resolution itself was in profound consonance with the views held by the Permanent Secretary, Robert Underwood Johnson himself. And Johnson in effect ran things, despite the status of the men at the top— Howells, then Sloane, later Nicholas Murray Butler; Johnson was the Academy's primary engine. A first-rate organizer and administrator, he single-handedly acquired an endowment for the Academy—or, rather, he acquired the friendship and loyalty of Archer Milton Huntington, an extraordinarily wealthy donor with a generous temperament and a serious interest in Spanish culture. Huntington, a railway magnate's son, owned the empty plot of land on West 155th Street (across the street from Trinity cemetery, a northern extension of the historic Wall Street church), and offered it free; he also pledged $100,000 in endowment funds if enough money could be raised by 1919 to build on the land. Spurred on by this promise, Johnson went in zealous pursuit of the extra money, but came back with empty pockets. Huntington extended the deadline; still no other large-scale benefactor appeared. Huntington withdrew his terms and supplied the building funds himself; in addition, he showered the Academy with periodic gifts ($475,000 in 1923, $100,000 in 1927, $500,000 in 1929), so that within a very short span a membership that was only recently being dunned for dues found itself cushioned and cosseted by prosperity.

At the annual meeting of 1925, Johnson spoke of Huntington as "a permanent friend of the Academy who desires to remain permanently anonymous." This was certainly true; yet Huntington—who quickly became a member of the Academy, and whose second wife, a sculptor, was herself eventually elected—was not without intimations of immortality. In an autographed poem dedicated to the Academy and entitled "Genius," and in a style reminiscent of Johnson's own, he wrote in praise of "this oriflamme of glory":

High mystery prophetic that men cry!
The splendid diadem of hearts supreme,
Who shape reality from hope's vast dream
And gild with flame new pantheons in the sky!
Thus are we led to nobly raise on high
An edifice of deeds that may redeem
The lowliness of being, 'neath the gleam
Of mists all colorless where life must lie.

(There was a follow-up stanza as well.)

Huntington was Johnson's organizational masterstroke–a funding triumph with recognizably lofty verbal credentials, capable of gilding new pantheons with cash. But Johnson's executive instincts pulled off a second administrative coup— in the shape of Mrs. Grace Vanamee, who was enlisted as the Permanent Secretary's permanent deputy in the fall of 1915. A widow in her forties, Mrs. Vanamee was a kind of robust Johnsonian reverberation: if he was exuberantly efficient, so was she; if he was determined that no concern, however minuscule, should go unresolved, so was she. Mrs. Vanamee was, in brief, an unflagging enthusiast. She is reputed to have been a woman of large dimensions (though there is no one alive who can claim to have set eyes on her), and even larger energies. Like Johnson, she could successfully concentrate on several activities at once. On the side, so to speak, Johnson oversaw New York University's Hall of Fame; Mrs. Vanamee directed the Organization of Soldiers' Families of America. A public lecturer herself, she was also chair of the Republican Women's State Speakers' Bureau and founder of the Women's National Republican Club; during the war she served as secretary of the Italian War Relief Committee, for which she earned a medal from the Italian Red Cross. Her career as celebrated Academy factotum (a combination of executive director and chief housekeeper) began in a "sordid little office" at 70 Fifth Avenue equipped with an ancient secondhand typewriter bought for twenty dollars. Huntington soon provided a more suitable venue, a building he owned on West 81st Street, which was rapidly refurbished with offices, an auditorium, and living quarters for Mrs.

274

Vanamee. There was, in addition, a President's Room decorated with a mahogany desk and green leather chairs and fine carpeting, at a cost of fifteen hundred dollars. Only two years later, when the West 155th Street edifice was ready to be occupied, all this would be dismantled.

But in the meantime, Mrs. Vanamee was in charge of caring for the now lavishly outfitted interim building—though not alone. A certain Frank P. Crasto emerges here as her indispensable assistant and sidekick; it is possible that he may represent our history's love-interest. (The archives, it goes without saying, are silent on this point.) Mrs. Vanamee's early widowhood was enlivened by an open and famously zippy character, and her correspondence with this or that member of the Academy occasionally bordered on the flirtatious. In the middle of so much dense Victorian formality, she was even capable of an indiscreet anecdote: if not for Mrs. Vanamee, posterity would still be in the dark about the Pinching of the Trowel. In her account of Marshal Foch and the West 155th Street cornerstone ceremony—"President Sloane almost white with excitement, Mr. Johnson radiant because his dreams had come true"—she describes how "the little Marèchal was tired and had to hurry away, and as he did so to our great amusement and consternation we saw that he had absent-mindedly thrust the lovely little silver trowel into his hip pocket, but we never saw it again."

This cheery neglect of reverence for the great French military leader did not extend to Frank P. Crasto, himself a military man. Mrs. Vanamee identified him as "a Captain in the Reserves [who] knows what it is to inspect buildings and equipment and to maintain discipline as well as order and cleanliness," and added, with the esteem due such things, that "he understands all about printing, and is an expert proof-reader." He was also found to be useful in handling the heavy work. Captain Crasto became Major Crasto, and Major Crasto was promoted to Colonel Crasto—ascending titles that Mrs. Vanamee noted with veneration. His maintenance responsibilities were perhaps less lofty than his officer status would suggest—at the Academy Board meeting of May 11, 1921, for instance, he reported that one hundred and thirty-eight of the three hundred and ten light bulbs at West 81st Street were out. Eventually he was raised to the post of Librarian; but his ascent in Mrs. Vanamee's affections had evidently occurred long before. In times of sickness they spelled each other. In 1923, when she was seriously ill in a Brooklyn hospital (but she lived until 1946), all inquiries concerning her condition were directed to the Colonel, and it was she who in 1925 packed him off on a recuperative steamer trip to New Orleans after a heart episode: "there is nothing pressing at the Academy," she urged. One gets the inescapable impression of a pair of turtle doves under the Temple's eaves.

Mrs. Vanamee, the Colonel, and, of course, the Permanent Secretary all moved on together to West 155th Street. Huntington carried out his plan to sell the West 81st Street building (he intended to use the profits as endowment funds) despite pressure from Wytter Bynner of the Poetry Society of America, who hoped to rent it as a meeting place for "all the Poetry Societies of America." The idea was discussed by the Academy Board early in 1922 and quickly rejected. Brander Matthews dismissed such a convention of poets as "a large body of very small people," and Robert Underwood Johnson declined to place "the Academy's stamp of approval on the lack of standards of the Poetry Society." (Its membership at the time included Stephen Vincent Benet, Carl Sandburg, and Edwin Arlington Robinson, all of whom Johnson scorned.)

It was in this same year that Sinclair Lewis, elected to Institute membership, angrily rejected it, unwilling to place *his* stamp of approval on the Academy or any part of it. Seven years later, accepting the Nobel Prize for Literature before the Swedish Academy in Stockholm, he excoriated its American counterpart: "It does not represent literary America of today. It represents only Henry Wadsworth Longfellow." (And in 1979 Witter Bynner had *his* revenge, albeit posthumously, with the establishment of the Academy's Witter Bynner Prize for Poetry.) The Academy was offended by Lewis but unruffled. The Board went on to review of roster of quotations that might be appropriate to stand as a frieze across the brow of the new building. Aperçus by Cicero, Lucian, Pericles, Plato, Aristotle, and Emerson were proposed, none of which satisfied—whereupon Johnson remarked that a member might be moved (he may have been thinking of himself) to write something original. The wording for the frieze was not determined until 1924, a year after the opening of the building. Brander Matthews made the selection: HOLD HIGH THE FLAMING TORCH FROM AGE TO AGE. When the architects asked for a second quotation, Matthews supplied them with ALL ARTS ARE ONE ALL BRANCHES ON ONE TREE. (The sources for both lines are unknown.)

The estimated cost of the finished Temple as presented to the Academy by the architects—McKim, Meade, and White, all three of whom were members—was $380,223.04, though the final bill probably exceeded half a million. The doors were heavy bronze. An early sketch of the façade before completion shows a pair of neoclassical sculptures in embrasures, and while these draped female figures, goddesses or Muses, at length vanished from the plans and were never executed, their spirit stuck fast. Standford White was the designer of New York University's neoclassical campus on University Heights, and Charles F. McKim presided over Columbia's Beaux Arts buildings on Morningside Heights; both were visionaries of an ideal acropolis conceived as an echo (or rebirth) of older cities grown legendary through literature and art.

It was the same echo that had sounded in Robert Underwood Johnson's ear since his days at Earlham College, a small Quaker institution in Indiana that emphasized Latin and "the human element of Virgil, Horace, Tacitus, Cicero." Even the college-boy jokes were in Latin: a classroom was dubbed *Nugipolyloquidium*, "a place of talkers of nonsense." Out of all this came the lingering faith that the classical is the eternal, and that the past, because it *is* the past, holds a sacred and permanent power—a view that differs from the historical sense, with its awareness (in contradistinction to Truth and Beauty) of evolution, displacement, violence and oppression, migration of populations, competing intellectual movements, the decline and fall of even contemporary societies and cultures. The achievement of such a serene outlook will depend on one's distance from strikes, riots, destitution, foreign eruptions, the effects of prejudice, immigrants pressing in at Ellis Island, and all the rest. Inland Earlham in 1867, when Johnson was a freshman there, is deservedly called "tranquil"—"Tranquil Days at Earlham" is a chapter in Johnson's autobiographical *Remembered Yesterdays*, self-published in 1923 (just when Marshal Foch was pocketing the silver trowel); and tranquility was the goal and soul of Johnson's artistic understanding. "We were charmed by the mountain scenery of the Gulf of Corinth, every peak and vale of which is haunted by mythological associations," he writes in a chapter entitled "Delight and Humor of Foreign Travel." "The Bay of Salamis gave us a thrill and at Eleusis we seemed to come in close touch with classic days, for here was the scene of the still unexplained Eleusinian mysteries." Living Greeks—at their rustic best, since "the urban Greek is undersized and unimpressive"—are admired solely as an ornamental allusion: "Some of them resembled fine Italian types, one or two reminding me of the elder Salvini," an Italian tragedian. More gratifying than these Greeks in the flesh are the crucial landmarks: "I stayed up until one o'clock at night to catch sight of the beacon on the 'Leucadian steep' which marks the spot from which Sappho is reputed to have thrown herself." "One may well imagine that three fourths of the time we spent in Athens was passed on the Acropolis."

This was the sensibility that dreamed and labored over and built the American Academy of Arts and Letters. Johnson came to this task—this passion—after forty years at *The Century,* the magazine that succeeded *Scribner's Monthly.* Its editor-in-chief was Richard Watson Gilder, a poet hugely overpraised by his contemporaries ("An echo of Dantean mysticism . . . He wanders in the highest realms of spiritual poetry") and wholly dismissed by their descendants. As editor-cum-poet, he was uniquely qualified to be mentor and model for Johnson, whom Gilder appointed associate editor in 1881. Gilder's own mentor and model was Edmund Clarence Stedman, himself a mediocre poet of the idealist school; both Stedman and Gilder were Academy members. Although

Alfred Kazin (a present-day Academician) describes Gilder as "a very amiable man whom some malicious fortune set up as a perfect symbol of all that the new writers [of the Twenties] were to detest," he was, for Johnson and his generation, the perfect symbol of all that belles-lettres and an elevated civilization required. Nor were Johnson and his generation misled. *The Century* was the most powerful literary periodical of its time, a genuine influence in the formation of American letters. In 1885, for example, the February issue alone carried—remarkably—excerpts from Mark Twain's *Huckleberry Finn*, Howell's *The Rise of Silas Lapham*, and James's *The Bostonians*. Gilder was a believer in purity of theme, which drew him away from certain subjects; Johnson was Gilder's even more cautious copy. In 1904, when, despite the editorial risk, Gilder wanted to publish Edith Wharton— he was shrewd enough to see that she was "on the eve of a great popular success"—Johnson demurred: Wharton had written stories about divorce. At Gilder's death in 1909 Johnson took over as editor-in-chief. The decline of *The Century* is usually attributed, at least in part, to his inability to respond to changing public taste and expectation. The trustees, at any rate, found him inflexible; he resigned in 1913.

He was then sixty years old, in full and effective vigor, with a strong activist bent and an affinity for citizenly service. He was an advocate, a man of causes. At *The Century* he had promoted the conservation of forests and was instrumental in getting Congressional sanction for the creation of Yosemite National Park. It was he who persuaded a coolly reticent General Ulysses S. Grant to set down an emotional memoir of the battle of Shiloh. As secretary of a committee of authors and publishers, Johnson lobbied for international copyright and fought against the pirating of foreign books. His ardor spilled over into nine volumes of verse, all self-published, on subjects both sublime and civic, often interwoven: "The Vision of Gettysburg," "The Price of Honor: The Colombian Indemnity," "The New Slavery (On The Expatriation by Germany of Civil Populations of Belgium)," "Armenia," "Henrik Ibsen, The Tribute of an Idealist," "To the Spirit of Luther:

On Learning of the Reported Appeal of Germany to Matrons and Maidens to Give Themselves 'Officially' to the Propagation of the Race, Under Immunity from the Law." There are poems on the Dreyfus Affair: "The Keeper of the Sword (Apropos of the Dreyfus Trial at Rennes)" and "To Dreyfus Vindicated." The talent may have been middling, but the goodwill, and the prophetic vigilance, were mammoth.

If, as Emerson insists, the shipbuilder is the ship, then Robert Underwood Johnson was, long before its founding, the American Academy of Arts and Letters. There can be no useful history of the Academy that fails to contemplate Johnson's mind. Whatever ignited his enthusiasm, whatever struck him as repugnant—these formed the mind of the Academy. It was not that Johnson was dictatorial—on the contrary, he was elaborately courtly, and punctilious as to protocol. (As Permanent Secretary, he sent himself a deferential letter announcing his election to the Academy, and, with equal deference, wrote back to accept the honor.) He did no violence to the opinion of others; rather, his opinion was generally the opinion of the membership, and vice-versa. It may have been the Muses themselves who nurtured such unanimity; or else it was the similarity of background of these cultivated gentlemen, similarly educated, similarly situated in society, each with his triplet of rhythmically interchangeable names, all of them patriots, yet all looking toward an older Europe for continuity of purpose—with one urgent European exception.

The exception was Germany in the Great War. The Academy, most notably in the person of Robert Underwood Johnson, threw itself indefatigably into the war effort against Germany, contributing $100,000 to Italy and over one hundred ambulances presented in the name of the poets of America. Though the hostilities had come to an end with the November armistice of 1918, the Academy's hostility remained white-hot into the following year, with the publication of its *World War Utterances*. Here patriotism over-reached itself into unrestrained fury. In an essay called "The Incredible Cruelty of the Teutons," William Dean Howells— the most benignly moderate of novelists—asked: "Can anyone say what the worst wickedness of the Germans has been? If you choose one there are always other crimes which contest your choice. We used at first to fix the guilt of them upon the Kaiser, but event by event we have come to realize that no man or order of men can pervert a whole people without their complicity."

Luminary after luminary joined the cry, under titles such as "Can Peace Make Us Forget? A Plea for the Ostracism of All Things German"; "The Shipwreck of Kultur"; "The Crime of the *Lusitania*"; "Germany's Shame." "The nation which had invited our admiration for its *Gemütlichkeit* instantly aroused our abhorrence for its *Schrecklichkeit*," wrote Brander Matthews. And Nicholas Murray Butler, condemning Germany's "principle of world domination," compared German conquest and subjection of peoples to Alexander the Great, the legions of Rome, Charlemagne, Bonaparte, and, finally, "the Hebrews of old." (As the author of Columbia University's notorious and long-lasting Jewish quota, Butler—quite apart from his Academy activities, where such views were never expressed—apparently also feared conquest by later Hebrews.) Woodrow Wilson, who had campaigned for the Presidency with the slogan "He kept us out of war"— to the disgust of his more belligerent colleagues at the Academy—now spoke of Germany as "throwing to the winds all scruples of humanity" while engaged in "a warfare against mankind." In his "Note on German Music and German Ideas," Horatio Parker, one of the period's nearly forgotten composers, could not resist making a plea for German music, especially Bach, Richard Strauss, and Mendelssohn ("It is as useless to deny the beauty and greatness of classical masterpieces by Germans as it is to deny the same qualities in their mountains"); nevertheless he concluded that "prejudice of the public and of officials in this country against *modern* German music is perhaps justifiable."

In these exhortations to hatred and ostracism, the Academy's impulse was no different from the anti-German clamor that was everywhere in the American street. From our distance, the bitter words may seem overreactive and hyperchauvinist. Still, reading these papers now three quarters of a century old, one feels a curious displacement of rage—a vertiginous sense of the premature, as of an hourglass set mistakenly on its head. The sinking of the *Lusitania*, merciless act of war though it was, was not yet Auschwitz. If Howells, say, had written as he did, not in 1918 but in 1945, after the exposure of the crematoria, how would we judge his judgment? It is sometimes an oddity of history that the right thing is said at the wrong time.

And it may be that, in the third decade of its life, many things were spoken at the Academy at the wrong time. When the war was over, Johnson turned his energies once again to the celebration of a type of high culture. And again there looked to be a displacement of timing. In 1919, race riots broke out in Chicago and a dock workers' strike hit New York; the eight-hour workday was instituted nationally; President Woodrow Wilson won the Nobel Peace Prize and presided over the first meeting of the League of Nations in Paris; the Red Army took Omsk, Kharkov, and the Crimea; Mussolini founded the Italian fascist movement; Paderewski became Premier of Poland. Henri Bergson, Karl Barth, Ernst Cassirer, Havelock Ellis, Karl Jaspers, John Maynard Keynes, Rudolf Steiner—indelible figures—were all active in their various spheres. Short-wave radio made its earliest appearance, there was progress in sound for movies, and Einstein's theory of relativity was borne out by astrophysical experiments. Walter Gropius developed the Bauhaus in Germany and revolutionized painting, architecture, sculpture, and the industrial arts. Kandinsky, Klee, and Modigliani were at work, and Picasso designed the set of Diaghilev's *The Three Cornered Hat*. Jazz headed for Europe; the Los Angeles Symphony gave its initial concert; the Juilliard School of Music opened in New York and the New Symphony Orchestra, conducted by Edgard Varèse, inaugurated a hearing for modern music. A nonstop flight across the Atlantic was finally accomplished. Babe Ruth hit a 587-foot home run. The Nobel Prize for Literature went to Knut Hamsun.

In short, 1919 was the beginning of a deluge of new forms, new sounds, new ventures, new arrangements in the world. And in such an hour the Academy undertook to mark the centennial of James Russell Lowell, who had died twenty-eight years before. In itself, the choice was pleasant and not inappropriate. A leading American eminence of the nineteenth century, a man of affairs as well as a man of letters, a steady opponent of slavery, Lowell was poet, critic, literary historian. He was vigorous in promoting the study of modern languages, which he taught at Harvard. He was, besides, *The Atlantic Monthly*'s first editor and (with Charles Eliot Norton) a founder of *The North American Review*. He served as American ambassador to the Court of Spain, and afterwards as emissary to Britain. His complete works—both verse and prose—occupy ten volumes. According to Lowell's biographer, Horace E. Scudder—member of the Institute and author of a laudatory *Encyclopaedia Britannica* article on Lowell that is virtually contemporaneous with the Academy's celebratory event—Lowell "impressed himself deeply on his generation in America, especially upon the thoughtful and scholarly class who looked upon him as their representative." Johnson unquestionably looked on Lowell as his representative; Lowell's career—poet, editor, ambassador—was an ideal template for Johnson's own.

The centennial program, subtitled "In Celebration of the Unity and Power of the Literature of the English-speaking People," was intended to emphasize the ongoing link with the Mother Country. To further this connection, invitations went out to, among others, Prime Minister Herbert Asquith, Robert Bridges (the Poet Laureate), Rudyard Kipling, James Barrie, Conan Doyle, Gilbert Chesterton, Gilbert Murray, Arthur Quiller-Couch, Edmund Gosse, Alfred Noyes, and John Galsworthy. Ambitious though this roster was (it ran after nearly every living luminary of that scepter'd isle), only the last two accepted and actually arrived—Galsworthy with the proviso that he would attend the gala luncheon "*so long as this does not entail a speech.*" Stephen Leacock came with a troop of notables from Canada, and Australia was represented by one lone guest.

Still, a demonstration of the unity and power of literary Anglo-Saxonism was not, as it turned out, the whole purpose of the centennial. Nor was it precisely as an act of historic commemoration that Johnson sought to honor Lowell. On February 13, 1919, a New York newspaper, *The Evening Post*, explained: "James Russell Lowell, who was born a hundred years ago next week . . . would not have liked Vers Libre or modern verse in general, says Robert Underwood Johnson . . . Mr. Johnson knew Lowell personally." The *Post* went on to quote the Permanent Secretary's reminiscences— "I remember hearing Lowell once say, when asked if he had read the latest novel, 'No, I have not yet finished Shakespeare' "—and followed with a considerable excerpt from the rest of Johnson's remarks:

> Mr. Lowell represented in himself, as it is sometimes necessary to remind the current generation, the highest plane of learning, scholarship, and literary art, the principle of which he expounded in season and out of season in his critical writings . . . His critical works furnish a body of doctrine in literary matters which is certainly preëminent in American criticism at least. In these days, when the lawlessness of the literary Bolsheviki has invaded every form of composition, it is of tonic advantage to review Lowell's exposition of the principles of art underlying poetry and criticism . . . No man studied to better purpose the range of expression afforded by the English classics or would have been more outraged by the random and fantastic productions which are classified with the poetry of the present time under the name of Vers Libre. While no doubt he recognized the force of Whitman, he refused to recognize him as a poet, and once retorted, when it was suggested that much of Whitman's poetry was between prose and poetry, that there was nothing between prose and poetry.

Johnson concluded with a pledge that the Academy would take on the "agreeable duty to endeavour to accentuate the treasures of American literature which have fallen into neglect," and hoped that the occasion would "incite our college faculties and their students to a study of the heritage which we have in the beautiful poetry and the acute and high-minded criticism of James Russell Lowell."

To suppose that the times were ripe for a return to the prosody of Lowell was a little like a call to reinstate Ptolemy in the age of Einstein. The Lowell centennial was not so much a memorial retrospective—i.e., an unimpeachable review of a significant literary history—as it was that other thing: an instance of antiquarianism. Or—to do justice to Johnson's credo—it was a battle-cry against the onrushing alien modernist hordes, the literary Bolsheviki.

The difficulty was that the Bolsheviki were rampant in all the arts. Young American composers—Virgil Thomson, Marc Blitzstein, Elliott Carter, Marion Bauer, Roger Sessions, Herbert Elwell, Aaron Copland, George Gershwin—were streaming toward Nadia Boulanger's studio outside Paris for instruction in harmony (much as young American writers were streaming toward Gertrude Stein's Paris sitting room for lessons in logic), and coming back home with extraordinary new sounds. Boulanger introduced Copland to the conductor Walter Damrosch (later President of the Academy at a time when its laces were far less strait), who joked about Copland's Symphony for Organ and Orchestra: "If a gifted young man can write a symphony like that at twenty-three, within five years he will be ready to commit murder." What Copland called the "jazz spirit," with its irregular rhythms and sometimes exotic instruments, was received by the more conventional critics as a kind of symphonic deicide—the old gods of rational cadence struck down by xylophones, tam-tams, Chinese woodblocks. Copland was charged with releasing a "modernist fury" of "barnyard and stable noises." "New York withholds its admiration," Virgil Thomson wrote of the critical atmosphere, "till assured that you are modeling yourself on central Europe."

But experiment was unstoppable: George Gershwin was blending concert music and jazz in works commissioned by Damrosch, and Serge Koussevitsky, conducting the Boston Symphony, was presiding over Copland's barnyard noises. Edgard Varèse, who came to the United States from Paris in 1915, reversing the flow, declared his belief in "organized sound," or "sound-masses," and employed cymbals, bells, chimes, castanets, slapsticks, rattles, chains, anvils, and almost every other possible percussion device, "with their contribution" as he put it, "of a blossoming of unsuspected timbres." His scores were often marked with "*hurlant*," indicating howling, roaring, wild and strident clamor; any sound, all sounds, were music.

In the prosperity and optimism of the Twenties, proponents of the "new" music were turning their backs (and not without contempt) on traditionalists like Frederick Shepherd Converse, Edward Burlingame Hill, George Whitefield Chadwick, Reginald DeKoven, Arthur Foote, Victor Herbert, and John Powell, all members of the Academy, and all continuing to compose in nineteenth-century styles. The maverick among them was John Alden Carpenter, nearly the only Academician to venture into blues, ragtime, and jazz. But in the world beyond the Academy, the matchless Louis Armstrong and other eminent black musicians were revolutionizing the American—and European—ear, and by 1927 Duke Ellington's band in Harlem's Cotton Club was devising original voices for trumpet and trombone. The Twenties saw an interpenetration of foreign originality as well: Sergei Rachmaninoff arrived after the Russian revolution, and in the winter of 1925 Igor Stravinsky appeared with both the New York Philharmonic and the Boston Symphony. Three years earlier, Darius Milhaud was lecturing at Harvard, Princeton, and Columbia. Ernest Bloch, noted for chamber music and an enchantment with Hebrew melodies, became an American citizen in 1924. Arnold Schoenberg, inventor of twelve-tone technique and a refugee from Nazi Germany, emigrated to the United States in 1933, but his influence had long preceded him.

Meanwhile, Henry Cowell, a native Californian, was not only trying out novel sounds on the piano—sometimes treating it like a violin—but was inventing a new instrument, the rhythmicon, "capable of producing very complex combinations of beat patterns." The quarterly Cowell founded, suitably named *New Music*, was hospitable to the work of the most arcane innovators, including Charles Ives—whose composition teacher at Yale in 1894 had been the mild but uncomprehending Horatio Parker. It is one of the ironies of the Academy's later history, and also one of its numerous triumphs over its older self, that grants and fellowships are now awarded to young composers in Charles Ives's name, and out of the royalties of his estate—though Ives's polytonality, quarter tones, and disjointed melody line would surely have appalled the Academicians of the Twenties. In February of 1923, Richard Aldrich, a member of the Institute since 1908, and music critic for the *New York Times*, wrote in a bitter column called "Some Judgments on New Music":

> It is nothing less than a crime for a composer to write in any of the idioms that have been handed down, or to hold any of the older ideas of beauty ... Any who do not throw overboard all the baggage inherited from the past, all transmitted ideas of melody and harmony, are reactionaries, pulling back and hindering the march of music ... Whatever is presented to [the receptive new audiences] as acrid ugliness or rambling incoherence is eagerly accepted as emanations of greatness and originality. It never occurs to them that it might be simple, commonplace ugliness.

These are lines that might have emerged from Robert Underwood Johnson's own inkpot. But it fell to John Powell, a Virginian elected to the Institute in 1924, to catch the Johnsonian idiom entire—the modernists, Powell said, were "nothing more or less than cheap replicas of the recent European Bolshevists." Powell was a composer of moods, beguiled by the picturesque and the nostalgic, especially as associated with Southern antebellum plantation life. The introductory wail of his *Rapsodie Nègre* is intended to capture a watermelon peddler's cry—a telltale image that, apart from its melodic use, may possibly bear some relation to his distaste for racial mixing and new immigrants. His musical preference was for what he termed "the Anglo-Saxon Folk Music School," and he shunned *Cavalleria Rusticana* and *Tristan und Isolde* not because he disliked opera, but because he disapproved of marital infidelity.

The new music, with its "acrid ugliness and rambling incoherence," may have been the extreme manifestation of what the Academy idealists were up against. Among the other arts, though, the idealists did have one strong ally, which steadfastly resisted—longer than music and longer than painting—the notions of freedom of form and idiosyncratic or experimental vision that modernism was opening up to the individual artist. Sculpture alone continued to profess public nobility and collective virtue in service to a national purpose. "Sculpture" meant statuary dedicated to historical uplift and moral seriousness. Even architecture, through its functional aspect, was more inclined to engage in individual expression—but virtually every statue was intended as a monument. The Armory Show of 1913, the catalyst that revolutionized American painting, barely touched the National Sculpture Society, which had settled on Augustus Saint-Gaudens and his successors, in their advance from marble to bronze, as "The Golden Age of American Sculpture." (Saint-Gaudens died in 1907.) Colossal multifigured structures, exhibition palaces (often fashioned from temporary materials and afterward dismantled), fountains, celebratory arches, symbolic themes indistinguishable from spiritual credos—all these were in full consonance with Robert Underwood Johnson's dream of an American Temple. Nearly fifty years before the Armory Show, the sculptor Erastus Dow Palmer had declared: "No work in sculpture, however wrought out physically, results in excellence, unless it rests upon, and is sustained by, the dignity of a moral or intellectual intention."

This dogma remained intact until the rise of the modernists, who repudiated not only its principles but its techniques. The Paris Beaux Arts tradition depended on studio assistants; a sculptor was a "thinker," a philosopher who conceived the work and modeled it in clay, after which lower-level technicians were delegated to carry out its translation into finished form. Modernism, by contrast, brought on a rush of hand carving—the kinetic and aesthetic interaction of sculptor with tools and material. But it was not until the Twenties were almost out that individual style began to emerge as a recognizable, though clearly not yet dominant, movement. It was a movement that purposefully turned away from Old

World models, and looked to the "primitive," to African and pre-Columbian as well as Sumerian and Egyptian sources. While the Academy itself clung to the civically earnest, advanced taste was (once again) headed for unfamiliar territory. Thomas Hastings, a Beaux Arts adherent elected to the Academy in 1908, had designed a Victory Arch—adorned with abundant inspirational statuary—for the soldiers returning after the First World War to march through. In 1919 it was executed in temporary materials, and the soldiers did march through it. But public sentiment failed to support a permanent rendering in stone, and the Arch was taken down. Monuments to a civil consensus were slipping from popularity; work steeped in lofty aims met indifferent, or perhaps jaded, eyes.

Yet the new sculptors were not recognized by the Academy, and the strikingly fresh shapes and experiments of the Twenties streamed past the Temple only to attract its vilifying scorn. Saul Baizerman, whose innovative studies of contemporary life, *The City and the People*, were hammered out between 1920 and 1925, was never invited into the Institute, while even more notable sculptors of the period had to wait for a later generation's approbation. Bruce Moore was not admitted until 1949; William Zorach became a member only in 1953, and Robert Laurent only in 1970, the year of his death. Within the Academy of the third decade, it was Daniel Chester French (admitted in 1908) who was preëminent: the prized sculptor of the Lincoln Memorial in Washington, D.C., the creator of a female *Republic* (with staff, globe, and dove) and of Columbia University's *Alma Mater*, himself a grand symbol of the grand symbolic statuary that preceded the modernist flood and was finally—if belatedly in the Academy—overwhelmed by it.

In a tribute delivered on French's death in 1931, Royal Cortissoz, an Academician who was art critic for the *New York Tribune* from 1891 on, observed with just precision that French "was thoroughly in harmony with [the Academy's] spirit" in a life "dedicated from beginning to end to the production of noble work . . . A beautiful seriousness of purpose animated him." As an example he offered French's figure of *Memory*, "a seated nude reminiscent of antique ideas." Cortissoz was reflecting exactly what William Milligan Sloane had prescribed in his address at the opening of the Temple in 1923:

> We are a company seeking the ideal . . . we do not forget that our business is conservation first and foremost, conservation of the best and but incidentally, if at all, promotion of the untried. We are to guard tradition, not to seek out and reward innovation . . . we are sternly bound as an organization to examine carefully any intellectual movement striving to break with tradition . . . Our effort in word and work must be to discover and cherish the true American spirit and keep it pure, in order to prevent inferior literature and art from getting the upper hand.

What, then, was Cortissoz about when he labeled modern art "a gospel of stupid license and self-assertion," if not preventing the inferior from getting the upper hand? Still another Academician, the painter and critic Kenyon Cox, wrote: "There is only one word for this denial of all law, this insurrection of individual license without discipline and without restraint; and that word is anarchy." The Armory Show, Cox announced, was a "pathological museum" where "individualism has reached the pitch of sheer insanity or triumphant charlatanism." Gaugin was "a decorator tainted with insanity." Rodin displayed "symptoms of mental decay." If Cortissoz thought Matisse produced "gauche puerilities," Cox went further, and condemned "grotesque and indecent postures" drawn "in the manner of a savage or depraved child."

Eleven years after the Armory shock, the Academy, still unforgiving in 1924, published three papers attacking "Modernist Art," one each by Cortissoz and Cox, and the third by Edwin Howland Blashfield. All three blasts had appeared in periodicals in 1913 and 1914, in direct response to the Armory Show, but the Academy—while asserting that modernism's influence was "on the wane"—saw fit to reprint them in the interests of dislodging "eccentricities" from "the tolerance of critics." Here again was Kenyon Cox: "The real meaning of the Cubist movement is nothing else than the total destruction of the art of painting"; Cézanne "seems to me absolutely without talent"; "this kind of art [may] corrupt public taste and stimulate an appetite for excitement that is as dangerous as the appetite for any other poisonous drug"; "do not allow yourselves to be blinded by the sophistries of the foolish dupes or the self-interested exploiters of all this charlatanry." And Cortissoz on the Post-Impressionists: "work not only incompetent, but grotesque. It has led them from complacency to what I can only describe as insolence"; their "oracular assertion that the statues and pictures are beautiful and great is merely so much impudence." Blashfield, finally, after deploring "a license to omit painstaking care, coherent thinking, an incitement to violence as compelling attention," simply ended with a cry of self defense: *there is no dead art.*"

Thus the Temple on the coming of the New. And thus the Academy's collective impulse toward vituperation—delivered repeatedly, resentfully, remorselessly, relentlessly; and aimed at the New in music, painting, sculpture, literature. And not only here. Whatever was new in the evolving aspirations of women toward inclusion and equality was repudiated. New immigrants (no longer of familial Anglo-Saxon stock, many of whom were to enrich American literature, art, and music) were repudiated. Any alteration of nineteenth-century standards of piety or learning was repudiated. In a 1922 address. Owen Wister, author of *The Virginian*, ostensibly lauding "the permanent hoard of human knowledge," offered a list of "certain menaces to our chance for great literature":

> We are developing a ragtime religion. Homer and Virgil were founded on a serious faith . . . The classics are in eclipse. To that star all intellect has hitched its wagon. Literature has become a feminine subject in our seats of learning. What female Shakespeare has ever lived? Recent arrivals pollute the original spring . . . It would be well for us if many recent arrivals would become departures.

Across the water Virginia Woolf, too, was speculating on

the absence of a female Shakespeare, though from another viewpoint. And in the very bowels of the Academy, in a letter to President Sloane on October 22, 1921, loyal Mrs. Vanamee herself—in the name of the logic of precedent—was protesting the exclusion of women:

> You will be astonished to learn that I found a volume of Institute Minutes which was once loaned to Mr. Johnson and in looking through it this morning we found a record of [Julia Ward] Howe's election to the Institute. It seems she was regularly [i.e., routinely] nominated and regularly elected for at that time [1907] there was no ruling against women's being elected to the Institute. Mrs. Howe's name has always been included among the names of "Deceased Members of the Institute." Of course this makes the ruling of yesterday entirely out of order.

Mrs. Vanamee recommended that "any record of what occurred" (meaning the entire set of minutes of the meeting ruling against admission of women) be expunged in a little act of hanky-panky. Accordingly, the culpable minutes were somehow spirited away, never again to emerge—but the issue continued to fester, and it would be another five years before enough ballots could be counted in favor of admission. Julia Ward Howe's membership—for the three feeble years before her death at age ninety-one—was argued against as "an error of procedure." Besides, as the author of "The Battle Hymn of the Republic" she was less a woman than a national monument, one of those ideal female symbol-figures specialized in by Daniel Chester French.

In the ballots of 1923—asking directly, "Do you favor the admission of women to the National Institute of Arts and Letters?"—sometimes a simple "no" was not enough to satisfy the spleen of an elderly gentleman born before or during the Civil War. "NO I DO NOT," roared the painter Whitney Warren. "A categorical NO," announced the composer Arthur Bird, and followed up with a tirade:

> To express my decided antipathy against this proposed

innovation you will notice that I have added *categorical*. I have lately in the Chicago Musical Leader ventilated my opinion on this subject in a short exposé. The occasion of a woman attempting to conduct the Philharmonic orchestra here at a symphony concert gave me a long awaited opportunity to mouth a short but vigorous sally . . . against the attempts of a certain clan of womanhood to try to do things the feminine gender is by nature utterly incapable of doing and hooting at those things for which it is by nature predestined. What on earth *have or ever will have women* to do with science, art and letters (in the highest sense of the words) or are they satisfied to play a very mediocre second fiddle? It is needless to hide the naked fact, conceal the plain truth, that the moment the fair sex drops its skirts, throws aside guiltiness, modesty, refinement, all that gentility that we know and love so much, *don the leather breeches, beat the drum*, then lackaday to all the poetry of this life, away with the sentiments so expressive in Heine's poem so prettily and cleverly translated by our Longfellow, "The sea hath its pearls," etc. Then we shall say "For women must work and fight, men weep and spin." Id est—the world turned upside down.

Tirades on the one hand, gloatings on the other. "I rejoice exceedingly," the writer James Ford Rhodes wrote in 1918 to Robert Underwood Johnson (who, surprisingly, favored women's admission), "that you were beaten on the women question. What would you do with the 'wimmin' at the dinners at the University Club? . . . A hysteria is going over the country, showing itself in women's suffrage and Prohibition." (The Temple may have been able to do without women at dinner, but it rarely permitted itself to do without booze, and regularly circumvented the Eighteenth Amendment— viz., "My dear Cass, Please send the bottle of Gin for the Institute dinner, carefully wrapped up so as to conceal its identity." "My dear Thorndike, Will you please send the bottle of Gin, carefully wrapped up so that it will not look suspicious.")

In the midst of all these fulminations and refusals and repudiations (always excepting the gin), there was, nevertheless, one moment early in the Academy's third decade that hinted at a glimmer of doubt, perhaps even of self-criticism. It was, in fact, a kind of bloodless insurrection or palace coup, and took place behind Robert Underwood Johnson's formidable back. The rebel in the case was Hamlin Garland, author of *A Son of the Middle Border*, a school classic of the last generation. Wisconsin-born, Garland grew up in the drudging privations of farm life, at home in the unpolished—and impoverished—regions of Iowa, California, and the Dakotas. Unlike Johnson (out of whom the last traces of Indiana had long since been squeezed), Garland could never have been mistaken for a formal Eastener. His perspectives were wider and more sympathetic than many of his colleagues'; he was a liberal who wrote seriously on social reform. His name was irrefutably linked with narrative realism, but he was a realist in the more everyday sense as well: he looked around and saw an Academy of fatigued and retrograde ancients stuck fast in a narrow mold. "We must avoid the appearance of a club of old fogies," he warned, and kept an eye out for a chance to invigorate the membership.

The chance came in 1920, when President Wilson (an Academy member since 1908) appointed Johnson to be Ambassador to Italy, and Garland stepped in as the Academy's Acting Secretary. In Johnson's absence, Garland's first target was Johnson himself: "We cannot become a 'one man organization,' no matter how fine that man may be." To Brander Matthews he wrote, "Now is the time to make the Academy known. If we let this chance pass we shall be a Johnson Institution for the rest of our lives . . . We can't be run by a volunteer member seventy years of age . . . We are called . . . that Johnson thing." He noted "the age and growing infirmity of many of our members who are losing interest in the organization" and "the fact that our membership is scattered as well as aged and preoccupied . . . We should draw closer," he advised, "and take the future of the Academy much more seriously than we have heretofore done . . . We must not lose touch with youth. We should not be known as 'a senile institution.' We must assume to lead in the progress of the Nation."

Yet Garland's ideas for Academy programs turned out to be less than revolutionary: "The Academy by a Lecture Foundation should offer to the Nation a series of addresses on American Arts and Letters in which the most vigorous propaganda for the good as against the bad should be carried forward. We should stand against all literary pandering, all corrupting influences"—an exhortation that might easily have been uttered by any of the old fogies had it not concluded with a call to "make it plain that we are for progress, that it is our plan to hasten and direct the advance. That we intend to recognize the man of genius whether in the Academy or not." He proposed the election of honorary foreign members, so that the Academy's "penumbra can extend throughout the world." As for the native membership, he warned against "the choice of a scholar who is known only to a few other scholars." "There is always the danger of electing too many men who are merely college professors. The Academy," he insisted, "cannot afford to elect a classicist in preference to the man of original genius." And there was only one kind of genius he really wanted: "The Academy membership must be kept predominantly literary or the Academy will lose power. The moment the Academy is over-balanced on the art side it loses standing, a result which may be unjust but it is true." He pushed for fame: "A man may be chosen who is recognized by the great public as a figure. Edwin Markham for example does not have to be explained. He is in Who's Who. Some of the Academy elections have to be explained even to members." He pushed for zeal: "men who will come to the meetings . . . Every time the Academy takes in a man who has a sort of contempt for what it is trying to do it weakens the organization." He pushed above all for the Academy as "an inspiration to young men," and called for the establishment of annual awards to "young workers in the five arts."

And as a final push, though Johnson was still in Italy, Garland considered how to suppress him on his return: "Johnson is ex-officio on all committees," he conceded, but "should not be Chairman." In the course of time Garland proposed an even more radical solution—the Academy should get rid of Johnson altogether: "The returning secretary is an old man, preoccupied (as the rest of us are) with personal work of his own. He cannot give his entire mind to the Academy and as he is a member, it is not desirable that he should. It is not a good thing to have any one member known as the manager of the organization. The managing Secretary should be an outside man on a salary."

At the end of the day Garland was happy to have Johnson back. The truth was that Johnson *could* give his entire mind to the Academy, and had always been eager to do exactly that. The administrative minutiae that Johnson reveled in ultimately made Garland grumble—he was clearly sick of contending with old-fogey letters like the two that arrived a month apart in the Fall of 1921, from Abbott Lawrence Lowell, the President of Harvard:

> I do not know whether I shall be able to be present at the meeting on November 2nd; but I want to suggest that it would be well for the Academy, which stands for Letters, to use the best English in its communications to members, and say "I shall," or "shall not, be present"— not "I will, or will not."

> I do not know what the duties of the Education Committee of the American Academy of Arts and Letters are. I am very glad to serve on the Committee; but it seems to me that it would be a great mistake for the Academy to attempt to do anything or express an opinion about education.

Like Lowell, the membership, reluctant to be more activist than they had been under Johnson, resisted Garland's pressure for broader concern and greater participation. "The lack of interest and cohesion is pitiful," he wrote to President Sloane. And to Matthews he complained, "I am just downright discouraged . . . The truth is we are a lot of 'elderly old parties' who don't care very much whether school keeps or not—we'd rather not if it involves any janitor work on our part . . . I cannot be a party to a passive policy." The Academy, it seemed, liked it well enough that Johnson ran a one-man establishment, and Garland himself was feeling more and more the imposition on his own literary productivity. "I am carrying so much of the detail work of the Academy at this time," he moaned one year into his service as Acting Secretary, "that I have no leisure for my own writing." Two years later he was in a state of full surrender, and could hardly wait for the finish of Johnson's ambassadorial stint. "As I see it now there will be no one but Johnson to carry on the work and I withdraw all opposition to him." And: "I've been a nuisance to little effect and shall turn the Office of Secretary over to Johnson the moment he reaches the building. It is a thankless task for any man."

Thankless for any but Robert Underwood Johnson. Though his beard may have grown whiter, he resumed his position at the helm as energetically as before: it was as if Italy had never intervened. Despite Garland's efforts to introduce notions of "progress," everything Johnson had left behind was still in place, every prejudice intact, the familiar projects ongoing: the preoccupation with standards of English diction; public addresses entitled "The Literature of Early American Statesmanship," "Kinship and Detachment from Europe in American Literature," "The Emotional Discovery of America," "The Relations of American Literature and American Scholarship in Retrospect and Prospect" (all these in 1924, to mark the Academy's twentieth anniversary); the annual Evangeline Wilbour Blashfield Lecture, in honor of the wife of Edwin Howland Blashfield, sculptor of *The Evolution of Civilization*. At her death she was eulogized not merely for "nobility of character" but more particularly for faith "in the furtherance of sane and useful movements in literature and the Arts."

Perhaps the most Johnsonian display of taste burst out in 1924, the year Robert Frost won the Pulitzer Prize for poetry and the Academy voted not to award its Gold Medal to anyone at all. According to the minutes of October 10th, Johnson protested this decision, "favoring as the recipient Miss Edith M. Thomas, whose seventieth birthday has just occurred. Mr. Johnson spoke in high appreciation of the substance and style of Miss Thomas's work, which he regarded as the summit of contemporary American poetry." Not that this was Johnson's first salvo on behalf of the summit. He had begun to urge Miss Thomas's cause six years earlier; apparently he regarded her as his most incendiary weapon in the war on free verse. "Aside from her professional merits and the nobility of her character," he pressed, "the spiritual tone of her work . . . would be all the more timely because of the widespread misconceptions in the public mind concerning the art of poetry, due to the vogue of formless, whimsical and eccentric productions, which by reason of their typographical form are generally classified as poetry by publishers, librarians, critics and readers. That the Academy should honor a poetic artist of so fine a strain as Miss Thomas would be to throw the force of its influence against the lawlessness of the time that has invaded all the Arts." And even by 1926—it was now four years since the landmark appearance of "The Waste Land"—Johnson was still not giving up on Edith Thomas: "I believe that in some respects she has seen more deeply and reported more melodiously the evanescent phases of the borderland of the soul than any other American poet except Ralph Waldo Emerson."

In 1925 the vote for the newly established William Dean Howells Medal, given "in recognition of the most distinguished work of fiction published during the preceding five years," went to Mary E. Wilkins Freeman for her depiction of "Old New England, New England before the coming of the French Canadian and the Italian peasant . . . The body of her work remains of the Anglo-Saxon order." (Other American fiction published in that *annus mirabilis* of 1925 included *The Professor's House*, by Willa Cather, who was elected to the Institute in 1929; *In Our Time*, short stories by Ernest Hemingway, never admitted to membership; *The Great Gatsby*, by F. Scott Fitzgerald, also never admitted; *Am American Tragedy*, by Theodore Dreiser, another non-member; *Manhattan Transfer*, by John Dos Passos, admitted in 1937; and *The Making of Americans*, by Gertrude Stein, who of all American writers was least likely to be nominated.) At the same time the vote in the Institute for the Gold Medal for Belles Lettres landed on William Crary Brownell, an Academy member who had the distinction of serving as Edith Wharton's editor at Scribner's. Wharton herself was still unadmitted. In 1926, the Gold Medal for Sculpture was presented to Herbert Adams, the Academician who had designed the Academy's bronze doors, with their inscription: GREAT MEN ARE THEY WHO SEE THAT THOUGHTS RULE THE WORLD. In 1927, William Milligan Sloane won the Gold Medal for Biography and History; Johnson had successfully nominated the Academy's President for the Academy's own award.

The Academy was also engaged in other forms of self-recognition. There was the question of bookplate, insignia, regalia—all the grave emblems of institutional Importance. The bookplate—an airy Pegasus rearing among clouds, framed by a wreath resting on a book, below which appears the Academy's motto: OPPORTUNITY, INSPIRATION, ACHIEVEMENT—was devised by the architect Henry Bacon and engraved by Timothy Cole. The airiness was Cole's contribution—"a delicate light style," he said, "that I have been at great pains to secure"—but Bacon rejected it, preferring the "heavy strong manner" of Piranesi, the eighteenth-century Italian neoclassicist. Bacon died in the middle of the dispute, so Pegasus continued to fly lightly, as Cole rendered him. No lightness attached to the issue of regalia, however—odd-looking caps and shroudlike gowns were supplied to the Academicians (a photograph attests to their discomfort) and then discarded. From 1923 on, there were various experiments with insignia; at one point the current small rosette was in disfavor for grand occasions, and a great floppy badge was introduced—a giant purple satin ribbon trimmed with gold scallops and tiny bows. (A box of these relics, accompanied by cards of unused ribbon, matching thread, and even needles and pins, is still being thriftily stored in the Academy's archives.) And there were Roman-style busts of the Academicians themselves: F. Wellington Ruckstull, an Academy sculptor, was commissioned to immortalize both Nicholas Murray Butler and Wilbur Cross, a governor of

Connecticut whose name, familiar as a highway leading to New England, may prove that asphalt is more lasting than bronze.

But it would be misleading to imply that the Academy was fixed only on itself in these years. One ambitious plan for the general enlightenment was to establish an art museum in every state lacking one. "The commanding motive," Johnson explained in 1925, was to bring "knowledge of the best painting and sculpture to populations that are not able to visit the great centers." Doggedly optimistic, Johnson traveled from city to city searching for donors and making speeches – "I am well, but a bit tired of my own voice," he reported to Mrs. Vanamee. The idea fell through, possibly because, as Johnson noted, "there is an impasse between the artistic and the commercial temperament." A second attempt to widen the Academy's purview—its affiliation with the American Academy in Rome—was more efficacious, and endured. And the course of public lectures the Academy launched in Boston, Cleveland, Chicago, Philadelphia and other venues frequently aspired to a global embrace: "The Literature of Japan"; "The Spirit of Italy"; talks on Scandinavia, France, Russia; and, following the war, an entire series on "The Failure of German Kultur" (though these were rather more punitive than embracing). Relations were kept up with the Belgian and French Academies. Letters of invitation—and homage—went often to British men of letters. In 1919, Maurice Maeterlinck, the 1911 Nobel Laureate, visited the Academy as an honored literary guest from Belgium. The novelist Vicente Blasco Ibáñez came from Spain.

Spain, Italy, Belgium, France, Canada, and Britain all sent laudatory messages to the Academy's William Dean Howells memorial meeting in March of 1921; Rudyard Kipling's contribution, representing England, brought a vigorous insight into the American literary past—with more conviction, possibly, than some of the narrowly Anglophile Academicians themselves (always conscious of what they saw as American marginality with regard to European models) could wholeheartedly summon. Despite the international tributes solicited from overseas, and despite the number of speakers and subjects ("Howells the Novelist," "Howells the Dramatist," "Howells the Humorist," etc.), some indeterminate trace of the intramural nevertheless clung to the Howells commemoration—a touch of the gentleman's club; Howells, after all, had been the Academy's first president. The event rises out of the record less as a national literary celebration than as an Academy period piece. The speakers, Academy members all, were once again identifiable by their common idiom—the idiom of backward-looking gentility, hence of diminishment. Press attention was meager.

Three years later, H. L. Mencken, in an article headlined "No Head for Howells' Hat" in the Detroit *News* of March 23, 1924, took up a different approach to Howells. (Howells had died four years before.) "Suppose," he wrote, "Henrik Ibsen and Anatole France were still alive and on their way to the United States on a lecture tour, or to study prohibition and sex hygiene, or to pay their respects to Dr. Coolidge . . . who would go down the bay in a revenue cutter to meet them . . . who to represent American literature?" Represent it, he explained, "in a tasteful and resounding manner." "So long as Howells kept his legs," Mencken went on, "he was chosen almost automatically for all such jobs, for he was dean of the national letters and acknowledged to be such by everyone. Moreover, he had experience at the work and a natural gift for it. He looked well in funeral garments. He had a noble and ancient head. He made a neat and caressing speech. He understood etiquette."

But the price of Mencken's esteem for Howells, however soaked in the Mencken satire, was disesteem for the Academy:

Who is to represent [American literature] today? I search the country without finding a single candidate, to say nothing of a whole posse. Turn, for example, to the mystic nobles of the American Academy of Arts and Letters. I pick out five at random: William C. Brownell, Robert Underwood Johnson, Hamlin Garland, Bliss Perry, and Henry Van Dyke. What is wrong with them? The plain but dreadful fact that no literary foreigner has ever heard of them—that their appearance on the deck of his incoming barge would puzzle and alarm him and probably cause him to call for the police.

These men do not lack the homely virtues. They all spell correctly, write neatly and print nothing that is not constructive. In the whole five of them there is not enough sin to raise a congressman's temperature one-hundredth of a degree. But they are devoid of what is essential to the official life; they have, so to speak, no stage presence. There is nothing rotund and gaudy about them. No public and unanimous reverence bathes them. What they write or say never causes any talk. To be welcomed by them jointly or severally would appear to Thomas Hardy or Gabriele d'Annunzio as equal to being welcomed by representatives of the St. Joe, Mo., Rotary Club.

On the heels of the Howells commemoration came the Academy's 1922 memorial to John Burroughs, the naturalist, a member since 1905. This was marked by a lengthy address entitled "The Racial Soul of John Burroughs," by Henry Fairfield Osborn (who was *not* an Academy member)—a talk of a certain brightness and charm until it discloses its dubious thesis: the existence of "racial aptitudes." "The *racial* creative spirit of man always reacts to its own historic racial environment, into the remote past." "Have we not reason to believe that there is a *racial soul* as well as a racial mind, a racial system of morals, a racial anatomy?" In short, it was his "northern heredity" that drew Burroughs to become "the poet of our robins, of our apple trees, of the beauties of our forests and farms," and "the ardent and sometimes violent prophet of conservation." There is no evidence that any of Osborn's listeners demurred from a theory linking conservation of forests to northern European genes. And a decade later similar ideas of race, less innocently applied than to an interest in robins, would inflame Europe and destroy whole populations.

In the spring of that same year—1922—the Academy

turned once again to Europe, anticipating Mencken's nasty vision of distinguished "literary foreigners" being welcomed at the docks by a Temple nonenity. The nonenity in this instance was not an Academician but rather a Mr. Haskell, unknown to history and apparently a Columbia University factotum sent to the pier by Nicholas Murray Butler to meet the S.S. *Paris*. Aboard were Maurice Donnay and André Chevrillon, Director and Chancellor respectively of the Académie Française. The pair had been imported to attend the three-hundredth anniversary of the birth of Molière—"In Celebration of the Power and Beauty of the Literature of France and its influence upon That of the English-speaking Peoples"—and were fêted at luncheons and dinners in New York, Princeton, Boston, Philadelphia, and Washington. The official Academy dinner included oxtail soup, appropriately dubbed "Parisienne"; the appetizer was a quatrain by Richard Watson Gilder:

Molière

He was the first great modern. In his art
   The very times their very manners show;
But for he truly drew the human heart
   In his true page all times themselves shall know.

The public meeting honoring Molière—or his latterday representatives—was held at the Rtiz-Carlton Hotel on April 25, 1922. A day earlier the visitors had been taken uptown to see the site of the new Temple, and then were conducted back to the temporary Academy building at 15 West 81st Street for tea and a speech by Butler: "I well recall that in his subtle and quite unrivaled study of French traits, our associate, Mr. Brownell, pointed out that while among the French the love of knowledge is not more insatiable than with us, it is infinitely more judicious . . . precision, definiteness, proportion, are certain marks of what is truly French." "The aim of the American Academy," he continued, "must for long years to come be to rescue a people's art and a people's letters from what is vulgar, from what is provincial, from what is pretense, and to raise a standard to which the lovers of the beauty of loveliness and the lovers of the beauty of dignity may, with confidence and satisfaction, repair."

Precision, definiteness, proportion were truly French; vulgarity, provinciality, pretense were truly American. The literary foreigners may have been flattered by what seemed to be homage born of New World insecurity, but since Butler's list of American flaws covered not only homegrown philistinism but also international modernism ("pretense"), the French were surely implicated in the latter. It was France, after all, that had produced Matisse and Milhaud and Jules Laforgue (who had influenced Eliot)—not to mention the French infatuation with jazz, and Paris's harboring of suspect American types like Gertrude Stein. And if the laughing ghost of Molière had come to the feast, would it have chosen to side with the deadly predictable purveyors of "the beauty of loveliness" or with the syncopated ironists of modernism?

In 1925 Robert Underwood Johnson was still incorribly at war with the new poets. The recoil from modernism he enshrined as a cause; and what was Johnson's cause was bound to become the Academy's cause, very nearly its *raison d'être*. (The first cracks in anti-modernism would not occur until late in the decade, and then—torrentially—in the 1930s and 1940s.) On November 23, 1925, in a letter to *Who's Who in America*, presenting himself as an incarnation of the Temple's eternality, Johnson requested that he be identified as "an antagonist of free verse and author of a criticism of it in an address before the Academy entitled 'The Glory of Words.'" "The modernists," he complained in that talk, "wish to exalt into poetic association words that heretofore have not been considered poetic... Naturally such an attempt is conspicuously deficient in the glory of words." The "metrical product of the revolutionists," he went on, was "unimaginative," "monotonously conventional," and "objectionably sophisticated—individualism run to seed." And: "They are determined to make silk purses out of sows' ears." "Because the Muses no longer rule there must be no allusion to Parnassus; the Muses are not 'factual' and must go by the board." "The chief promise of poetry is to express the pervasive and permanent spiritual forces of all time."

Although Johnson's zeal on behalf of Miss Thomas had failed to win her an Academy honor, his fight against Robert Frost did not abate. To Booth Tarkington he wrote:

I am very strongly opposed to Frost's nomination on principle (I have never met him and have no personal feeling) . . . I think both he and Edwin Arlington Robinson who has been nominated are in the main mediocre in their work . . . they are not worthy of consideration for the Academy . . . We have other men in the Institute who ought to be put forward for the quality of their poetry—Percy McKaye, Clinton Scollard, Richard Burton, Brian Hooker, Don Marquis, Charles deKay and John Finley. Each one of these men has done beautiful work.

To our ears these are largely unrecognizable minor deities. Johnson's own Parnassus has not gathered them to its bosom. And if Polyhymnia, having anointed (sparingly) Edward MacDowell and Victor Herbert, remains cool to Frederick Shepherd Converse and George Whitefield Chadwick, while smiling palely on Horatio Parker chiefly for his connection with Charles Ives, what of the painters' Muse? Edith Thomas as poet and John Powell as composer may be confined to the category of antiquarian curios, but (for instance) Joseph Pennell and Childe Hassam are not. (Anyone examining the superbly evocative Pennell drawings that accompany Henry James's *Collected Travel Writings*, reissued in 1993 by the Library of America, will be stirred by what we call permanence in art: that which cannot "date.")

Repeatedly infuriated by the encroachments of new modes of literary expression and helpless before its tide—Robinson and Frost were both admitted to the Academy, in 1927 and 1930 respectively—Johnson was determined that the Temple should make an indelible statement at least in the graphic arts. One effort toward that end, the attempt to put a museum in every state, fizzled. A second idea both survived and prospered: this was to establish a collection by Academicians and other American painters. Johnson worked closely with the earliest Committee on Art, then known as the Committee on Art Censorship—a name that may suggest the prescriptive tastes of its three members: the painter and critic Kenyon Cox, the sculptor Herbert Adams, and the architect Cass Gilbert. Paintings were solicited from private collectors and through bequests. Since one of Johnson's motives was to promote and augment the influence of the Academy, it is no wonder that portraits dominated, or that the collection was based, by and large, on the products of its own members. Johnson was relentless in going after contributions, especially from the freshly widowed wives of deceased Academicians. The collection expanded to cover etchings, lithographs, engravings, small sculptures, photographs, memorabilia, and manuscripts.

To display the Academy's riches, the year 1927 saw four public events: separate exhibits honoring Academicians Childe Hassam, Timothy Cole, and Joseph Pennell, and an "Exhibition of Manuscripts Representing the First Century of American Independence"—which included the notebooks of John Burroughs and letters by Academy members Henry Adams, Charles Francis Adams, Thomas Bailey Aldrich, Julia Ward Howe, William Dean Howells, Thomas Wentworth Higginson (the very Higginson who had chided Emily Dickinson for "spasmodic" and "uncontrolled" verse), Henry James, Henry Charles Lea, Edmund Clarence Stedman, and Richard Henry Stoddard. Manuscripts by Emerson, Hawthorne, and Whitman were also on exhibit. As a mendicant on behalf of the Academy, Johnson was astoundingly tireless, and his solicitations ended only with his death in 1937. With Johnson gone, the Academy's policy for both artists and writers (and for musicians and composers as well) moved from mainly self-reflecting acquisition to outward-looking prodigality: awards to the young at the start of their careers.

A few days after the Timothy Cole event, Huntington presented the Academy with a gift of $100,000 as an endowment for future exhibits. The permanent collection, and the new plan for ongoing showings by painters, were designed to set a standard for American cultural aspiration. So were the concerts and recitals sponsored by the Academy during the decade of the Twenties: what was to be emphasized,

George Whitefield Chadwick urged, was "the development of *American Music* (not by foreign musicians, no matter how accomplished)." But the pressure for indigenous American achievement—a sign of the early Academy's sense of its own inferiority before the age and weight of Europe's cultural cargo—was nowhere more pronounced than in the preoccupation with American speech. President Sloane warned of "a stream of linguistic tendency, prone to dangerous flood and devastating inundation," alluding no doubt to the postwar immigration. Yet native-born journalists were almost as perilous a threat as foreigners spilling into the country: "How are we to justify the diction of the press," William Roscoe Thayer inquired, "through which pours an incessant stream of slang, vulgarism, grammatical blunders, and rhetorical crudity?" Responding, the press—in the shape of the Boston *Herald* of December 15, 1926—pretended to take up the case of an instance of ambiguity in the use of "is" and "are," which was being placed before the Temple for adjudication: "After having brought half the dilettantes and intellectuals of the nation in futile disagreement, one of the worst sentences ever written will soon arrive at the Academy of Arts and Letters in search of further trouble."

Further trouble? Such playfulness—or mockery—could hardly sit well with the Permanent Secretary. The function of the Academy, Johnson grandly noted, was to reject "invasions from the ribbon counter" and to "stand against the slovenly, and for the dignified and effective use of words." This meant also the *sound* of words. In a radio talk invoking the Academy's various causes, Mrs. Vanamee testified to the excitements of clear enunciation:

There is a medal for good diction on the Stage which was awarded to Walter Hampden in 1924 and last spring to Miss Edith Wynne Matthison whose perfect diction was never more perfectly in evidence than in her superbly simple and touching acceptance of the medal from the hands of Robert Underwood Johnson, the Secretary of the Academy, and after he and its Chancellor,

Dr. Nicholas Murray Butler had paid high tribute to Miss Matthison's work.

Mrs. Vanamee was plainly not in line for a medal honoring Style.

The ribbon counter, along with the Academy's defunct ribbon badge, has vanished; it is a different Academy today. For one thing, though born of the Institute, the Academy has swallowed up its progenitor. What was once two bodies, joined like Siamese twins in any case, is now a single organization—diverse, welcoming, lavishly encouraging to beginners in the arts. Yet what Hamlin Garland remarked on long ago remains; a quantity of seasoned gray heads—few of whom, however, are polemically inclined to retrogressive views. Crusty elitism is out. The presence of women goes unquestioned. Ethnic parochialism is condemned. No one regards experiment as a revolutionary danger. And by now modernism, which seventy years ago seemed so disruptive to the history-minded, is itself an entrenched tradition with a lengthening history of its own—even fading off into the kind of old-fashionedness that derives from repetitiveness, imitation, overfamilarity. Modernism has grown as tranquil as Robert Underwood Johnson's Parnassus; and what postmodernism is, or will become, we hardly know.

Do these white-bearded, high-collared gentlemen of the Academy—who live out the nineteenth century's aesthetic and intellectual passions right up to the lip of the Great Depression—strike us as "quaint"? Condescending and unholy word! Unholy, because it forgets that death and distance beckon us, too: our turn lies just ahead. Possibly we are already quaintly clothed, as unaware that we are retrograde as Kenyon Cox and Royal Cortissoz before Matisse, or Robert Underwood Johnson in the face of T.S. Eliot and Mariane Moore. Despite our ingrained modernist heritage, we may, after all, discover ourselves to be more closely linked to the print-loyal denizens of the Twenties Temple than we are to the cybernetic future. If a brittle and browning 1924 Mencken clipping testifies to the cultural irrelevance of the official humanists of two generations ago, consider these comments on "post-textual literacy," quoted in a recent issue of the *New York Times*: "The typewriter shaped our current view of literacy. Now we're finding new computer tools that honor visual-audio thinking as opposed to textual thinking." "Digital video, with vast possibilities for manipulating images, exercises the mind." "Today people think of print as the only kind of writing. There will be a different kind of literacy based on a melange of digital information—the entire stream of all the things that flow into our mind from our computers." These words may herald the Armory Show, so to speak, of the year 2000. They bring a similar disorientation to fixed expectations. The loss of text, if it occurs, may be as cataclysmic for us as Cubism was to the votaries of Beaux Arts.

And if time has reduced Robert Underwood Johnson and his solemnly spiritualized colleagues to toys for our irony, what does that signify? Probably that (given our modernist habits) we value irony more than dignity, and what does *that* signify? The "mystic nobles," as Mencken called them, of the Academy's third decade lacked irony; but they also lacked cynicism. When they sermonized on "nobility of character," they believed in its likelihood, and even in its actual presence. When Johnson honored "Beauty changeless and divine," he took it for granted that the continuity of a civilization is a sacred covenant. A review of *American Poetry: The Nineteenth Century*, a pair of Library of America volumes published in 1933 and edited by John Hollander, a contemporary Academician, adds this perspective: "Just as the spare acerbity of early modernism must have looked bracingly astringent to writers and readers grown weary of nineteenth-century rotundities, so today . . . these relics of another age are deeply refreshing."

We who are postmodern inheritors of the violent whole of the twentieth century no longer dare to parade—even if we privately hold them—convictions of virtue, harmony, nobility, wisdom, beauty; or of their sources. But (setting aside irony, satire, condescension, and the always arrogant power of the present to diminish the past), the ideals of the

Temple, exactly as Johnson conceived them, *are* refreshing to an era tormented by unimaginable atrocity and justifiable cynicism. Nor are those ideals precisely "relics." Suppose Johnson had chosen Frank Lloyd Wright as architect for the new building, what might the Academy have looked like then? If it is good to have the Guggenheim Museum's inventiveness, it is also good to have the Academy's Venetian palace, just as Stanford White and Charles McKim dreamed it.

Or what if the Academy's art committee had allied itself with, say, Alfred Stieglitz's "291" gallery, the heart and muscle of the modernist cause? What if Robert Frost and Charles Ives had been admitted to membership in 1918? Or H.L. Mencken?

Such speculations instantly annihilate the history of the Temple's credo between the Great War and the Great Depression. Worse, they wipe out the name and (noble) character of the redoubtable Robert Underwood Johnson, and who would want that?

METAPHOR AND MEMORY

NOT LONG AGO I was invited to read some tale of mine before an assembly of physicians. I was invited not because I knew anything about disease or medicine or physiology, but precisely because I knew nothing at all. And the doctors, on their side, were not much concerned with tales or their tellers, unless the writer were to come to them with an interesting complaint. But a writer standing there in dull good health, reading aloud from a page, with not so much as a toothache or a common cold or even a mild rash, with no visible malady other than word-besottedness, could hardly serve. To the lives of doctors, given over as they are to the hard sad heavy push against mortality—what salve or balm or use might a word-besotted scribbler be? For a writer to turn up among doctors without a rash was rash indeed.

These doctors, however, had a visionary captain, or viceroy, or prince, who had read his Emerson. Emerson in "The American Scholar" noted what he called the "amputation" of society, each trade and profession "ridden by the routine of . . . craft": "The priest becomes a form; the attorney a statute-book; the mechanic a machine; the sailor a rope of the ship." And the doctor a CAT scan.

In response, the captain of the doctors formulates an Emersonian idea: an idea of interpenetration: of cutting through the dividing membrane: of peopling one cell with two temperaments. He will set the writer down among the doctors, the fabulist among the healers. The purpose of the experiment will be to increase the doctors' capacity to imagine. The doctors, explains their captain, too often do not presume a connection of vulnerability between the catastrophe that

311

besets the patient and the susceptibility of the doctors' own flesh: the doctors do not conceive of themselves as equally mortal, equally open to fortune's disasters. The writer, an imaginer by trade, will suggest a course of connecting, of entering into the tremulous spirit of the helpless, the fearful, the apart. In short, the writer will demonstrate the contagion of passion and compassion that is known in medicine as "empathy," and in art as insight.

This, then, is the plan. The writer, though ignorant of every scientific punctilio, will command the leap into the Other.* That is how tales are made.

Yet the writer is cautious, even frightened. Here among the doctors, the redemptive ardor of literature begins to take on a vanity. How frivolous it seems, how trivial—vanity of vanities! The doctors are absorbed by blood and bone; each one, alone in his judgment, walks the fragile bridge between the salvation into life and the morbid slide toward death. The writer is as innocent as a privileged child before all this, a sybarite of libraries, a voluptuary of print. The doctors, by contrast, are soaked in the disinfectant fetor of hospitals, where the broken and the moribund swarm in their cold white beds. What gall, to suppose that a dreamer of tales can bring news of the human predicament to the doctors on their dread rounds!

All the same, I had my obligation; I had been summoned to tell the doctors a story, to speak out of the enlarging lung of chronicle. And so, not suspecting what would come of it, I began to read out a narrative about a sexually active faraway planet where the birth of children is no longer welcome, and finally, for prurient technological reasons, no longer possible. The most refined intellectuals on that planet are those least willing to bear children—not only because children interfere with the *tidiness* of any planet, but also because the intellectuals have discovered that children interrupt: they interrupt careers, journeys, vacations, appointments, games, erotic attachments, telephone calls, self-development, education, meditation, and other enlightened, useful, and joyous pur-

* A term now grown severely stale, but I have been unable to discover a substitute.

suits. A number of children manage to get born in any case, illicitly and improbably, and I wish I could tell you how these children turned out, and what happened to that sophisticated though unlucky planet afterward; my intent, however, is not to disclose the destiny of the children, but rather the behavior of the doctors. Perhaps it is enough to mention that in my story everything ended in barbarism and savagery.

Now you can hear even from this truncated, raw, bare-bones, tablet-sized account that the story I had chosen to present to the doctors was part parable, part satire, outfitted in drollery and ribaldry, in deepest imitative tertiary debt to the history of literary forms—Kafka, Swift, Chaucer; drenched, above all, in metaphor. The tale of a lascivious planet too earnestly self-important to tolerate children could only have been directed against artifice and malice, sophistry and self-indulgence; it could only have pressed for fruitful-ness and health, sanity and generosity, bloom and—especially—continuity. My story, I thought, was a contrivance that declared itself on the side of life; and therefore, presum-ably, on the side of the doctors themselves. In the lovely lists of parable, how light the lance, how economical, how sudden! To be able to unfold artifice and malice and self-indulgence, fruitfulness, health, sanity, generosity, bloom, continuity—and never once the need to drag these blatant carcasses of heavy nouns across the greensward! The power and charm of fable are in the force of its automatic metaphor-ical engine, and in bringing metaphor to the doctors, surely I was obeying their captain, and opening the inmost valve of the imagining heart?

But among the doctors something was rumbling just then—a stirring, a murmuring, an angry collective hiss. The doctors, their captain included, were not simply discontent; they were all at once ranked before me as a white-coated captious tribe, excited, resentful, bewildered, belligerent. They accused me of obscurantism, of having mean-spiritedly resolved to perplex. They wanted—they demanded—the principles of ordinary telling. They wanted—*this* is what they wanted—plain speech. They were appalled by metaphor (the shock of metaphor), by fable, image, echo, irony, satire, obliqueness, double meaning, the call to interpret, the call to penetrate, the call to comment and diagnose. They were stung by what they instantly named "ambiguity." They protested, they repudiated, the writer's instruments and devices as arcane, specialist, oracular, technical. Before the use of the metaphor they felt themselves stripped and defenseless: they complained that the examining tables had been turned on them; that their reasoning authority had fallen away; that they stood before the parable as a naked laity; that I had sickened them.

And so I had. I had sickened the doctors—or at least the intrusion of metaphorical thinking had.

Now the argument may be urged that physicians are themselves abundantly given to metaphorical speech and thought; that they live every hour under the raucous wing of the Angel of Death and Crippling, whose devastating imagery they cannot deny, and whose symbols they read cell by cell, X-ray by X-ray; that ambiguity and interpretation are ineluctably in the grain of their tasks; that all medical literature, however hidden in obscure vocabularies in abstruse journals, is, case after case, a literature of redemption through parable: new cases remember past cases. And, finally, that no cast of mind is more surrendered to the figurative than the namers of organs: the color-bearing circular diaphragm of the eye, that flower of the mind's eye called *iris* after the rainbow goddess; the palisades cells and the goblet cells; the pancreatic islets of Langerhans, the imagination's archipelago.

But dismiss all this. Say that the doctors have rejected metaphor as not of their realm—as inimical to their gravity. They do it because they have one certainty: they know that, whatever else they may be, they are serious men and women. They may be too frail, as their captain proposed, to enter into psychological twinship with the even frailer souls of the sick; but the struggle to heal, the will to repair the shattered, the will to redeem and make whole—this is what we mean when we speak of lives lived under the conscientious pressure of our moral nature. And metaphor, what is metaphor? Frivolity. Triviality. Lightness of mind. Irrational immateriality. Baubles. To talk in metaphor to serious men and women, indeed to talk *of* metaphor to serious men and women, is to disengage oneself from the great necessary bond of community: it is to disengage oneself from the capacity to put humanity before pleasure, clear judgment before sensation, useful acts before the allure of words. It is to cut oneself off from the heat of human pity—and all for the sake of a figure of speech.

If the doctors think this way—if a great many other serious men and women think this way—it may be, first, because they associate metaphor with writers and artists of every sort, and, second, because they associate writers and artists with what we always call "inspiration." It isn't only that doctors like to keep away from inspiration on grounds of science and empiricism and predictability. Nor is it, for serious people, mainly a matter of valuing stability over spontaneity, or responsibility over elation. Something there is in inspiration that hints of wildness—a wildness even beyond the quick unearned streak of "knowing" that brings resolution without warning. Serious people are used to feeling an at-homeness in their minds. Inspiration is an intruder, a kidnapper of reason, a burglar who shoots the watchdogs dead. Inspiration chases off sentries and censors and monitors. Inspiration instigates reckless cliff-walking; it sweeps its quarry to the edge of unfamiliar abysses. Inspiration is the secret sharer who flies out of pandemonium.

All these characteristics do suggest that inspiration is allied to the stuff of metaphor. Isn't metaphor the poetry-making faculty itself? And where does the poetry-making faculty derive from, if not from inspiration? It is in fact a truism to equate poetry and inspiration, metaphor and inspiration. Though truisms are sometimes at least partly true, my purpose is to tell something else about metaphor. I mean to persuade the doctors that metaphor belongs less to inspiration than it does to memory and pity. I want to argue that metaphor is one of the chief agents of our moral nature, and that the more serious we are in life, the less we can do without it.

Begin, then, with the history of inspiration. Inspiration is one of those ideas that can, without objection, claim a clear

315

history; but never the history of poetry. Its genesis is in natural religion, or, rather, in the religion of nature. To come to Emerson again: in an essay rather unsuitably called "History"—it might more accurately have been named "Anti-History," since it annihilates the distinction between Then and Now—Emerson recounts a picturesque conversation with "a lady with whom I was riding in a forest [who] said to me that the woods always seemed to her *to wait*, as if the genii who inhabit them suspended their deeds until the wayfarer had passed onward; a thought which poetry has celebrated in the dance of the fairies, which breaks off on the approach of human feet." Now that is a very pretty story, but only because in Emerson's day the woods around Concord were safe, and the civilization of genii and fairies long finished. Inspiration may end in daydream or fancy, but it sets out in terror. For us Pan is all poetry, a charming faun with a flute; among the Greeks he caused panic. Fairies and all the other spirits of natural religion were once malevolent powers profoundly feared. Devout Athenians on the third day of the important Anthesterion festival took the ceremony of frightening away the spirits as a somber religious duty. Emerson, reading history as benign nature, reads natural religion as a sublime illumination—"The idiot, the Indian, the child and the unschooled farmer's boy," he announces, "stand nearer to the light by which nature is to be read, than the dissector or the antiquary"—whereas for its historical adherents, its flesh-and-blood congregants, the religion of nature was mainly panic, dread, and desperate appeasement of the uncanny. Poetry, including Emersonian poetizing, seeps in only after two millennia have exhausted and silenced the fairies; only after the great god Pan is indisputably, unexaggeratedly, dead. In natural religion there are no metaphors; the genii are *there*; the poetry is not yet born.

The genii are there, potent and ubiquitous. They are in the birds and in the beasts, in the brooks, in the muttering oaks— the majestic Zeus himself got his start as a god who spoke out of the oak tree. Divinity lives even in a notched stick. In natural religion, there is nothing that is not an organ of omen, divination, enthusiasm. But when we reflect on this "enthusiasm"—a Greek locution, *én theos*, the god within—there is one instance of it so celebrated that it comes to mind before all others. The syllables themselves have turned into the full sweetness of poetry: the Oracle at Delphi; the sound of it is as beautiful as "nightingale." The cult of the Eleusinian Mysteries remains a secret, a speculation, to this day; we know only that there was immersion in a river, that sacred cakes were eaten, a sacred potion drunk, and the birth of a holy infant proclaimed. The exalting ritual performed by the initiates, shrouded all through antiquity, had no public scribe or record-keeper. The events at Eleusis continue inscrutable. But about what went on at the shrine of Apollo at Delphi almost everything has been disclosed. We can still follow its process, and there is nothing metaphoric in any of it.

Apollo was a latecomer to Delphi. Earthquake-prone, the place had once belonged to Gaea, the earth-goddess, and the shrine was built over a gorge, or pit; a sort of saucer in the ground, within sight of the mountains of Parnassus. Excavations have uncovered no crack or opening of any kind in the floor of the saucer, but a certain gas was said to issue from a hole in the earth: the narcotic stench of decomposition—below lay the carcass of the terrible python Apollo slew. An underground stream flowed there, prophetic waters called Kassotis; these too had narcotic properties. The agent of divination—the enthusiast, the sibyl possessed by the god—was at first, apparently, a young virgin. Then the rules were changed, no one seems to know why, and now the votary had to be a respectable, often married, woman of at least fifty—she was, however, required to dress up as a maiden. This was the Pythoness, or Pythia, Apollo's oracle, the incarnation of everything we mean, in our own civilization and language, by inspiration.

Her method was to induce frenzy. She chewed the leaves of a narcotic plant, drank from the narcotic spring, breathed in the narcotic vapor. A number of attending priests, called the Holy Ones, members of important local families, waited until she seemed on the brink of seizure, and then led her to a tripod, the seat of the god's speaking. These notables already had in hand the question the god was to treat. The answer came, in the moment of possession, from the mouth of the sibyl either as howls or as murmurs—cascades of gibberish flooded the shrine. Here is how the Swedish novelist Pär Lagerkvist imagines the moment of possession:

It was he! He! It was he who filled me. I felt it, I knew it! He was filling me, he was annihilating me and filling me utterly with himself, with his happiness, his joy, his rapture. Ah, it was wonderful to feel his spirit, his inspiration coming upon me—to be his, his alone, to be possessed by god . . .

But the feeling mounted and mounted; it was still full of delight and joy but it was too violent, too overpowering, it broke all bounds—it broke me, hurt me, it was immeasurable, demented—and I felt my body beginning to writhe, to writhe in agony and torment; being tossed to and fro and strangled, as if I were to be suffocated. But I was not suffocated, and instead I began to hiss forth dreadful, anguished sounds, utterly strange to me, and my lips moved without my will; it was not I who was doing this. And I heard shrieks, loud shrieks; I didn't understand them, they were quite unintelligible, yet it was I who uttered them. They issued from my gaping mouth, though they were not mine. It was not myself at all, I was no longer I, I was his, his alone; it was terrible, terrible and nothing else!

How long it went on I don't know. I had no sense of time while it was happening. Nor do I know how I afterwards got out of the holy of holies or what happened next; who helped me and took care of me. I awoke in the house next to the temple where I lived during this time, and they said I had lain in a deep sleep of utter exhaustion. And they told me that the priests were much pleased with me.

That, of course, is the drama of fiction. The priestly role was more intellectual, and certainly political, and lends itself less to theatrical reconstruction. When the Pythia's vatic fit was over, the priests had to take up the task of interpretation. It is conceivable that their interpretations were composed in advance, since the questioner's predicament had been submitted in advance, and often in writing. Being both human and bureaucratic, the priests now and then accepted a bribe in exchange for a politically favorable interpretation. Still, they were without doubt men of no small gifts; they were in fact devoted to their ingenious versifying, and would sometimes set their interpretations in the meter of Homer or Hesiod, or else in succinctly ambiguous prose that, no matter what the future brought, was always on the mark. The replies of the oracle were famously broad, ranging from family-court matters to statecraft. The priests, like most priests everywhere, were conservative: when much of Greece seemed ready to give up the practice of human sacrifice, the Delphic Oracle had nothing to say against it, and the priests continued to approve it.* There were some liberal decisions

---

* But current anthropology, I am told, has it that human sacrifice was, in fact, never practiced in Greece at all. This view diverges sharply from the scholarship of, say, sixty years ago. The thirteenth edition of the *Encylodpaedia Britannica*, for instance, describes the Thargelia festival, an agricultural celebration, as "a purifying and expiatory ceremony. While the people offered the first-fruits of the earth to the god in token of thankfulness, it was at the same time necessary to propitiate him ... Two men, ... the ugliest that could be found, were chosen to die, one for the men, the other (according to some, a woman) for the women. On the day of the sacrifice they were led round with strings of figs on their necks, and whipped on the genitals with rods of figwood with squills. When they reached the place of sacrifice on the shore, they were stoned to death, their bodies burnt, and the ashes thrown into the sea (or over the land, to act as a fertilizing influence). The whipping with squills and figwood was intended to stimulate the reproductive energies of the [sacrificial victim], who represented the god of vegetation, annually slain to be born again. It is agreed that an actual human sacrifice took place on this occasion, replaced in later times by a milder form of expiation."

Apparently it is no longer agreed, and the claim is as dated as an old encyclopaedia article tends to become. But whether human sacrifice was actually or only symbolically practiced in Greece, the issue—the concept as applying to the imagination of a civilization—is still very much to the point. In the history of comparative culture, what counts is whether the idea of human sacrifice is present at all, in any embodiment, even that of legend, and what this might portend (since both pity and pitilessness require teaching) in the necessary nurturing of pity.

Consider the nature of the internalization of the same idea at the dawn of Judaism, in its earliest hour: Judaism's first social task, so to speak. The story of Abraham and Isaac announces, in the voice of divinity itself, the end of human sacrifice forever afterward. The binding of Isaac both represents and introduces the supreme scriptural valuation of innocent life. The sacrifice of Isaac never occurred and was not permitted to occur—the image and the

nonetheless: the occasional manumission of slaves, for instance. Delphi, the fount of inspiration, was in essence the seat of pragmatism. Santayana, recalling that Plato too identifies madness with inspiration, and acknowledging that the "aboriginal madness" of the oracle could produce "faith, humility, courage, conformity," yet marvels that "the most intelligent and temperate of nations submitted, in the most crucial matters, to the inspiration of idiots."

All this does not mean to insinuate—it would be an untruth—that because the oracle's infusion of the god-spirit at Delphi had nothing to do with our idea of religion as conscience, Greece was a society that paid no attention to the moral life. We know otherwise, from Socrates, Plato, and Aristotle preëminently; we know otherwise from Greek drama, Greek poetry, Greek history, Greek speculation. What else is the story of Antigone if not a story of conscience? What else is tragedy if not moral seriousness? And beyond these, the mind of science, the mind of art, are Greek. There is not one Greece, but a hundred: heroes side by side with slaves, reason side by side with magic, the self-restraint of Epictetus side by side with sensuousness. It is the Greeks, W. H. Auden reminds us, "who have taught us, not to think— that all human beings have always done—but to think about our thinking." If one nation can be measured as more intelligent than all other nations that ever were, or were to be, that is how we can measure the Greeks. And the priestly interpretations at Delphi were themselves grounded in an immensity of human understanding: ambiguity is psychology; ambiguity is how we sort things out, how we decide. "Nothing in excess" is a Delphic inscription.

Yet what was missing in the glory that was Greece was

---

possibility are wiped out once and for all. A heavenly instruction directs Abraham to the ram in the thicket—after which the idea of human sacrifice in the service of the divine is never again broached in the line of Jewish thinking (and without a moment's regression in a people well known for backsliding).

The ram in the thicket is the herald of metaphor—a way station to the ultimate means of God-encounter, which will more and more distance itself from the altar (a literal-minded device that will finally vanish) to become purely verbal and textual. And metaphor, as I hope to show, is the herald of human pity.

metaphor. Perhaps this statement shocks with its instant absurdity. You will want to say, What? A nation of myth, and you claim it has no metaphor? Aren't myths the greatest metaphors of all? And surely the most blatant? Or you will want to listen again to the priestly interpretations at Delphi: aren't these, in their fertility of implication, exactly what we mean by metaphoric language?

The answer in both instances, I think, is no. Remember that mythology took on the inwardness of poetry only when the gods were no longer efficacious, only after they had ascended out of the reality of their belief-system into the misted charms of enchantment. And even now, when we read that Apollo slew the python, what do we learn? We learn that snakes are dangerous and that the gods are brave and strong. For Apollo's constituents, the aversion to snakes—and also their strange sacredness—was confirmed; so was the reverence for Apollo. If there is a lesson, it is either that the bravery of the gods ought to be emulated; or else that it is hubris to suppose the bravery of the gods can be emulated. But why, you will say, why speak of "learning," of "lessons"? Do we go to the gods for schooling, or for self-revelation? Look, you will say, how humanly resplendent: each god represents an aspect of human passion. Here is beauty, here is lust, here is wisdom, here is chance, here is courage, here is mendacity, here is war, and so on and so on. Isn't that metaphoric enough for you?

Observe: there is no god or goddess who stands for the still small voice of conscience.

As for the Delphic riddles: they were recipes, not standards. They were directions, not principles. Nor was there any consistent social compassion inherent in their readings. The oracle remembered nothing. The voice of conscience did not speak through the god at Delphi, or through any of the gods. Moral seriousness could be found again and again in Greece, especially among the geniuses; it could be found almost anywhere, except in religion, among the people. The reason is plain. Inspiration has no memory. Inspiration is spontaneity; its opposite is memory, which is history as judgment. When conscience flashed out of Greece, as it did again and again, it did so idiosyncratically, individually, without a base in a community model or a collective history. There was no heritage of a common historical experience to universalize ethical feeling. To put it otherwise: there was no will to create a universal moral parable; there was no will to enter and harness metaphor for the sake of a universal conscience.

By turning their religious life into poetry, we have long since universalized the Greeks. They are our psychology. But that is our doing, not theirs. The Greeks, with all their astonishments, and in spite of the serenity of "Nothing in excess," were brutally parochial. This ravishingly civilized people kept slaves. Greeks enslaved foreigners and other Greeks. Anyone captured in war was dragged back as a slave, even if he was a Greek of a neighbouring polis. In Athens, slaves, especially women, were often domestic servants, but of one hundred and fifty thousand adult male slaves, twenty thousand were set to work in the silver mines, in ten-hour shifts, in tunnels three feet high, shackled and lashed; the forehead of a retrieved runaway was branded with a hot iron. Aristotle called slaves "animate tools," forever indispensable, he thought, unless you were a utopian who believed in some future invention of automatic machinery. In Athens it was understood that the most efficient administrator of many slaves was someone who had himself been born into slavery and then freed; such a man would know, out of his own oppressive experience with severity, how to bear down hard. A foreigner who was not enslaved lived under prejudice and restriction. Demosthenes tells about the humiliation of a certain Euxitheus, a prosperous Athenian whose citizenship suddenly came under a cloud because his father happened to be overheard speaking with an un-Athenian accent. Euxitheus had to prove that his father had in fact been Athenian-born, or his own status would drop to that of resident alien, stripping him of his property and his rights, and endangering his freedom. That the Greeks called all foreigners "barbarians" is notorious enough; but it was not so much a category as a jeer. It imputed to all foreign languages the animal sound of a grunt or a bark: bar-bar, bar-bar.

So there is much irony in our having universalized Greece

through poetizing it. The Greeks were not only not universalists; they scorned the idea. They were proud of despising the stranger. They had no pity for the stranger. They were proud of hating their enemies. As a society they never undertook to imagine what it was to be the Other; the outsider; the alien; the slave; the oppressed; the sufferer; the outcast; the opponent; the barbarian who owns feelings and deserves rights. And that is because they did not, as a society, cultivate memory, or search out any historical metaphor to contain memory.

We come now to a jump. A short jump across the Mediterranean; a long jump to the experience of another people, less lucky than the Greeks, and—perhaps because less lucky—collectively obsessed with the imagination of pity; or call it the imagination of reciprocity. The Jews—they were named Hebrews then—were driven to a preoccupation with history and with memory almost at the start of their hard-pressed desert voyage into civilization. The distinguished Greeks had their complex polity, their stunning cities; in these great cities they nurtured unrivaled sophistications. The Jews began as primitives and nomads, naive shepherds as remote from scientific thinking as any other primitives; in their own culture, when at length they established their simple towns, they had no art or theater or athletics, and never would have. A good case can be made—though not a watertight one—that the Jews did not become students and scholars until they learned how from the Greeks—surely the classroom is a Greek innovation. And, finally, the Jews carried the memory of four hundred years of torment. Unlike the citizen-Greeks, their history did not introduce civics; it introduced bricks without straw, and the Jews who escaped from Rameses' Egypt were a rough slave rabble, a mixed multitude, a rowdy discontented rebellious ragtag mob. A nation of slaves is different from a nation of philosophers.

Out of that slavery a new thing was made. It should not be called a "philosophy," because philosophy was Greek, and this was an envisioning the Greeks had always avoided, or else had never wished to invent, or else had been unable to invent. I have all along been calling this new thing "metaphor." It came about because thirty generations of slavery in Egypt were never forgotten—though not as a form of grudge-holding. A distinction should be drawn between grudge-holding and memory; they are never the same. As for grudge-holding, it was forbidden to the ex-slave rabble. The helping hand, says Exodus, reaches out to your enemy. If you meet your enemy's donkey or ox going astray, you must bring it back to him. If you happen on your enemy's donkey collapsed under its burden, you may not pass by; you must help your enemy relieve the animal. The Egyptians were cruel enemies and crueler oppressors; the ex-slaves will not forget—not out of spite for the wrongdoers, but as a means to understand what it is to be an outcast, a foreigner, an alien of any kind. By turning the concrete memory of slavery into a universalizing metaphor of reciprocity, the ex-slaves discover a way to convert imagination into a serious moral instrument.

Now a fair representation of the Delphic Oracle is not the work of a minute; this we have seen, and it is a paradox. Inspiration, which is as sudden and as transient as an electrical trajectory, takes a long time to delineate, possibly because latency (a hidden prior knowing) and unintelligibility (the mysterious grace that surpasseth understanding) are in its nature. It is in the nature of metaphor to be succinct. Four hundred years of bondage in Egypt, rendered as metaphoric memory, can be spoken in a moment; in a single sentence. What this sentence is, we know; we have built every idea of moral civilization on it. It is a sentence that conceivably sums up at the start every revelation that came afterward. It has given birth and tongue to saints and prophets, early and late. Its first dreamers are not its exclusive owners and operators; it belongs to everyone. That is the point of its having been dreamed into existence at all.

The sentence is easily identified. It follows sixteen verses behind "Love thy neighbor as thyself," but majestic as that is, it is not the most majestic, because its subject is not the most recalcitrant. Our neighbor is usually of our own tribe, and looks like us and talks like us. Our neighbor is usually familiar; our neighbor is usually not foreign, or of another race. "Love thy neighbor as thyself" is a glorious, civilizing, unifying sentence, an exhortation of consummate moral beauty, difficult of performance, difficult *in* performance. And it reveals at once the little seed of parable: the phrase "as thyself." "Thyself"—that universe of feeling—is the model. "*As* thyself" becomes the commanding metaphor. But we are still, with our neighbor, in Our Town. We are still, with the self, in psychology. We have not yet penetrated to history and memory. The more compelling sentence carries us there—Leviticus 19, verse 34, and you will hear in it history as metaphor, memory raised to parable:

> The stranger that sojourneth with you shall be unto you as the homeborn among you, and you shall love him as yourself; because you were strangers in the land of Egypt.

Leviticus 24, verse 22, insists further: "You shall have one manner of law, the same for the stranger as for the homeborn." A similar injunction appears in Exodus, and again in Deuteronomy, and again in Numbers. Altogether, this precept of loving the stranger, and treating the stranger as an equal both in emotion and under law, appears thirty-six times in the Pentateuch. It is there because a moral connection has been made with the memory of bondage. Leviticus 24, verse 22, demands memory, and then converts memory into metaphor: "Because you were strangers in the land of Egypt." Bondage becomes a metaphor of pity for the outsider; Egypt becomes the great metaphor of reciprocity. "And a stranger shall you not oppress," says Exodus 23, verse 8, "for you know the heart of a stranger, seeing you were strangers in the land of Egypt." There stands the parable; there stands the sacred metaphor of belonging, one heart to another. Without the metaphor of memory and history, we cannot imagine the life of the Other. We cannot imagine what it is to be someone else. Metaphor is the reciprocal agent, the universalizing force: it makes possible the power to envision the stranger's heart.

In the absence of this metaphoric capability, what are the consequences? The Romans originally had a single word, *hostis*, to signify both enemy and stranger. Nowhere beyond the reach of the Pentateuch did the alien and the home-born live under the same code; in early Roman law, every alien was classed as an enemy, devoid of rights. In Germanic law the alien was *rechtsunfähig*, a pariah with no access to justice. The Greeks made slaves of the stranger and then taunted him with barks. There have been, and still are, religio-political systems that have incorporated the teaching of contempt, turning the closest neighbors into the most despised strangers—a loathing expressed in words like "untouchable," "dhimmi," "deicide." In our own country, slavery thrived under the wing of a freedom-proclaiming Constitution until the middle of the last century. And in 1945, a British camera on a single day in a single German death camp just liberated photographed a bulldozer sweeping into five pits five thousand starved and abused human corpses at a time, a thousand to a pit, all of them having been judged unfit for the right to live.

By now you will have noticed that I have been quoting Scripture—a temptation that is always perilous, not only because it is a famously devilish pastime, but also because it induces the sermonizing tone, which for some reason always seems to settle in the nasal cavities. For this I apologize. My intended subject, after all, has not been national character or ethics or religion or history; it has not even, appearances to the contrary, been Matthew Arnold's fertile delta: Hebraism and Hellenism. What I have been thinking of is *language*—explicitly the work of metaphor.

And it is time now to ask what metaphor *is*. One way to begin is to recognize that metaphor is what inspiration is not. Inspiration is *ad hoc* and has no history. Metaphor relies on what has been experienced before; it transforms the strange into the familiar. This is the rule even of the simplest metaphor—Homer's wine-dark sea, for example. If you know wine, says the image, you will know the sea; the sea is for sailors, but wine is what we learn at home. Inspiration calls for possession and increases strangeness. Metaphor uses what we already possess and reduces strangeness. Inspiration belongs to riddle and oracle. Metaphor belongs to clarification and humane conduct. This is the meaning of the contrast between the Oracle at Delphi and the parable of servitude in Egypt. Inspiration attaches to the mysterious temples of anti-language. Metaphor overwhelmingly attaches to the house of language.

Should it, then, seem perplexing that both the oracle and the parable are identically dedicated to interpretation? The chief business of the priests at Delphi is practical interpretation. The incessant allusion to Egyptian bondage is again for the purpose of usable interpretation. And still the differences are total. Because the Delphic priests must begin each time with a fresh-hatched inspiration, with the annihilation of experience, they cannot arrive at any universal principle or precept. Principles and precepts derive from an accumulation of old event. Delphi never has old event; every event in that place is singular; the cry from the tripod is blazingly individual, particular, peculiar unto itself. From the tripod rises the curse of nepenthe; amnesia; forgetting; nor is it the voice of the race of humanity and its continuities we hear. The tragedy of the Delphic priests is not that their interpretations are obliged to start from gibberish. After all, what goes in as raw gibberish comes out as subject to rational decision, and it is more than conceivable that social principles might be extracted from a body of such decisions. But the priests think consciously only of their own moment. Their system is not organized toward the universalizing formulation. The tragedy of the priests is that, cut off from the uses of history, experience, and memory, they are helpless to make the future. They may, in a manner of speaking, "prophesy," with whatever luck such prophets have,* but they

---

*A parenthetical bemusement. Nowadays much of American literature is included in this Delphic fix. Certain novelists claim that fiction must express a pure autonomy—must become a self-sufficient language-machine—in order to be innovative; others strip language bare of any nuance. These aestheticians and reductionists, seeming opposites, both end inevitably at the gates of nihilism. A certain style of poetry is so far committed to the exquisitely self-contained that it has long since given up on that incandescent dream we call criticism of life. Abandoning attachments, annihilating society, the airless verse of self-scrutiny ends, paradoxically, in loss of the self. A certain style of criticism becomes a series of overlapping solipsisms—consider those types of "deconstruction" that end only in formulae. Insofar as these incommunicado literary movements are interested in interpretation at all, they have their ear at the Pythian tripod.

cannot construct a heritage. They have nothing to pass on. They cannot give birth to metaphor; one thing does not suggest another thing; in a place where each heart is meant to rave on in its uniqueness, there is no means for the grief of one heart to implicate the understanding of another heart. In the end, inspiration and its devices turn away from the hope of regeneration.

Metaphor, though never to be found at Delphi, is also a priest of interpretation; but what it interprets is memory. Metaphor is compelled to press hard on language and storytelling; it inhabits language at its most concrete. As the shocking extension of the unknown into our most intimate, most feeling, most private selves, metaphor is the enemy of abstraction. Irony is of course implicit. Think how ironic it would be, declares the parable of Egypt, if you did *not* take the memory of slavery as your exemplar! Think how ironic your life would be if you passed through it without the power of connection! Novels, those vessels of irony and connection, are nothing if not metaphors. The great novels transform experience into idea because it is the way of metaphor to transform memory into a principle of continuity. By "continuity" I mean nothing less than literary seriousness, which is unquestionably a branch of life-seriousness.

Now if all this has persisted in sounding more like a lecture in morals than the meditation on language it professes to be, it may be worth turning to that astonishing comment in T. S. Eliot's indispensable essay on what he terms "concentration" of experience. "Someone said," says Eliot in "Tradition and the Individual Talent," " 'The dead writers are remote from us because we *know* so much more than they did.' Precisely, and they are that which we know." He is speaking of the transforming effect of memory. The dead writers have turned metaphoric; they contain our experience, and they alter both our being and our becoming. Here we have an exact counterpart of biblical memory: *because you were strangers in Egypt*. Through metaphor, the past has the capacity to imagine us, and we it. Through metaphorical concentration, doctors can imagine what it is to be their patients. Those who have no pain can imagine those who suffer. Those at the center can imagine what it is to be outside. The strong can imagine the weak. Illuminated lives can imagine the dark. Poets in their twilight can imagine the borders of stellar fire. We strangers can imagine the familiar hearts of strangers.

Permissions and Acknowledgements

Some of the essays in this collection were originally published in the following periodicals: *Commentary, Harper's, Moment, Ms. The New Criterion, The New Republic, The New York Review of Books, The New York Times, The New Yorker, Partisan Review,* and *Salmagundi.*

Grateful acknowledgment is made to the following for permission to reprint previously published material:

Harcourt Brace Jovanovich, Inc.: "Ruth" by Cynthia Ozick from *Congregation: Contemporary Writers Read the Jewish Bible,* edited by David Rosenberg. Copyright © 1987 by Harcourt Brace Jovanovich, Inc. Reprinted by permission of Harcourt Brace Jovanovich, Inc.

Johns Hopkins University Press: "A Translator's Monologue" by Cynthia Ozick from *Prooftexts.* Volume 3, 1983. Reprinted by permission of the Johns Hopkins University Press.

"A Drugstore in Winter" first published in the *New York Times Book Review,* 21 January 1982. "Washington Square, 1946" published as "The First Day of School: Washington Square 1946", in *Harper's,* September 1985. "Alfred Chester's Wig" first published in the *New Yorker,* 30 March 1992. "Cyril Connolly and the Groans of Success" first published in the *New Criterion,* March 1984. "The Lesson of the Master" first published in the *New York Review of Books,* 12 August 1982. "On Permission to Write" first published as "Writers Domestic and Demonic" in the *New York Times Book Review,* 25 March 1984. "The Seam of the Snail" first published as "Excellence", in *Ms.,* January 1985. "Portrait of the Artist as a Bad Character" first published as "Good Novelists, Bad Citizens" in the *New York Times Book Review,* 15 February 1987. "George Steiner's Either/Or" originally a talk at a conference, "Art and Intellect in America", at Skidmore College, April 1980. Published (in somewhat different form) in *Salmagundi,* Fall 1980–Winter 1981. "Of Basilisks and Barometzes" first published as "The Library of Nonexistent Classics", in the *New York Times Book Review,* 12 April 1987. "The Muse, Postmodern and Homeless" first published in the *New York Times Book Review,* 18 January 1987. "Crocodiled Moats in the Kingdom of Letters" first published as "Science and Letters—God's Work and Ours" in the *New York Times Book Review,* 27 September 1988. "Literature and the Politics of Sex: A Dissent" first published in *Ms.,* December 1977. "Innovation and Redemption: What Literature Means" conflated from: "Some Antediluvian Reflections", *American Journal,* Vol. 1, No.1 (1 December 1971); "Where are the Serious Readers?", *Salmagundi,* Summer–Fall 1978; "What Literature Means", *Partisan Review,* Vol.49, No.1 (1982). "Literature as Idol: Harold Bloom" first published in *Commentary,* January 1979. "Sholem Aleichem's Revolution" first published in the *New Yorker,* 28 March 1988. "Ruth" from *Congregation: Contemporary Writers Read the Jewish Bible,* edited by David Rosenberg, Harcourt Brace Jovanovich, 1897. "The Way We Live Now" first published as "More than a Victorian" in the *New York Times Book Review,* 1 January 1995. "Isaac Babel and the Identity Question" first published in the *New Republic,* May 1995. "A Question of Our Speech—The Return to Aural Culture" first published in *Partisan Review,* Fiftieth Anniversary Issue, 1984–5. "Annals of the Temple: 1918–1927" first published in the *New Criterion,* September 1995. "Metaphor and Memory", the Phi Beta Kappa Oration, Harvard University, Spring 1985. Published as "The Moral Necessity of Metaphor", *Harper's,* May 1986.